The Glory Road

THE GLORY ROAD

A GOSPEL GYPSY LIFE ★ ★ ★ ★ ★ ★

Anita Faye Garner

The University of Alabama Press ★ Tuscaloosa

The University of Alabama Press
Tuscaloosa, Alabama 35487-0380
uapress.ua.edu

Inquiries about reproducing material from this work should
be addressed to the University of Alabama Press.

Typeface: Janson

Cover image: Photography courtesy of the author
Cover design: Lori Lynch

Cataloging-in-Publication data is available from the Library of Congress.
ISBN: 978-0-8173-2091-1
E-ISBN: 978-0-8173-9350-2

For

Leslie Ray Jones,
who is the other half of this story

My daughter, Cathleen Fern,
Grandpa Ray's "Little Chickeeter"

My granddaughter, Caedan Ray

Contents

Musical Houses

Photographs follow page 136.

Author's Note

The youngest child in this story prefers not to be named. She'll be called The Baby when she's mentioned. Some additional names were changed in the telling of these stories. Events are retold in a voice in keeping with the times and places in which they occurred.

Chapter 1

Route 66

Bossier City, Louisiana, 1955

Leslie Ray took sick all of a sudden at Paw Paw's house in Bossier City. We were looking right at him when he fell. First he sat down hard by the side of the road, then he crumpled up and rolled over in the front yard and stayed there.

A few minutes before, he was playing Work Up with some of our cousins in Floyd's lot across the street. Floyd, Paw Paw's double-first cousin, bought the big lot intending to plant some onion experiments he and Paw Paw were keen to explore. Instead, they moved their onion operation to the slope of the Red River levee just down the road, and except when the river flooded, their onions grew just fine.

I was out there playing too until Mother called me over to sing "Jesus and Me" because she didn't feel like singing the high part.

Leslie was about to be sixteen and overnight he was as big as a man. Maybe because he was the tallest or because we were company, the other cousins let him boss everybody around. I seldom got to play games with him and his friends at home anymore, but here at Paw Paw's, the fact that I was a couple of years younger didn't matter, so they let me play too.

Paw Paw's little white house overflowed that summer with kinfolks coming to visit because our Daddy, Raymond, the firstborn of ten, was in town. With his brothers and sisters and their wives and husbands and kids, we took up a lot of room, inside and out. The front steps stacked up with Joneses, buzzing with music and storytelling and chicory coffee and sweet tea and biscuits and ham.

Uncle Leonard called me.

"Nita Faye, come on over here and sing."

Reluctant to surrender my position in the outfield, I took my time climbing over people to get up to the top step by Mother. Uncle Leonard reached down and lifted me the rest of the way up.

He plunked me down beside her and picked up his fiddle, starting the introduction to a song we sang everywhere our family performed—in church, under revival tents, at Singings, in concerts, and on the radio.

I was tired of singing anywhere and especially weary of duets with Mother, but we sang anyway, by request, for the assembled relatives. We only got through the first few words of the song and right then is when Leslie Ray fell.

The twins, Chicken and Big Boy, Daddy's brothers, ran over to him. They hollered to Grammaw Jones and she came outside carrying a quilt. Uncle Leonard tossed the quilt to the twins, who spread it in the bed of the truck and hoisted Leslie Ray onto it.

Uncle Fred one-arm vaulted over the tailgate and landed in the back of the truck next to my brother. The truck took off, spewing dirt behind it.

Mother asked Daddy's sister, who was standing in the doorway, where they were going, where they were taking Leslie Ray, and Aint Teensie took her sweet time answering, making her point with her tone, which said what anybody with a lick of sense knew.

"Well, Fern, I expect to the *doctor*. Do you want to go? I'll take you."

"No thank you. I'll wait for Raymond."

Aint Teensie knew when she offered that we didn't go to doctors, that Mother would wait for Daddy to sort it out when he returned. Since our parents believed in faith healing only, in an emergency they would call on believers to pray, to cast out whatever affliction troubled us, but no doctor would be involved.

Daddy was at a church convention over in Shreveport. Somebody must've rushed over there to let him know about Leslie. He came home, took in what happened, and went straight to the phone, calling up preachers, asking them to set a prayer chain in motion, then we piled into our car to go to the hospital.

The Jones men in the truck had been directed to the emergency room. By the time we arrived, several church people were already there, some of them standing close together, holding hands, praying, voices murmuring on the same note, syllables indistinct and rhythmic, turned into a spoken song. Strangers turned to look at the source of the hum, and I hoped that Leslie, wherever they'd taken him, couldn't hear this and wouldn't know about it.

In the emergency room, a clump of Jones brothers stood around. Daddy walked over and they took a step away from everybody and spoke quietly together. Then Daddy came back for Fred, the brother-in-law who was the owner of the truck that brought Leslie to the hospital. They appeared to be having a tight-lipped talk that ended with Daddy patting Fred on the shoulder in a not altogether reassuring manner.

Daddy turned to the group gathered nearby and, sliding into the language employed by Southern preachers, a combination of romance and Bible phrases, he said, bless your hearts, maybe all y'all didn't know, we don't take our young'uns to the hospital.

Some of these people, bless their hearts, *did* know, and I silently thanked the uncles for taking on Daddy that way, the twins and a brother-in-law racing to get their nephew medical attention before Daddy came home.

Nobody thought our parents were right to deny us medical care. Some of Daddy's people prayed often but also went to doctors. Still, Daddy and Mother were both ordained ministers and theirs was a respected profession. Nobody in Daddy's family voiced differing opinions, at least not in our hearing.

In the hospital cubicle, Leslie Ray was looking even more pale than when we got there.

Daddy said, "Son, we're gonna get you out of here now."

Leslie protested, "They said it might be my appendix. It might burst."

"No it won't. Not with the Lord on our side."

Leslie kept his eyes closed and he took so long to answer, I thought he might really be dying, but then he spoke, quiet and clenched and angry.

"I want to stay here."

Daddy's posture changed in a way that might not be perceptible to someone who didn't live with him. The welcoming face he shared with the world receded just a bit and froze in place, and it was evident he regretted having to remind his boy who he belonged to.

"Naw, son, I *said* we are leaving. Church people will meet us back at Paw Paw's house and we are gonna stay right there and pray through for as long as it takes until the Lord delivers us from this."

Leslie Ray and I had never been anywhere near a hospital. We were both born at home and early on we learned our family wouldn't be doing business with such places. While my brother still lay on a bed that was raised up and looked more like a table, we waited for whatever hospitals do next, surrounded by people in white, wearing shoes that made no sound, moving around inside a small room made of curtains and filled with smells we'd never smelled. Even in this alien environment, we'd have chosen to trust our fate to these strangers, but Daddy had spoken.

It was our experience so far that people prayed but people also died. We were sure seeing a doctor might prevent some of the dying. Whenever we asked about someone who'd passed away under circumstances that seemed out of season, in a way that wasn't described as peacefully going to sleep, Daddy answered, "It was the Lord's will." At funerals where our family participated with words and music, he said to the bereaved, "The Lord called him home."

It was not going to be all right with me for the Lord to call my brother home. I prayed my own prayers, which were more like threats. I said to Jesus, don't you dare let him die. I mean it.

It was our habit to sit up with each other when one was sick. When I didn't feel good, Leslie Ray would stay nearby, and I would do the same with him.

They'd say, "Nita Faye, you go on to bed now," or "Leslie Ray, your sister will be fine. Jesus will watch over her through the night." But as soon as they left, we would pop right back up and sit until we both fell asleep.

Louisiana wasn't the first place we needed medical care. There were health episodes in Arkansas, in Texas, in Georgia, and in Oklahoma, and whichever one of us was sick eventually returned to good health and our parents gave the Lord the credit.

Daddy checked my brother out of the hospital and back we went to Paw Paw's house. Leslie Ray's fever went down. His appendix didn't burst. Maybe it wasn't his appendix at all. That's where the pain was, he said, but we would never know for sure, because Daddy whisked him out of there before tests were completed.

Finally everybody at Paw Paw's went to sleep that night. Some went across the road to stay at Floyd's house. Jones cousins were scattered through the rooms, stretched out on pallets made of quilts, taking up most of the floor space. I got up and dragged a quilt over to the floor by the couch where they put Leslie Ray. I thought he was asleep, but he turned toward me so I could hear him.

"I'm gonna go."

"When?"

"Soon as I get well, I'm taking off."

This was not even a new verse in our same old song. We were always going to run away. Our plans to leave started as soon as Leslie Ray came home from the first grade in Americus, Georgia, and sat on the floor next to me in the hallway, the place we'd chosen for our private conversations in the small parsonage, backs against the wall, legs straight out in front of us, dripping juice from fresh tomatoes all over ourselves.

He told about other kids at school, what they wore, what they talked about, and how different we were. We learned other kids didn't travel so much, didn't give away their toys each time they left a place, and they never had to sing on the radio on Saturday mornings. From then on, he always said he had a plan. He didn't really have a plan, but over the years we discussed every possibility for getting away.

It was better to talk about a different life even if we didn't know how to get one. Where would we go? How would we get there? Who would take us in? If someone did, would they let us stay? Of course not. Daddy and Mother would come get us and we'd be right back where we started.

The trip to the emergency room made us ashamed, demonstrating to our relatives that Daddy would risk our lives for some deal between him and his God, something he'd committed us to. This latest vivid example frightened us, proving that though a particular kind of stomachache can send people to the hospital, your parents were allowed to take you home without treatment, even if you didn't want to go home.

Leslie Ray ate a little more each day and eventually he climbed off the couch in Bossier City and into the back seat of the car, and we continued to Gramma K's house in California as the winds of change blew across Route 66 whispering, *Fair warning*.

Chapter 2

California

We would soon be in Glendale, where our Mother and her Mother could add some new colors to the bruises they inflicted on each other during every tearful I-miss-you-so-much-what-do-you-mean-by-that visit.

Leslie Ray didn't say a word more than he had to on the long drive west and the front seat assumed it was because he was still feeling poorly, but I knew otherwise. The back seat where we folded ourselves up tight was crowded with cold, irrefutable anger.

When we traveled The Glory Road on revival tours, our big old cars were gospel tanks for Jesus, enlisted in the war on sin. Since we always headed out stuffed to the top with battle provisions, and though the distance between front and back seats was substantial, we were both so tall now, there was no place for our legs.

Travel, always a source of physical discomfort, was worse this time with Leslie offering no conversation. I scooched over close to the door on my side to give him more room. He answered anything addressed to him, but volunteered nothing that could be construed as neighborly. It's a long way from the Deep South to California when your best friend's not talking to you.

My brother was already using silence as an escape before we stopped in Louisiana, but now the quiet was the kind of withholding that crackled with aggression.

He studied self-control, talked about it, and as a little boy, he boasted to his buddies that he could make himself do anything. He could make himself throw up just by thinking about it, though he hated to do it so much that he only used it in extreme circumstances, such as getting out of church three Sundays in a row.

Within the first hundred miles, Leslie asked Daddy to pull over several times. I didn't know if he was really sick or if he was doing it on purpose. Every time we stopped, Daddy insisted on praying for Leslie's healing, and every time Daddy prayed, Leslie grew more agitated, so whether he willed it or not, he stopped throwing up for the rest of the trip. Daddy thanked the Lord.

When we stopped in Gramma K's driveway, she took a look at Leslie and escorted him inside, leaving the rest of us to straggle after. Gramma didn't have much truck with girls, but the firstborn son of a Southern family was worthy of her time and trouble. If the South should rise again, surely Leslie Ray would be king, and she'd be glad to knit a crown for him.

That is only barely a joke. Gramma could sew anything that needed sewing. Years ago in Arkansas, she had made all her daughter's dresses from donated piece goods and fashioned curtains from anything she could piece together. When her first husband ran off and left her out in the country with three kids, she became a tailor for hire. She could make a whole suit for a man and you would never know he didn't buy it at J.C. Penney. In California, most of her tailoring clients came from expensive men's stores.

We wrangled our suitcases and boxes inside while Gramma made up the front room couch for Leslie Ray with a fresh sheet and topped it off with one of her ugly knitted blankets. As beautiful as her tailoring was, her knitting was the opposite. She patted the spot and motioned for him to lie down.

Mother called me aside and told me to get the car keys from Daddy and go out to the trunk and hide the mate to this blanket, which we'd been using to wrap around the amplifier when we traveled. Our blanket was made by Aunt Birdie, Gramma's sister in Arkansas. The two of them competed in all categories of homemade goods. One of them must have sent the blanket pattern to the other, and it wouldn't do for Gramma to see where ours had ended up.

There were enough of us in constant motion on Route 66 to carry goods back and forth between California and the South so the sisters could sample each other's canning and pickling and quilting and knitting and crocheting. Gramma felt her creative output was superior to Birdie's and often expressed that opinion behind Birdie's back with comments like "I don't know what Birdie was thinking, picking those colors, but she does try."

Gramma announced there was a pot of something on the stove ready for us, biscuits were keeping warm in the oven, and we could help ourselves to the desserts on the big platter on top of the stove. Leslie slept for hours before he ate anything.

After a couple of days he was his usual self when only the two of us were in the room, but when Daddy or Mother came through, he fell back into the habit of keeping his eyes closed when he responded to them. After everybody else went to bed, Gramma stayed in her big chair by the couch where she and Leslie talked in private whispers. Something odd was going on. I fretted over it and couldn't stand not knowing if he was working on some new plan without me, so late one night after Gramma finally went to bed, I crept out and sat on the floor next to him and asked.

"Are you still sick?"

"I don't feel good."

"Do you feel *real* bad or just *some* bad?"

"I'm not getting back in that car. I want to stay with Gramma. She says I can."

"No!"

"Shhhh"

"That's not fair. If you get to stay, I get to."

"They're not gonna let you. You have to sing." He was diplomatically leaving out the other fact, that Gramma hadn't invited me to live in California. Only him. "Go to bed. I'll see if we can both stay here."

I still liked to believe that when he said he was working on a plan, he might really come up with one, so I went off to the rollaway bed on the back porch.

The next day while Gramma was making supper, she called me to the kitchen.

"Nita Faye, come in here and help me. I need you to take the bones out of the chicken in that pot."

The practice in our family was to drop a stewing hen, sometimes whole, sometimes rough-cut into a few large chunks, into a pot to simmer, bones and all. Later, if company was coming, somebody might pick out the bones, but when it was just family, you dished up your chicken and dumplings and either ate around the bones or picked the meat off before you started eating. Having been raised with chicken bones served up with soup or stew or dumplings, I asked who was coming over.

"Nobody. Your brother doesn't like bones in his bowl, so go pick some chicken off for him."

I said to her nicely, while leaning out far enough to show Leslie the eye-roll he deserved, "No m'am. I'm not doing it."

"That's how your brother likes it."

"He can take the bones out then."

"He's been sick."

"He's not that sick."

From the couch, Leslie said, "Gramma. She doesn't need to do that. I can do it."

"Well okay if you feel up to it. Nita Faye, why are you so mean to your brother?"

Leslie Ray was on the couch, clutching a pillow, laughing hard. He threw the pillow at me. I threw it back and landed it perfectly, right on his face. Gramma looked from one of us to the other, and it took a second for her to comprehend that if her favorite grandchild wanted chicken and dumplings with no bones, she'd have to be the one to see to it.

When we set out on this trip weeks before it was with a dual purpose. First, because Gramma K lived in California, we visited when we could, and second (or first, depending on who was making the list) Mother would be performing at a concert. She was booked on the bill with several country and Southern gospel stars at El Monte Legion Stadium, where Cliffie Stone broadcast his *Hometown Jamboree*.

Even though it was on television and Daddy was still working out whether television was a sin, he said yes to the show because his wife was testifying through her music and also because he was crazy about her. Since they'd both found Jesus, their agreement was that no matter where she sang she would carry forth the banner, witnessing by singing the gospel. She had already made the leap into television by singing over at Brother Daly's Tabernacle in New Orleans.

Raising his wife required all the reassurances Daddy could muster and so far it was taking up a good deal of his time on this trip. Gramma was thrilled her daughter would be singing on television in California but no amount of church music was going to be enough for her. Gramma said gospel would never make Mother famous.

Mother was wound up tight about the TV show and that was no small problem. She was high-strung during the best of times. Added pressure sent her spinning off. Her latest concern on this trip seemed to be what to wear.

Since becoming a preacher's wife, Mother's low-cut sweetheart necklines had been raised a bit higher. She brought out one of the dresses under consideration to show Gramma and hung it on the back of the door. Too plain for television, Gramma said. She plunged into a jewelry box on her vanity table and pulled out rhinestone clips. The two of them continued picking through all the sparkle on display. Mother grabbed an especially large piece and attached it to her dress, using the clip to gather the fabric downward, almost back to her former honky-tonk dip.

She looked in the mirror and said, "Could you just D-I-E!"

Gramma held out matching earrings. Big earrings with so many stones they would tax the earlobes of a timid woman. As soon as Mother saw the earrings in Gramma's hand, she snapped.

"Mother! You know I can't wear jewelry. I gave Raymond my word."

"You're not dressing for church right now. You're singing on a program where a lot of stars wear custom outfits. I guaran-damn-teeya every woman there will have on something like this."

There was no denying how much Mother wanted to wear those earrings. Here was my thinking. What I'd have done in her place. I'd have taken that jewelry with me and clipped them on just before singing. Then anybody who wanted to say something about it could just go ahead. It'd be too late. Mother didn't do that.

Every time we stayed awhile at Gramma's house, Daddy managed his mother-in-law, Zula K, with sweet talk about her garden and her special recipes. She didn't like to make breakfast and she relished whatever Daddy offered of a morning, so he made breakfast every day. The two of them turned it into an almost-pleasant ritual.

Mother's nerves took another turn, as they always did, and from the couch Leslie Ray exhibited symptoms of similarly coiled reflexes. His deference to his preacher father, already changing before we left the South, seemed in danger of disintegrating entirely at the slightest provocation. He was snippy with everyone except me and Gramma K. The two of them continued to spend time alone together talking and then falling silent when anyone came near.

I couldn't sense how it came about, and whether it involved Gramma K and Mother or just Daddy and Leslie Ray or which combination of them, but Leslie Ray was denied his request to stay in California.

When we left, he was in the car with the rest of us, but not really. That trip brought our family discord into the open for all to see, but we could have told you everything that happened had been a long time coming.

Gospel Gypsies

Chapter 3

All-Day Singing with Dinner on the Grounds

Hot Springs, Arkansas, 1951

By the summer of 1951, when I was ten and Leslie Ray was twelve, we were sick and tired of being little evangelists. We'd had our fill of traipsing around from state to state in the Deep South performing with Daddy and our unusual Mother.

We had recently been led to believe, no we'd been *promised*, that we wouldn't have to travel anymore, since Daddy had just taken on a new church to pastor in Murfreesboro, less than a hundred miles away. We'd barely unpacked at the parsonage, yet here we were, headed to Hot Springs with a car full of instruments so The Joneses could perform their unique musical selections.

Mother wrote songs with a beat, combining styles into something that soon would be called rockabilly. Daddy brought her from honky-tonks to church and she promised to perform only church music, but even when she sang a hymn, Sister Fern rocked in the name of the Lord. The way she sounded and the way she looked created ripples wherever we went, and at functions like this big Singing, it was always possible that ripples could turn into waves.

By any name, Mother and Daddy's music was becoming more popular, setting in motion an interminable round of Musical Houses. When our parents played it in church, it was called Southern gospel, a distinction used by white people singing the same songs as Black people, who called their church music gospel without the other word attached to it.

Both of them dreamed out loud, so there was no mistaking who wanted what. Mother's dreams were quite specific: a recording contract, a pink Cadillac, and a mink stole. Though Daddy was a performer too, it was clear his heart was in small churches. We were on his side. It was her music, after all, that kept us on the road.

I wouldn't blame you if you saw the loudspeakers on top of the big old sedan that crawled through town and thought to yourself, *There goes some politician trying to get elected.* In our part of the world, people running for office relied on the same methods we gospel crusaders used, so did bail bondsmen and anybody else with something to sell. By now our efforts didn't seem so much the sacred calling Daddy proclaimed as a sideshow to be avoided.

When the speakers began to blare, my brother and I were inside one of those cars, slunk so far down you couldn't see us, our bodies folded as near to flat as we could achieve, kissing the floorboards in an effort to deny any connection to the people in the front seat.

We cringed while our family's name barked out of the speakers, when it was The Joneses trumpeted as the group who'd be appearing at the All-Day Singing at the campgrounds outside Hot Springs. But wait a minute folks, this very day The Joneses will also perform even earlier, at a certain time on a street corner.

We were the parade out in front of the circus, drumming up business for the main event. We were old enough by then to know that not everyone lived the way we did, not even all true believers did. Oddities, that's what we were.

Playing the most portable of our instruments, a guitar and one of the smaller accordions, Brother Ray and Sister Fern opened with a blues-i-fied, country-ish, honky-tonk interpretation of an old hymn, which was immediately rewarded with applause from the crowd, sputtering on long enough that I was almost able to escape, but Daddy began playing the intro to the song I was required to sing, and called out to my retreating back, "Nita Faye, come on up here and sing your song."

By the time I reached the microphone, Leslie Ray had melted into the crowd. He would be blocks away after paying some kid a nickel to hand out the rest of the handbills about the Singing.

I sang "Then Jesus Came," a dramatic song Daddy seemed to find effective when sung by a child. The crowd at this street meetin' said amen and some of them clapped, possibly for me but more likely for Jesus, then Daddy delivered a brief version of his time-is-running-out-for-you-sinners sermon. With the closing prayer finished, Daddy asked, "Do you know where your brother is?"

Before I had a chance to lie, Leslie Ray magically reappeared to break down the equipment and we transported everything to Hot Springs.

In a clearing in the piney woods at the campgrounds, the All-Day Singing with Dinner on the Grounds was already declared a success before a single note was sung. Hundreds of faithful Southern gospel fans packed the tabernacle during the summer heat wave, chatting and fanning and stomping and clapping, stirring up the humid air one way or another while they waited for the music to start.

Rousted from our beds at dawn in the parsonage, we drove in near darkness. Mother, who was rarely awake before late morning, displayed uncharacteristic calm about the early departure time. She responded to Daddy's front seat conversation in a pleasant tone while in the back seat we two young travelers stewed.

My brother and I helped carry our family's accoutrements to the porch behind the huge old wooden building which formed the centerpiece of the Hot Springs Campgrounds. Daddy bounded up the steps ahead of us, clutching a guitar by the neck in each hand. Mother was still out in the car listening to the tail end of "Mona Lisa." He hollered back over his shoulder toward the field where the car was parked.

"Sugar, you better come on now. You run that battery down and we won't be gettin' back home tonight."

If you looked around, you'd see her smile and waggle her fingers at him from the car window. She never left the car while a favorite song was playing and he never expected she would.

I stomped up the plank steps behind Daddy, harboring stormy thoughts and toting the fat leatherette binder that held our music. It was my opinion that nothing good could come from this trip. We hadn't even tuned up yet, and already our presence at this Singing felt like a betrayal.

Leslie Ray grunted no thank you at the men who offered to help him carry the amplifier. He was adept at hauling the heavy brown box up and down stairs without jiggling any of its tubes. He let the amp lean against him at a certain angle when it needed to, turning the delicate speaker cloth inward so it rested on his pants leg, protecting the treble clef that formed the decoration in the front. Dragging his leg up each step with the weight of the amplifier attached, he moved like an old man wearing a cumbersome brace, but if something came loose anyway, he knew how to fix it.

Daddy deposited his guitars, and when he spied friends arriving he hurried toward them, taking the steps two at a time. The greetings, the hoots and hollers, carried up to my brother and me while we set up.

When we met people from outside the South, we were surprised to find they thought we all sounded alike. Every kind of drawl from every part of the Deep South made an appearance at a Singing like this one, represented by evangelists and singers and musicians who traveled several states the way our family did.

Though Daddy and Mother weren't raised all that far apart, the way they said certain words was different. Take the word "your," an example we heard all day every day. When Daddy said to go see what your Mama wants, it came out "yore Mama." When Mother said the same word, it was "yoh-ah." Her language contained very few hard sounds. Words meant to end in an "r" sound were most often missing the "r." She'd call you to bring her a glass of "wah-tuh," even if she was closer to the sink than you were.

Among this group, Brother Cecil Janway and Daddy were the youngest and the two closest friends. Both played instruments and sang. Both were handsome young farm boys turned evangelists who began their ministries at the same time, depending on music and personal charm and religious zeal to bring converts to their Pentecostal sect.

Both of them alternated between traveling and pastoring churches. Preachers and singers and musicians who traveled in revivals were said to be working "The Evangelistic Field." Sometimes that was us. Mother liked this part of our lives best. Preachers who were invited to pastor churches that needed considerable growth or renewed commitment were called "Pioneering Pastors." That's where Daddy excelled.

In his teens, Brother Janway had already set new standards for rowdy hymn playing. Honky-tonk pianists heard about him, went to see him in revivals, and left carrying with them some Cecil Janway trademarks, mimicking the way he jumped up and down off the piano bench and used his elbows once in a while to chase a big fat run all the way down to the other end of the keyboard.

When Daddy waded into the group of colleagues, teasing one, hugging another, lifting the distinguished Reverend Nathan Franks completely off the ground, his enthusiasm turned a gathering into a group of buddies wearing grownup church clothes but acting like kids.

These men were smooth performers and they dressed for it, in pleated slacks and skinny belts, colorful ties over crisp, white shirts, shoes polished to a high gloss. In the heat, most had left off their jackets and still they were a dashing bunch who looked like an Arrow shirt ad, if anybody wanted to line them up in a row and take their picture.

We'd been off the revival circuit for several months and everybody had questions for him.

"You old reprobate. Where you been? We were huntin' for you at the Singing in Biloxi."

Daddy started in with a glowing endorsement of the joys of shepherding his new flock. He talked about the sweet, sweet congregation.

"I feel like the Lord sent me to them. They've been needing a Pentecostal pastor over there."

His pride was unmistakable as he spelled out his personal hopes for our new church. Leslie and I wanted like anything to believe it was true, that the pastoring would become more important than her music. It wasn't her music we minded. It was the moving around that mattered.

Why were we at another Singing today? Why did Daddy bring his guitars to accompany Mother onstage when he'd preached a sermon just last Sunday about blooming where you're planted? Wasn't it Brother Ray himself who recently planted us in Murfreesboro?

He'd join her on a couple of duets, then it would be just her.

A musician asked Daddy, "Where's Sister Fern? We need to get together on her songs."

Brother Daly, pastor of a large and prosperous church in Amarillo where we often conducted revivals, asked, "You got the kids with you? My girl's wantin' to see Nita Faye."

"She's right over yonder." Daddy pointed at me.

I heard him but I didn't turn around and wave at him the way I normally would, the way manners dictated. I was there against my wishes and I meant to make that clear, while avoiding a noticeable break in the rules of behavior, which, when breached, could land you in the car without dinner on the grounds, resulting in an absence of ambrosia or coconut cake or banana pudding, which were the only good parts about being there.

Brother Daly came over anyway.

"You singin' today, Nita Faye?"

"Nossir."

"How 'bout you, Leslie Ray?"

"I don't sing anymore."

He said it as if it was an ordinary answer, when in fact it was a major new development in our family's business. My brother had only recently announced to our parents, "You can't make a person sing."

Any way you turned that sentence around in your head, it was true. From the time my brother closed his mouth tight when he was meant to be singing his part, there were no longer four members of the singing family called The Joneses. Daddy said Leslie was being contentious and asked him to keep his feelings to himself while everybody prayed about it.

Brother Daly turned back to me, not realizing my brother declining to sing was more than a crack in our family's foundation. It was the start of a chasm. No one else seemed fully aware of how angry Leslie Ray really was.

"Well, Nita Faye, we got people all the time asking to hear you sing. You come on back to Amarillo soon as you can."

I said to him "I sure will" the way you answer an invitation you don't plan to accept. I had begun serious consideration about declaring myself no longer a musical warrior for Jesus, in much the way my brother announced his retirement, but though I envied Leslie's temper and certain freedoms he earned with it, I wasn't yet prepared for Daddy's disapproval.

I unzipped the music case and plopped the sides down on an old table somebody had set up and in the process accidentally made a much noisier task of it than was required. Leslie Ray squatted behind the amplifier, rummaging in the pocket in the back, pulling out extension cords and a roll of tape.

"Nita Faye, you better simmer down."

He had recently adopted the language of our elders when correcting me. Some of Mother's music fell to the floor, also probably accidentally, and when I bent to pick it up, I didn't bother to put the songs back in order.

"You're gonna get in trouble."

Firstborn sons in a Southern family were always in charge of the younger ones, even if the age difference between them was less than two years.

"Ig-nernt," I replied.

"*You're* ig-nernt."

Our balance was restored.

Every sound from the grounds behind us funneled toward us, so with my back turned, I knew when Mother was out of the car because conversations changed. Pauses between words grew slightly longer. Good Christian men were allowed to stare, as long as they kept talking while they did it.

They watched her pick her way across the dirt parking area and then through the carpet of pine needles, staying up on her toes to keep her high heels from sinking in as she slowly reached the grassy area where musicians and singers and preachers mingled.

She either did or didn't know how much her back porch swayed when she minced along like that, but she didn't quit walking that way even after her mother pointed it out to her. Gramma K is the one who called it her back porch.

Daddy said not to repeat that and, besides, Gramma's got no business saying such things in front of kids. Still, it seemed that if a woman's own mother mentioned the way she walked and if it was true, well then.

Musicians from all over heard about Singings and stopped by to play. They found each other at these events and formed quick backup bands. Sometimes a musician from a local honky-tonk arrived to play for church folks in the audience who, because they were like the people he came up with, made him feel at home.

Players rotated on and off the stage and all at once there'd be several horns, some fiddles, banjos, mandolins, accordions, harmonicas, tambourines, drums, guitars plugged into any available amplifier, and so many keyboardists they could trade off all day long and not run out of talent. I never heard a single complaint about an excess of musicians. Everybody knew which keys they sang which song in and that seemed to be all any of the performers needed to know.

Musicians who didn't claim to be religious still knew most of the songs performed by well-known Southern gospel quartets. Mother was one of the few singers writing new music, and though she huddled only briefly out on the grounds with some humming and a few minutes spent picking up the chord changes, when she came onstage with these bands, you'd think they'd always worked together.

At every stop we were greeted by prodigal and prodigiously talented homecoming players. Church was often where they first made music, and though music was their ticket to the outside world, they reconnected with the source while they roamed the Southern states just like we did. Church people respected good music, no matter who played it. They put it right up there alongside home cooking and the Word.

Outside, Daddy fell back into old conversations, talking about the business details of a traveling ministry, sharing experiences gathered in cities and small towns and back roads. He was enjoying himself and would stay right there with that bunch, reminiscing until time for the opening song.

In these brief encounters, crucial information about expenses versus income was exchanged. They alerted each other about good and bad host pastors and music promoters, and which radio personalities were most likely to invite you into the studio to play and sing.

We knew the call letters of each station, and whether the studio was located in town or out by the antenna shack. We were on a first-name basis with every disc jockey who admired the kind of music The Joneses played. These men received our photos on Christmas cards and personal notes from Sister Fern, who handled our rolling publicity office from the front seat as we traveled. We spent money we couldn't afford on the occasional long-distance telephone call to let them know when we'd be nearby.

The condition of the roads was the subject of much discussion among the legions who traveled in the Lord's work. Potholes out in the country waited a long time for repair, while legends built up around them, increasing in size with each retelling. According to the storytellers, the roads they traveled boasted potholes big enough to swallow up whole tractors. Touring performers added their tales of axles that snapped late at night on a particularly rough stretch. The skillful navigation required for life in the evangelistic field made it a triumph to arrive at one's destination with both family and vehicle intact.

Daddy reassured us again on the way to Hot Springs that now we were pastor's kids and we wouldn't be traveling bumpy roads in the future. We were only visiting the Singing today because Mother had a new song. By tonight we'd return to our new home.

A few months back we'd moved into the parsonage where in the vacant lot between the house and the church our lives changed. A freshly planted garden grew alongside Leslie Ray's rabbit pens and pigeon cages. We had a chicken coop and a giant weeping willow tree with branches fluttering almost to the ground, creating a cozy space underneath I claimed as a playhouse.

A few steps from these homey installations, in no more than a minute, we could be in church, then turn around and go the other way and walk to school. Such convenience was previously unknown, and this was clearly how we were meant to live. Not in a car. We were not meant to complete homework on the road and send it back to a school where we knew no one. This move happened at just the right time. We needed friends of our own and we were prepared to do battle to stay in that house.

Our town was country all the way from the outer edge where a road led to a creek and back in the other direction to the cluster of buildings around Courthouse Square. It was nothing like the bustle of Texarkana where we kept an apartment as headquarters while we traveled.

As the group of performers outside grew, Mother joined a huddle of famous gospel quartets. She chatted and smiled inside the gathering of harmony singers including The Revelators, famous in the Southern gospel world, and the main reason for the size of the waiting crowd.

Singers emerged from the parking lot carrying their jackets, duplicated in fours and fives in matching colors, some with shiny lapels, some with a strip of sparkle down the side of a sleeve, and the group expanded, milling around, with one after another of the men reluctantly putting on their coats over shirts already damp in the morning heat.

As music makers donned their performing apparel, the cluster of them opened out into one giant flower with petals unfurling in all the colors of the rainbow and Mother in her red jersey dress was the bright and obvious center.

Daddy looked over the heads of his group of evangelists and pastors and beamed at Mother. He motioned for her to join him. There he stood, a tall handsome young preacher looking like Sunday morning, watching his Saturday night wife in her red dress ambling closer.

Daddy called to Leslie Ray and me to come around front with them. We followed reluctantly, impatient to escape our parents and make our way to the other side of the building where food preparations were underway.

Alongside these campgrounds were acres of forest with just enough space cleared to form parking lots, now filled with the cars and trucks that brought hundreds of people here today. It was the large area where food was unloaded that beckoned us. Inhaling the mixture of piney air and the dust kicked up by our Sunday shoes and the familiar fragrance of the best recipes of church cooks, we were intoxicated with the sights and the sounds and the prospect of temporary freedom.

Workers buzzed around long tables made of planks laid across sawhorses. Men carried washtubs of sweet tea. My brother and I yearned to be with the other preachers' kids and musicians' kids and singers' kids and volunteers' kids running up and down the rows, chasing each other, pestering churchwomen for a taste of something, a deviled egg, a chicken wing, a chunk of watermelon.

We waited impatiently while Daddy and Mother read every word on every piece of paper on the bulletin board out front. It wasn't a real bulletin board. Notices were tacked directly onto the side of the building and then a skinny wooden decorative frame was built around them. After too many postings were nailed onto the wood, someone always came along and took pains to arrange them artistically.

Pictures of today's performers occupied the most prominent space in the center, while all around the edges of the photos, scraps of paper were tacked up with appeals for rides to and from other events, with offers of overnight lodging in Christian homes, and on a piece torn off a paper bag, there was a hello from a friend in one town hoping to find someone from another town on the grounds.

Kousin Karl, the most famous disc jockey in the region, befriended Mother a while back, inviting her to sing live on his programs, when the rest of the music he played was from records. He had the final say about booking acts for this Singing. The Joneses were invited early on, and Mother told Gramma K on the phone she'd sent Karl her new picture in case he found a place for her as a solo act.

On the wall was a list of performers and the day's lineup telling when each person would take the stage.

"The Joneses Sing" was the first listing after the midday dinner break. It was a good spot on the bill. Performers at an All-Day Singing didn't want to be the closing act because fans who had a long drive home began filtering out by midafternoon.

There was the same picture of Brother Ray and Sister Fern Jones from the woodcut we used to promote our revivals, the two of them posing with most of the instruments they played, including several guitars splayed out in a semicircle, displayed against their biggest accordion. There was also a new picture of Mother alone, with a starburst drawn around the type announcing, "Special Attraction, Sister Fern Jones."

Staring at her likeness on the side of the building, she whispered to Daddy, "Honey, look!" She wrapped her arms around his chest and laid her head against his double-breasted seersucker suit. He rested his cheek on her curls and patted her on her back porch.

Chapter 4

The Joneses Sing

Kousin Karl took the stage and the crowd shook off their post-dinner torpor, ready to be entertained. He welcomed everyone back and made a few announcements, ending by reminding us there'd be plenty of food left out there at suppertime, then after the crowd rustled and scraped and quieted some, he hollered, "Ladies and gentlemen—THE JONESES!"

Daddy called out the key to the pickup band. A piano player started off and the crowd laughed as they caught on to what was happening. Brother Janway eased in from the side, chasing the first piano player away. He bounced around, playing some boogie-woogie first, then slid into the intro to the familiar song Daddy and Mother were about to sing.

Daddy paced, guitar strap slung over one shoulder, strumming and grinning as he walked over to the piano shaking his head, pretending to be shocked at Brother Janway's antics. The two buddies always had fun up there and their schoolboy foolishness had everyone smiling.

When Mother joined Daddy onstage, he moved over next to her and leaned in so close it looked like he was about to kiss her, then he stepped away again, always in motion before returning to share the mic with her. They started off on one of Daddy's favorites, "By and By," with Mother taking the lead and him singing harmony.

Daddy was always a crowd-pleaser yet it appeared to be accidental. He never held on to a note any longer than he had to. When Mother sang alone, she laid every ounce of emotion she could muster into a note before sending it out to the audience.

They finished their duet and it was time for her solo. The band kept vamping but she didn't jump in right away. She whispered to Daddy and he said something to the other musicians and then they launched into the introduction to her newest song.

She usually started off a solo spot with familiar songs first, like "Precious Lord," but I recognized the opening bars to "Keeps Me Busy," a song she'd been writing and rewriting late at night. As soon as she began the first verse, Brother Janway got everybody clapping and bouncing around in their seats.

Mother grinned at him and egged him on and then the people in the crowd closest to the edges of the stage kept getting louder. People in back stretched around to see what the commotion was about. There was movement from the steps made of rough planks that rose straight from the pine needles to deposit performers onstage. Striding up these steps, two on each side, wearing their matching jackets, came the famous Revelators Quartet!

These stars who'd already finished their performance should have been on their way to their next show but they waited to join in on Sister Fern's number. This kind of collaboration only happened with big names and she wasn't that big yet. I wondered how Mother had managed it. You could never tell how she worked these things out, but eventually you came to believe she always would. She was about to sing a song she'd just written and her backup singers were one of the most famous quartets on the circuit.

Stars like The Revelators performed just before the midday meal then rushed outside to sell merchandise. They had to, to keep their heads above water in their chosen profession. They gobbled a plate of food, complimenting the cooks who hung around nearby, then disappeared as soon as they'd sold enough sheet music and photographs. Even when admissions were paid at these events, ticket prices were low, and with the number of acts, there wasn't much to divide once the utility bills were paid.

As the crowd returned inside for the afternoon performances, the headliners' friends and family members broke down their display tables. Even the youngest children carried boxes and stowed them in the trailers parked nearby, and as soon as they were done selling and signing, they took their leave, carrying plates of food and mason jars of sweet tea the churchwomen pressed on them. But not this time. Today The Revelators were onstage, ready to sing two by two at their mics. Mother had her own spot in the center. She sang and The Revelators answered back.

Just can't catch up with my praises to the Lord

To the Lord

His blessings never ever are a few

Not a few

He keeps me day by day, He answers when I pray

The Revelators clustered together then, looking at a small piece of paper one of them held. Of course. They didn't know the words.

Here they came, all of them together, Mother and the handsome men in their shiny coats.

And He will surely do the same for you

She took a step back from the microphone, always an indication she was fixing to let loose.

Wellllllllll

The crowd roared right back at her. She sang.

Keeps me busy

The Revelators kept up with her all the way, singing first harmony then unison, clapping and grinning, all of them and Mother together sounding just like a record on the radio.

Busy busy
Countin' my blessings
Keeps me busy busy busy thanking the Lord

The song that started out bouncy was about to end up downright rowdy. A guitar player stepped over toward Mother to take a solo, filling the tabernacle with his blues style, volume turned up, sounding like every honky-tonk he played. The drummer kept pouring on the flourishes. Brother Janway was grinning and messing around way down at the end of the keyboard, making impressive runs through the high notes and lingering there for a while during the applause.

Mother and The Revelators had to keep singing the ending over and over because the crowd kept demanding it. Then they had to start over and sing the whole thing again and by then the crowd was singing it with them.

Chapter 5

Afterglow

Every musician still present at the end of the long day participated in playing one or two favorite hymns so we could sing ourselves out the door.

Hundreds of us sang "Precious Memories" standing up, reaching over for a stranger's hand, swaying.

Precious Memories, how they linger
How they ever flood my soul
In the stillness of the midnight
Precious sacred scenes unfold

A preacher pronounced the benediction and reminded us to be sure to pick up our dishes before heading home. Daddy was in a hurry to leave. He urged us toward the car. We said bittersweet goodbyes to people we knew from our touring lives, to church people we'd met in revivals, and to preachers and singers and musicians and evangelists who treated us like their own when we came to their towns. Saying goodbye was always sad, but this time there was something to look forward to at the end of our trip. We had our own house to return to instead of a motor court or an apartment.

We were all tired, but the two of us in the back seat weren't relaxed, not after Sister Fern's big success we'd just witnessed. Daddy had accepted the new pastorate with his wife in full agreement, we thought, and he'd tell anyone who was interested that yes, Sister Fern certainly was settling into being a fine pastor's wife. How, then, to explain the conversation in the front seat on the way home?

Mother asked, "Raymond, do you think my hair looked frizzy today—all this humidity?"

Daddy answered the way he always did.

"No, Sugar, your hair's not frizzy. It's curly is all."

He paused and turned to give her a sweet look.

"You've got beautiful doll baby curls."

I was busy with my usual travel diversion, a grocery bag filled with paper dolls I could dress anywhere. At the back of every *McCall's* magazine was a page devoted to Betsy McCall. I carefully cut out the Betsy printed each month, which I pasted onto cardboard. The clothes for her were so tiny, it took painstaking devotion to prepare those dolls for travel with their wardrobes.

As an experienced gospel traveler, I could change them into several outfits with a degree of expertise, and even include the smaller pieces such as a nurse's cap and shoes, without losing an accessory or missing a word of the conversation from the front seat. In addition to my paper dolls, my bag held a perfumed handkerchief, which both Gramma K and Mother insisted I have with me at all times, and extra bobby pins for the ones that would wiggle their way out of my hair during the day.

Leslie Ray toted his own diversions. He picked up one of his funny books, and even though it was nearly dark, he started to read. In a while, he would lay the book down and pick up his drawing pad. He and Mother were both good drawers and both were secretive about what they were putting onto paper. As we moved on toward dusk, I could hear Leslie Ray better than I could see him.

His pencil scraped, and his gum eraser whooshed. Scratch, scratch, brush, brush, brush. I could see the side of his hand moving, impatient, wanting his work to be perfect, faster. No use asking what he was drawing. If I asked, he'd say none of your beeswax, but later, in a day or two, at home I'd find his pad laying open and that meant wherever I found it, even if I went nosing around in his room uninvited, it was okay to see it and mention it.

Daddy returned to church talk.

"I'm plumb tickled Brother Booty and Sister Coker came today. They're not used to having a pastor traveling around to Singings. I'm mighty proud of our little congregation."

Leslie Ray said, "Brother Booty thinks Mother's pretty."

Mother was delighted.

"No! Did he say that?"

I said, "I like Sister Coker. She let me have ambrosia before dinner."

Leslie Ray hissed, "Ig-nernt. Don't tell them that."

In the hush of the prolonged summer dusk, nobody spoke for a while.

Then Daddy said, "I can't wait to get home."

He was going over his day-before-the-Lord's-Day list.

"Nita Faye? Pay attention now. You've got communion cups to fill tonight. Leslie Ray, don't you have some shoes to polish before church tomorrow?"

"Yessir," each of us mumbled, because we were required to acknowledge all communications aimed at us by any adult. We didn't need reminding. Church rituals were also our family's personal rituals. There was no such thing as being off duty.

Every Saturday night was given over to Sunday. All was preparation for the Sabbath. Whether we were traveling in revivals or pastoring a church, we preacher's kids had a list of chores to help prepare both the family and the worship structure. Daddy schooled us in those functions before we knew what any of them meant. By now we could set up a church or tent or storefront for any kind of service.

Mother said, "Hon, did you see Kousin Karl talking to me? He says the people in Hot Springs loved my music. He wants me to sing my new songs on *Kousin Karl's Korral*. He's got so many listeners!"

And there it was, what we were afraid we'd hear if Mother performed at today's Singing. It took all the fun out of the day and it knocked the wind out of us, thinking what could happen if the front seat conversation kept going along those lines.

Mother wanted to start singing away from home again. She said so to everybody, no matter how often Daddy gently reminded her that a preacher's family needed to be keeping some things private.

This life our Mother wanted, we couldn't let it happen. After living in the parsonage for just a few months, our lives had changed irrevocably. Leslie Ray and I each had a room of our own. We had freedom to roam around town. We saw the same faces every day. We worked in the garden with Daddy, something we had seldom done before.

In the back seat, I was near panic. I couldn't see Leslie Ray's face in the dark anymore, but I knew he was paying equally close attention.

Daddy said, "Sugar, *Kousin Karl's Korral* is all the way in Little Rock. Now how'm I gonna preach in Murfreesboro and get you to a radio program in Little Rock? I got old people and sick people to visit. I can't be taking all that time away from church. We talked about this. We decided we can't be singing out of town all the time. Our congregation's too new."

She put on her pout.

"They like my songs, Raymond. I've been working so hard to get them to hear my songs. I'm just gonna have to learn to drive, that's all there is to it."

She turned around.

"Leslie Ray, is my hair frizzy in the back? Leslie Ray! Are you reading funny books again? I don't think a preacher's boy ought to be reading funny books."

"Daddy reads the funny papers."

"Boy, what I read in the newspaper is none of your . . ."

Leslie Ray pretended he didn't hear him, but he put down his funny book and talked directly to Mother, duplicating almost exactly the tone Daddy used with her, but leaving out the sweet look.

"Your hair's not frizzy in the back. No ma'am."

He lifted a chunk of her long curly hair, which had fallen over the back of the seat and held it up for her to see.

"See? These are curls, not frizz."

"Well it *feels* frizzy."

She rummaged around in the satchel on her lap.

"Here Leslie Ray. Take this Vaseline and put some in the back of my hair. Rub it between your hands real good first."

He groaned.

"Moooother . . . make Nita Faye do it. She's a girl."

I asked her, "Why don't you quit trying to plaster it down and just let it fluff up if it wants to?"

Her head whipped around so fast it took both Leslie Ray and me by surprise. Her tone of voice lashed.

"Did your Grandmother say that to you? Did she?"

"No m'am," I lied.

"Gramma K didn't say a thing about your hair."

Of course we lied about Gramma. It didn't take much to see the advantage in being on her side. We were unhappy where we were and she was unhappy with the choices her daughter made, so Gramma was our perfect ally.

"Your Gramma's always been jealous of my hair."

She faced forward again and took in a jaggedy breath.

Leslie Ray whispered, "You stupid idiot. Now you got her started."

Indeed, Mother began to uncoil an old story dipped in venom.

"Made me cut off every bit of it when I was twelve for no reason, made me take the scissors to my own hair."

She paused to sniffle as she fished out from her lap a pretty handkerchief edged in bright pink crochet, a gift from the same Gramma she denounced. The sniffles always accompanied the telling. They came at different points in the story, but they always came. Nothing was required yet from anyone in the car, nor was there any need to check to see what Daddy was doing. He was looking straight ahead without expression, acting as if he hadn't heard this story a million times.

"My hair was beautiful. People said so all the time. That woman will do anything to make my life miserable. The devil's got ahold of her with the drinking and cussing and card playing and dancing. Now she's turning my own children against me. And me trying to do the Lord's work. She's plain hateful. Hateful. Every time we let you kids go stay with your Gramma, you come home acting like heathens—"

Was she going to add our last California visit onto her hair story? What did she know about it anyway? Neither of us had said a word about anything that happened.

"—just like heathens. Lord knows we'd rather leave you in a good Christian home but you'd think your own flesh and blood would respect the way you're raising your kids."

Mother hadn't brought up our recent stay in California in a while, and whenever she did, we were on guard, because it was all true. What our Mother was speculating about really had happened. Gramma led us down her sinful path to our everlasting delight, then encouraged us to lie about it.

In the front seat, Mother was on to other topics.

"Raymond, do you think Kousin Karl was flirting with me?"

"Well who wouldn't, Doll Baby?"

A subtle change in tone alerted the back seat. Mother was using her cozy voice with Daddy but there was serious intent now.

"Raymond, honey, we should hold revivals again. Go back into evangelistic work."

And there it was, her campaign declared.

"You know we can't do that, Sugar. We just now took on this new assignment. We've got a lot of building to do."

"But honey, think how many more souls you can bring to the Lord in revivals. You know how many people come down to the altar and get saved when you preach."

She laid it on thick, in language he liked to hear.

"And so many healings and people filled with the Holy Ghost. And baptisms."

He sounded weary. The back seat paid attention. If Daddy got tired of resisting and if she persisted, then we knew the whole plot of this story, start to finish. We'd lived through it before when we pastored awhile then hit the road again leaving everything behind. During an extended visit at Gramma's house, where the two of us stayed for months while our parents traveled, we heard her interpretation and nothing about it was reassuring. Gramma K said the more Mother sang, the more people wanted her to sing, and touring was the only way singers get to be well known enough to get a record contract, and when they get their contract, they have to tour some more. Revivals were the religious equivalent of a tour schedule. That was how Mother became a favorite in person and on the radio. The more revivals we held, the more we traveled. The more we traveled, the more fans were introduced to Sister Fern.

Revivals meant saying goodbye and every goodbye was more painful. As soon as we adjusted to a new town, new school, new friends, we lost them when we drove away. We now recognized Mother's ambition as the biggest threat to the life we wanted to live.

I had my own room now and cans of paint to turn it whatever color I wanted it to be. Leslie Ray had his animals out back and was running a clandestine used funny book business. We each had a door of our own we could close when we wanted to. These small gains imparted a sense of dignity to our lives that we couldn't define, but that we knew we didn't have before.

The new pastor asked his wife, "And who would take care of our church?"

"Well, Cecil Janway could do it for a while. Yes! Raymond! Brother

Janway! Everybody loves him. He plays our kind of music. He could hold a revival for a few weeks while we travel. Or Brother Thompson. The way he plays guitar—it'll be just like we were there. And we can trade pulpits with them later—pay them back."

It came out all in a rush, but we knew Mother had thought about this, planned on it, turned it every which way in her mind, and above all, she knew who she was dealing with and just how to approach him.

When we asked our parents why we had to be evangelists and travel all the time, the answer was they were called to preach the gospel wherever God led them. We told Daddy many times that we were very sorry it was our particular family the Lord called on so often.

Daddy didn't take long to respond to Mother's suggestion.

"Naw, Doll Baby, pastoring's what we're doing right now."

"But all I said was I agreed to settle down while—"

"Sugar," he warned, "I have asked you not to talk about that in front of—"

She was about to begin again, but he cut her off.

"Fern. Hush. We can't travel right now."

We were rapt. He said Fern. Not Doll Baby or Sugar or My Little Elberta Peach or Big Eyes or Mama-gal. Daddy seldom called her by her name and he seldom called her down in front of us. This time he said Fern and she paused. He said hush and she did.

I didn't have to guess what Gramma K would think about this turn of events. All I had to do was be still and Gramma would repeat it again, right there in my head.

Pay attention, Hotshots. She's not done yet. When your Mama wants your Daddy to change his mind, she'll find a way. They only stopped traveling because of her condition. Soon as she's feeling better, you kids'll be yanked out of school again, you wait and see.

We heard "her condition" but paid it no mind since it was unlikely we could distinguish a medical need from her mercurial behavior we'd seen often over the years. Besides, we were consumed with our own situation.

I whispered to Leslie, "I'm not going. We just planted the garden. If they say we're moving again, I'm running away."

Gramma chimed in, crowding into the back seat with her warnings.

Your Mama's gotta sing, and she needs to be up there in front of more people than you've got in that little bitty church. She'll figure out a way to get your Daddy out of there.

I said to Leslie Ray, out loud this time, "When we get home, I'm going over to the Cokers' house. She's bringing home some supper for us from the Singing."

"No you're not. I'm going."

"Nuh-uh. I am."

Daddy said, "I don't want either one of you crossing that field after dark. There's snakes in that field."

While we sorted out our individual yearnings, a storm snuck up on us. Thunder rumbled loud. Lightning cracked. Mother shivered and scooted over closer to Daddy. She was afraid of storms.

Daddy said, "I'd just as leave you two get on with your chores. It's fixin' to start in raining good and hard. I'll drop y'all off at home and then *I'll* go over to the Cokers'."

I poked Leslie Ray.

"What?"

He sounded annoyed but he was still a conspirator in the dark. We whispered again but we didn't need to. After years of riding in back seats we knew they didn't always listen to our conversations. From my brother I sought reassurance we both knew he couldn't guarantee.

"You swear?"

"Swear what?"

"We're not leaving?"

"I already *said*. We're not leaving. She might go to Little Rock or Hot Springs to sing on the radio, but we're not going on the road anymore."

"Swear."

With his face turned toward the dark outside the car window so I couldn't tell for sure what he was thinking, he said, "I *swear*." Then he asked, "What kind of gum you got?"

"Juicy Fruit. What kind've you got?"

He said Dubble Bubble and he gave me some.

Chapter 6

Little Sinners

Glendale, California, 1950

Our Mother and her Mother didn't like each other. We didn't know how or when the feuding between them began. We were born into it. It was as immutable a circumstance of our birth as our red hair or where we lived or what our family did for a living or how Mother and Daddy's love affair affected our lives.

Mother and Gramma K talked bad about each other to everybody else then cried real tears whenever a car took off with one inside, headed away from the other one. They sought each other's company and after each visit they decimated the memories they'd just created. Battle lines between Gramma K and Sister Fern were drawn, and whichever way you turned, you'd better step lively or you'd find yourself knee-deep in their mess.

Mother's explanation for Gramma K was "the devil's got ahold of her," but Mother eventually said that about each member of the family in turn. She always seemed fairly knowledgeable about what the devil was up to.

Fate does seem to love a twist and even the youngest person in the back seat could appreciate the next turn of events. When Leslie was eleven and I was nine, someone looked at our school records and told our parents we couldn't keep mailing in homework from the road. So far a generous description of our education would be "sketchy." We pastored in Arkansas, then went on the road again, pastored in Georgia, then got back on the road, pastored in Texas, then left again. Though we registered in several schools, we didn't spend much time in any of them.

We did our homework at kitchen tables in motor courts or in the homes of pastors and mailed the work back to teachers. They sent new assignments to our post office box in Texarkana where a friend sent them to us general delivery in whatever town we'd visit next.

When the edict came down declaring we had to stay in a classroom for a while, it was the first time we'd ever heard of anyone in authority giving instructions to a preacher. In our world, preachers had the final say. Daddy and Mother discussed options while we whispered in suspense, wondering how this situation could possibly be resolved. Where would we go to school?

Gramma K turned out to be the only relative who'd agree to take in two kids and get them to school every day, so our parents set out with us on Route 66 to drop us off in Glendale, California, at the home of a woman who liked to have a good time in a much different fashion than they condoned.

Gramma was the leader of our dissenters' choir, head of our Greek chorus, so of course we believed she would also be the solution to our problems. We were ecstatic when Daddy and Mother informed us that, against their wishes, we would be separated from them for quite a while.

Our growing discontent was fanned into a conflagration during that stay. The months we spent in California forever widened the gap between us and them. At Gramma's house, we witnessed much of what Daddy preached against every Sunday, cocktails and dancing and card playing and cigarette smoking and cussing, and we enjoyed every minute of it.

During our short family visits to California through the years, Daddy maintained equanimity, chiming in only when matters of sin were concerned, but we were certain if he knew the details of our new everyday life in Glendale, he would be likely to abandon his efforts at peacemaking with his mother-in-law and yank us out of there immediately.

Daddy and Gramma K treated each other with grudging respect. They both liked growing things, and because Daddy was the best gardener, Gramma deferred to him, seeking his advice about the large patch in her Southern California backyard that wasn't supporting the crops she wanted.

They were equally accomplished cooks. Both came from poor Southern families and knew how to turn nothing into something delicious. After Daddy moved away from his own sharecropping family, he went to Roosevelt's CCC camps, then worked as a cook until he announced his new calling.

During every visit to California, Brother Ray and Zula K cooked together, and when Mother wasn't present, if you squinted just so, you might even think they were friends. Daddy was a born diplomat and Gramma wrapped herself in the raiment of the Southern Flirt whenever she chose. When it was just the two of them in the kitchen without Fern, as long as the subject of religion was avoided, it could be downright pleasant to wander in there while they held forth.

The months we were scheduled to stay at Gramma's without our parents promised a happy eternity. The prospect of living in the home of an actual sinner would be the most glorious feature of our respite. On Route 66 as we drove closer to California, the future we imagined was illustrated on billboards. Citrus-colored signs suggested life could be rows of palm trees and giant bowls of native-grown, plucked-from-your-own-backyard California fruits and dates, and everything was surrounded by ocean.

For our arrival, Gramma made her famous fried pies, but instead of the usual abundance of peach and apple we were used to in the South, there were fragrant half circles of golden crust, crimped and crispy around the edges, filled with apricots, cooling on the shelf above the burners of her new O'Keefe & Merritt stove.

Gramma's stove was the center of life on Raymond Avenue. It was the most beautiful stove we'd ever seen, a giant fit for royalty, with two ovens, a griddle down the middle, and every surface that wasn't meant for cooking was white and shiny, polished until it glowed. The apricots were proof a confirmed Californian was in charge. Nobody in the South made apricot fried pies.

The minute our parents told us goodbye, Gramma declared herself unbound from their rules. She started in immediately about how she didn't agree with the way they raised their children. We were thrilled to hear it. We didn't agree either. This trip couldn't have happened at a better time. We'd packed our suitcases with a list of complaints about life on the road and a bunch of questions for Gramma about how it got that way.

Gramma K preferred to believe she didn't drink at home, but every evening she eased into her big chair in front of the TV and implored one of us to pour her a little Mogen David wine from the bottle under the sink. She kept special sets of tumblers for this purpose, with the names of Las Vegas casinos on the side, collected over many weekend gambling trips.

"All I want is a little taste. Be sure to put some water in it."

We learned immediately that if we left out the water, family secrets flowed faster.

"Thanks, Hotshot." (We were both "Hotshot.") "Know why your Mother hates me?"

Leslie was older and quicker.

"She doesn't *hate* you."

"Oh I know she talks behind my back. Your Mother blames me for everything. Because I divorced your Grandaddy. Well I had to work and I needed her to take care of her sister and brother. She hated staying home with them. She tells people I was a roundheel, running around with this one and that one."

"What's a roundheel?"

"I'll tell you later. Acting like I didn't have a right to have a date once in a while. Go pour Gramma a little more and put some water on top."

It was my turn to refresh her glass and Leslie had taught me how.

"They want to go gallivanting all over the place and the school tells them you two'd better show up, so here they come, bringing you to California."

That stung.

I said, "But we *like* to stay with you, Gramma. Don't you *want* us to stay here?"

Leslie Ray said, "This is my favorite place in the whole world. I'm going to the picture show every day. I wish I could live here."

This was what she wanted to hear. Leslie Ray, firstborn son in our family, was the prize. The competition for his favor between Mother and her Mother grew each year. It was a fact he knew and I knew. He neither sought it nor exploited it and therefore I couldn't blame him for it.

"Well, I would *love* that, Hotshot."

He wanted to leave his parents' home and live with her. She won this round.

"But I'm *sure* your folks would miss you a *lot*."

She might have thought she was sounding generous, but it didn't come out that way. In fact it came out sounding so put-on a toddler could spot it.

Chapter 7

Queen of the Southern Transplants

Gramma was very young and very poor when her children were born in Arkansas. Both Gramma and Fern were in their teens when they started having their babies, and Gramma was still not anywhere close to matronly.

She acted like a young girl, teasing every man she encountered. We could see how Mother might have followed the same path had she not fallen in love with a poor country boy who wanted to be a preacher and therefore her every smile, every move was closely observed.

Gramma enjoyed hearing people say "Zula, this can't be your daughter." She reminded people she was in her teens when she had Mother. Our Mother enjoyed hearing people say "Sister Fern, you can't possibly have a son this big!" Leslie Ray was tall, which at first glance made him appear more mature. Mother liked to remind everyone she was only sixteen years older than him. Daddy liked to add, "And now I'm raising both of you." Mother and Daddy always laughed at this exchange and we didn't.

Gramma K and Mother both kept a distance from other women. They employed Southern-speak with liberal uses of "bless your heart" and "aren't you precious to think of me." In our family, women who felt a need to say something mean couched it in ways that transmitted both sugar and heat so the listener would feel unable to complain about the one without tossing out the other. Gramma K could have taught classes.

These two powerful women saved their best performances for men. Each of them received a good deal of attention and craved even more. Both of them were curvy. Gramma, at 5'7", said she'd been the tallest woman at normal school, where in the 1920s she studied to be a teacher. Fern, at 5'11", could have been carved on the prow of a Viking ship.

Gramma didn't resemble any grandmothers we encountered in church circles. She was divorced. We didn't know another divorced person, and having one in our own family was thrilling. It was something we bragged about until Daddy heard about it and reminded us divorce was a sin.

Gramma K wasn't the beauty Fern was, but she was a handsome woman who enjoyed all the frippery Mother had dispensed with in the name of religion. Gramma favored bold colors and sparkly jewelry. Her hair was thick and wavy, cut short in a chic modern do exactly the opposite of Mother's, whose curls were bobby-pinned in front into the shape of a heart, or as close as she could get them on a humid day.

Gramma was never seen in public without full makeup and red polish on her fingers and toes. She wore high heels and didn't leave home without a spritz of Prince Matchabelli Potpourri or her other favorite fragrance, White Shoulders.

We were, of course, eager to find out more about what regular sinners did on a day-in, day-out basis, and any Sunday at Gramma's house was a good place to start. She lit up her Lucky Strikes. When music started, she danced right where she was standing, with one hand on a hip and the other wagging a finger in the air, executing a slip-sliding, hip-shaking dance she called truckin'. She moved from the kitchen stove to the back porch pantry and back again without losing track of the rhythm or the pot she was stirring. If a man walked into one of her dancing moods, he'd need to stay long enough to twirl her around before she'd feed him supper.

She had a good singing voice like all the people on both sides of the family. When Gramma K visited us in the South, she went to the radio station with us and appeared on the family show. When we were at her house, we sang Ink Spots and Mills Brothers hits with her, and she taught us the words to every blues song about anybody who was ever done wrong. Her favorite was "St. Louis Blues," because she said, every word was true.

If it hadn't-a been for powder and all that store-bought hair
That man of mine, he wouldn't-a gone nowhere
Got the Saint Louis Blues, just as blue as I can be
Cause that man's got a heart like a rock cast in the sea

She sang that right in front of Uncle Jim, her second husband, the one who hadn't done her wrong. His reaction was to puff on his pipe and smile. James Kalbaugh, with his cardigans and cultivated manners, claimed to enjoy her wit and seldom reacted to her rants. One of her favorite targets was her first husband, Charlie Salisbury, who fooled around on her. Though that happened so long ago, she'd already divorced him and moved to California before we were born, she still talked about it.

Uncle Jim dealt with his wife in his own way. He traveled a lot. He had legitimate reasons sometimes, but he seemed to decide that extended absences were good for the marriage. He was a claims advisor, traveling to mining locations, often abroad. Sometimes he came home and handed Gramma checks for thousands of dollars, but when he hadn't done so in a while, we all heard about it.

From his favorite chair he watched our comings and goings with his mean Chihuahua, Pedro, in his lap. Pedro snarled at everyone for committing the sin of walking by. He especially didn't like Gramma leaning too close to her husband, so of course she made sure to do that.

Uncle Jim never participated in conversations that included negatives about our parents, and we knew how difficult that must be, living right there next to the woman who initiated so much of it. Peaceable, that's what he was, and we appreciated him for that.

Zula K was only accidentally and occasionally grandmotherly, and only offered a glimpse of that when she was in her kitchen, cooking and feeding Southerners who migrated to California. She wasn't a clasp-you-to-her-bosom grandmother. Her apron wasn't meant to inspire an image of feminine kitchen rituals, but rather to protect fancy dresses from cooking endeavors. She stirred and simmered and baked awhile, then burst out through the dining room door, truckin', flirting with the brother-in-law of some Southern relative who'd recently arrived and was told to look up Zula as soon as you can.

She kept a party going every Sunday afternoon. Her house in Glendale was the first stop when you arrived on the West Coast. She stayed in touch with all our relatives from the South and kept track of which suburbs the transplants occupied. If you wanted to know where Virgie's girl from Odessa went, ask Zula K. She'd give you Mildred's address and phone number and a bit of gossip about Mildred's last relationship. Hint: He was a no-account and good riddance.

She was the supplier of references for all Southern transplants. Her phone book, a metal oblong with a slider that pointed to every letter in the alphabet, got a lot of attention. Stop the sliding tab on any letter, the top would pop open, and you'd discover a resource.

Relatives on Mother's side were settling in from Pasadena to Ventura, with a few sprinkled around in Orange County, and anyone newly arrived from the Deep South could be found wherever Gramma's phone book pointer stopped.

She welcomed them all, turning out homemade noodles cut into strips which Leslie Ray and I draped to dry on cheesecloth hung over the backs of chairs. There was roast pork with smoky barbecue sauce, cornbread and sage dressing, fried okra, chicken and dumplings, our favorite fried pies, and dark dense gingerbread she made with blackstrap molasses smuggled into California from the South. Every Sunday Gramma's house filled with magnificent aromas and every corner was occupied by someone who drawled the way we did.

Every week we took in the same show. When she was done preparing a huge meal, she urged a roomful of people to come on in and serve themselves. Everyone filled bowls and plates and found places to sit in the dining room or living room, and still Gramma was in the kitchen.

Someone called to her.

"Zula, come on in here and eat with us."

"Oh, y'all go on ahead. Start without me. I'm just going to finish up a couple of things and then I'll sit down."

She wouldn't take a bite until after the next portion of her show. She singled out a man in the room, generally the one person she wasn't sure was in love with her yet. She walked over to him as he ate.

"How is it?"

She wiped her hands on her apron, giving the appearance of awaiting this important person's opinion.

"It's good, Zula, real good."

"Are you sure? Does it have enough salt? Because I might not have put in enough . . ."

She leaned forward to watch him take another bite.

"No, it doesn't need a thing."

Now she executed some rather startling eye-to-eye contact.

"I'd be so proud to know *you* enjoyed it."

"Oh I do. I do."

The two of them, the cook and the food appreciator, occupied a bubble together for a moment, and a nearby wife didn't take offense because she didn't know she should. Gramma attracted men everywhere she went.

Our Mother was pretty and had an outstanding figure and she didn't have to work to be noticed, but like her Mother, she was aware of who was and wasn't paying attention at any time, and once in a while she might send a little extra effort in a specific direction, displaying something approximating vulnerability, which didn't match the drive and ambition and iron will of either of these women we knew.

We watched Gramma K and Mother engage in similar performances, and we talked about it when we were alone, but it didn't affect us much until later, when the two of them turned disturbingly serious in their competition for the one male in their lives who was most difficult to persuade, who was not prepared to be anyone's prize. Leslie Ray had his own plans.

Chapter 8

Truths and Dubious Wisdom

When something needed to be decided and Gramma said, "Go build us a pot of coffee," it was likely we were eventually going to hear a yes and she was teasing us, asking for one more thing then one more thing, postponing doling out the good news. We raced each other to the kitchen to make the coffee.

She always took her coffee in a favorite cup, with sugar and cream. She stirred and tasted, then sent one of us back to the kitchen to get her one of those biscuits from this morning. She told Leslie Ray, go slice me an onion real thick. He asked, regular or Vidalia? Always Vidalias when she could get them.

We returned with a hefty biscuit, spread with butter, salt and pepper, and a thick slice of onion served on one of the flowery saucers she collected. Only after she sipped a bit would she announce a plan for the day. It might be that we would go to Bob's Big Boy on Colorado Boulevard and eat supper in the car with the tray attached to our window. Or maybe tomorrow we would spend the day at Bullock's Wilshire and have lunch at Van de Kamp's, or on the weekend we might go to Knott's Berry Farm, or the two of us could go to the picture show at the Alex Theatre. Sometimes the good news would be that Uncle Jim and Gramma K would take us grocery shopping late at night at Bill's Ranch Market in Burbank, a place we loved so much, a grocery list could occupy hours.

She promised to keep taking us places and showing us things if we swore not to tell. Of course we swore. Many of our activities were the subjects preached against by Reverend Jones. Gambling, for instance, according to Daddy, was on a long list of iniquities invented by the devil to tempt us. Gramma loved to bet the horses. She read the Green Sheet and believed everyone should learn to handicap. We went with her to Hollywood Park and Santa Anita.

Some Saturdays we stayed at the Alex on Brand Boulevard through multiple showings of every picture show, until Uncle Jim pulled up in front to collect us. We watched the same movies so many times we lost count. *Cinderella* came out that year and I loved it, but equally important were movies that allowed me to consummate my filmic relationship with Mr. Gene Autry by sitting in a picture show watching him on the screen.

Some weekends all we wanted to do was watch television. Contrary to

Daddy's predictions, we did not feel the fires of hell lapping at our backsides while we sat on the floor for hours with our faces pointed toward the glowing box. Leslie liked to watch Gorgeous George wrestle. I watched Spade Cooley or *Hometown Jamboree* on Saturday nights. Uncle Jim asked if I wanted to sing on TV like Molly Bee and the answer was no, I don't but Mother does.

Though our parents performed only religious music in public, we were allowed to sing anything we wanted at home and in the car. We learned every new song as soon as it came on the radio, and despite Daddy preaching against television, Mother set a goal for herself of bringing one of her own songs to a show in California. She offered many arguments to Daddy on this subject while we toured. He never told her a for-certain no, but he repeated that television was not in the same business as our family.

Mother called us up in California every week, excited to find out if the songs we were listening to were the same as what she was hearing.

"What's playing on the radio out there? Tell me all of them."

"'Slow Boat to China,' 'Dear Hearts and Gentle People,' 'My Foolish Heart,' 'Harbor Lights'—"

"Which version?"

"Bing Crosby."

"Do you know it yet?"

"Sure."

"Let me hear what key you're in."

I sang the first line.

"Just a second," she said, then she found the key and strummed her guitar. "Okay, keep going."

I sang the next line, and before I came to the end of the phrase, she joined in with a harmony part and we finished the song on the telephone. If this sounds like a girlfriend talking to a girlfriend, then that's about right. I was nine that year and Mother was twenty-seven, going on thirteen.

Nearly every Friday night Gramma K and Uncle Jim, Leslie Ray and I dressed up to go to Damon's Steak House, where we had cocktails before dinner. Uncle Jim and Gramma ordered mixed drinks with colorful names. Leslie and I had the virgin versions. Nothing we had experienced so far matched the glamour of Friday nights out.

Back at the house, we fetched Gramma some wine. After a couple of drinks at the restaurant, she was already talkative, and after some Mogen David, downright loquacious.

"Your Mother and Daddy weren't always so holy. They were normal when they met. She was fifteen. Looked like a grown woman when she was twelve. Snuck out at night, lied about her age, sang in juke joints. Your Daddy was so handsome, all the girls were after him. He was a gentleman too, danced with every woman at the town dance on Saturday nights, every single one, the young ones and the old ones. Of course he danced with me so I'd let him keep seeing Fern. They were something. Best looking couple on the floor. Crazy about each other. Never did understand how Raymond put up with your Mother."

A little more wine.

"Don't you know she turned up pregnant and I had to sign papers so she could marry him when she was sixteen?"

No, we hadn't known Mother was pregnant before they married but now we did. We were cloistered children with no idea what to do with this information. In our world a woman with a growing belly was going to "get a baby" and we didn't really care how.

"They wouldn't let her stay in high school, so she went to night school, pregnant and all. Got her diploma. Made straight As too. Leslie Ray, you came along and the first thing they did was get religion, repent for their sins. Now *everything's* a sin."

We sat there on the floor, hanging on every word, fascinated by our parents' lives before Jesus.

"I thought your Mama would die when Raymond said no more fingernail polish, no more picture shows. And her just a kid herself. They don't even dance together anymore. That's a sin now too. One thing they sure can do is have babies. Nita Faye, you were born next and they never slowed down, just kept dragging you two all over the country."

I needed to correct an important point.

"We're gonna quit traveling. Daddy says he's taking a church to pastor so we can go to school all the time."

"Your Mama won't stay put. She needs to sing on the radio and she loves those big crowds y'all have in revivals."

Leslie Ray started his protest. "But Daddy said—"

Gramma continued, "You two best not count on staying in one place. I don't know what your daddy's saying to you—"

We both started to jump in. She raised her hand for quiet.

"But I can tell you for a fact when your Mama wants Raymond to change his mind, she'll find a way. Course, if they *do* stay out on the road maybe you'll get to come visit me again."

While we wanted to believe Gramma K was on our side, it became clear during our stay that her first allegiance was to her continuing feud with her daughter. Theirs wasn't temporary spite. It was full-time, full-blown war, with each coveting something the other held and casualties littering the field.

Gramma was bossy and peevish and she talked bad about our parents and she was, of course, the most interesting person we knew. We wanted to stay with her forever.

Chapter 9

Our House

Murfreesboro, Arkansas, 1951

Gramma was wrong. Daddy did accept the pastorate in Murfreesboro. Though her prediction about that missed the mark, her other stories, embroidered around the edges with inflammatory opinions, took up an enormous amount of room in the car on the way from California back home to the South.

They sent Mother's sister, Aunt Freddie, to pick us up, and we spent several days on Route 66 trying to adjust to our once-again circumscribed existence. It was a tearful journey away from the most freedom we'd tasted. Hundreds of miles went by with both of us immersed in a thick soup of gloom.

Gramma said if Daddy and Mother found out about all the things she let us do in California, they wouldn't let us stay with her again. We swore we'd never tell and we didn't, but by the time we returned to our real lives with The Joneses, it was too late for un-knowing. We were complicit little sinners headed straight to hell and we made no attempt to correct our downward slide.

We became actors pasting together an intricate system of untruths to keep our parents from learning the details of our California adventures. We also had new plans. We'd seen more of the world than our church life afforded, and we now knew exactly what we would do the minute we gained our freedom. Leslie Ray would be an architect. He carried a pad and pencil with him on his paper route and stopped to sketch buildings that interested him. He said he might also be a piano player. When he told Daddy about the buildings he was drawing, Daddy responded, "Well, son, I reckon the Lord will decide whether he needs any more architects but I can tell you for a fact he can always use piano players."

I gave up my initial dream to be a toe dancer when it looked like I'd be tall like the rest of our people. My new goal was to return to California to sing with Gene Autry on his radio program, which he would rename *Gene and Nita Faye at Melody Ranch* as soon as people caught on I wasn't a threat to Mrs. Autry.

"This isn't really our furniture," I told my new friend, Ruby, as I showed her around. We didn't have furniture of our own, and I didn't want her to think I was trying to put on airs, pretending we did. This was furniture borne into the parsonage on the good will of church members eager to welcome their new pastor.

I had only rudimentary knowledge of how friends behaved and what they talked about because I'd never stayed in one place long enough to have a friend. I had made the acquaintance of daughters of evangelists and pastors, but I saw them only when we passed through their towns. A while back, I was almost ready to call Margaret Daly my best friend, even though we only saw each other in Amarillo when my family held revivals, but then she told me I should serve Jesus however my parents decided and that I should quit complaining about it so I stopped writing to her.

Ruby nodded and smiled and made kind comments as I took her through each room of the parsonage. Much of what I showed her was in questionable condition. I recognized these kinds of furnishings from parsonages we occupied briefly in the past. Some of the pieces had stayed too long in the spare room of a farmhouse with the door kept shut to conserve heat in the winter, maybe the room that somebody's Aunt Cricket lived in until she crossed over. A few pieces contained evidence of time spent closer to the outdoors than originally intended, maybe on somebody's porch where the weather had its way.

There was always at least one big old chair, the kind with wooden arms and legs but upholstered in something flowery. The center of the seat was sprung and it sank a little when you sat down. Every parsonage we occupied had a similar chair, and though the fabric was faded, it was surprisingly comfortable exactly because of the years of use the seat cushion had already experienced.

Most evangelists who came off the revival circuit didn't own furniture unless their families held on to a house for them in some town they might choose to occupy once they no longer traveled. No one was holding a house for us anyplace except right here, right now.

The only personal possessions Leslie Ray and I traveled with were my Betsy Wetsy doll and his football. We got them for Christmas in Atlanta, Texas, where we pastored a church with a dear congregation who treated us like family. That year we were told there was no money for gifts but maybe there would be an orange and some candy in our stockings. In our house, there was no talk of Santa. Christmas was to celebrate Baby Jesus and gifts were not essential.

But then on Christmas day there came a knock at the door and like magic, two wrapped boxes with big bows were presented by a church member. Leslie got a football and I got a doll. His football went flat without provocation but it was still displayed on the top of the chest of drawers in his room. My Betsy Wetsy doll came with her own bottle. Her eyes closed to display long eyelashes, and as soon as the water drained from the bottle into her mouth, she wet her diaper. Ruby thought Betsy was the most intriguing creature, and since Betsy arrived with two diapers, there was a lot of drinking and wetting as we began our friendship.

Except for these two prized possessions, we weren't allowed to transport toys from one location to the next. Each time we moved, we went to the home of someone poorer than us where Daddy insisted we hand over everything we'd played with.

Now that we were each in our own rooms, it felt safe to put Betsy Wetsy on a shelf over my chest of drawers. It was no longer a requirement for me that she drink and wet and have her diaper changed. It was enough to know she could. She occupied a position of respect, and perhaps it would not be considered bragging to introduce her to Ruby that day.

Ruby's house, a quick walk away, was furnished even more sparsely than ours. I met her at school the day she arrived in the fifth grade. She told Miz Flowers she couldn't be there for the whole term. Her family traveled even more than we did. Her people were itinerant pickers, moving from crop to crop, renting living space in each town while they worked, then leaving all but essentials behind, exactly the way we did. She also hadn't spent a lot of time in classrooms, but was more self-assured than I was. Though I'd been performing in front of people all my life, I never got used to changing schools and was miserable each time. Ruby didn't seem to be. When she was introduced to the class, she took the desk assigned right in front of me, turned around, and said, "I like your hair. Want to come to my house after school?"

This must be how friends behaved. I was ecstatic. I told her it was my turn to take care of the laundry after school.

"I have to get permission."

"Let me know when."

She turned back around to face Miz Flowers.

I tapped her on the back and whispered, "You can come to my house but we have to be quiet. Mother has sick headaches."

All the women in Mother's family had them. They tallied days spent in darkened rooms. When Gramma K or Aunt Freddie or Mother had headaches, they weren't interested in household routine and sometimes required reminding about what needed to be done.

Mother had different moods, and if I brought someone home, I couldn't be sure which one we'd find. Sometimes when she came out of the bedroom, she was happy, giddy even, she and Daddy chasing each other around the house and laughing about it, but sometimes not.

I could tell Ruby about these things because we were a perfect match. Ruby lived in a house with its own emotional ups and downs. Her Daddy drank. I didn't tell her the part about my own Daddy having say over who I called friend because I didn't want her to feel bad about her people being unbelievers, and also I hoped to seem like a normal person to her, a person who could have someone over to play after school.

I put my faith in this ordinary house filled with old furniture. Now that we lived like other people, Ruby might not notice the odd parts and our family could start to rank higher on a scale of who's normal and who's not. I was committed to copying the behavior of new people I met, hoping in this phase of our lives we Joneses would soon clang the bell up at the very top where the sign read "Ordinary" and the light blinked "Congratulations!"

Ruby, on the other hand, expressed no desire to change her life. She displayed no disappointment at not having things to call her own and evidenced no frustration about her family's constant packing and traveling. Smart as a whip she was, and also resigned, far beyond our mutual ten-year-old experiences, to not wanting anything she couldn't have.

I downplayed my own aspirations, which seemed completely unrealistic in comparison to her lack of them. If *not* having dreams and plans was normal, then that's what I would pretend, too, in front of everybody except Leslie Ray.

The parsonage furniture was put into place to serve our family just before our arrival, along with linens and cooking utensils and every small thing needed to set up housekeeping, all of it contributed by members of our new congregation, who finished carrying the last items inside at the moment we pulled up in front from our last revival tour.

In our denomination, pastors accepted donations of goods and services. All donations received were considered tithes. When church people couldn't contribute 10 percent of their income because there was no actual cash income, church leaders were instructed to accept whatever was given, and it was duly credited to the church member's annual pledge or tithing account.

It was most often the case that not much cash transferred from their hands to ours, so we lived on donations. We adapted to hand-me-downs and wove the region's agricultural output into our meals.

When the Cokers butchered, we had meat. Brother Booty stopped by with personal deliveries from his dairy (and lingered for a chance to chat with Sister Fern at home). We feasted on fresh churned butter and used his farm's thick cream to top our breakfast fruit, or to turn leftover rice into pudding, or we whipped up cream with the hand beater to plop on top of anything. Brother Booty's dairy allowed us to lighten Mother's strong coffee to our preferred shade. As far back as we could remember, my brother and I were allowed to drink coffee, provided we stuck to half coffee and half cream.

Daddy said what a blessing to have such generous farmers and big-hearted Christians in our church and that we would be well fed in our new town. Mother said yes, that certainly was true, but she would also appreciate it if the Good Lord would move on the hearts of someone to donate some pretty yard goods, and if that happened, she would make me a new school dress. In every place Daddy pastored, he asked church members to pray for the loan of a used piano for Sister Jones.

There was seldom cash for new shoes, none for the eyeglasses a teacher said I suddenly needed in order to read the blackboard, or for any other purchases reliant on money changing hands. Still this was, in my opinion, the finest residential situation we'd experienced. Before coming to Murfreesboro, we had *stayed* many places, or we had *visited* around, but this time Daddy said we would *live* here. That was the big difference. I made an effort to appear casual in front of Ruby about what I considered my extreme good fortune to have a closet in which to hang my clothes.

Soon after we moved in, I learned that this house, even though it had a full back porch with a working washing machine, was nothing special in the eyes of our townspeople. It was, indeed, quite a modest building, two rooms wide and no more capacious than it absolutely had to be, but within our family's brief experiments at settling down, this was a hallmark.

There were two important houses we passed on our way to school. One was traditional brick with well-kept landscaping around it, and the other was a white two-story with gingerbread trim. The brick one was owned by Doctor Duncan and the white one by the Anthonys, a prominent local family. These were the kinds of houses that caught people's attention and the occupants were known all over the county because of the interesting lives they lived. Either of these homes could have been set down in a magazine with a caption beneath the photos telling about the fascinating goings-on inside. These homes existed in another world.

Our house wasn't even as big as those occupied by other people of modest means. We learned that some poor people own things. While we toured and were invited into homes in several Southern states, I figured this phenomenon of poor people owning things didn't happen because they had once been rich before they were poor, but because their parents and grandparents lived in one place for a long time and their belongings stayed right there with them.

In other people's houses, things were loved, and if not exactly loved, at least they were kept for decades, because many of those things had been used from day to day by people with the same last names who once lived at that same address.

I didn't yet view our lack of household belongings as a liability, but it hurt Mother's feelings that her family lived with tables and chairs and lamps and beds that somebody else didn't want. Daddy saw it differently. He looked at the way church people got together to provide housing and dishes and linens and an icebox and an old stove and he saw Christianity in action.

Mother said if we had been living in a house these past years instead of a rented apartment and motor courts and other people's parsonages, if she'd had any funds for buying things for a home, she certainly wouldn't have decorated her house like most people.

Her decorating style ricocheted off her insecurities. Her embarrassment about being poor and her terror of this condition lasted a lifetime. She was attracted to everything new. Her fear of poverty had already chased her across several Southern states since her own childhood, and it certainly wasn't allayed by living among things that didn't belong to her.

She shuddered.

"All this dark old furniture. I don't know how anyone can stand it."

She was drawn to shiny objects, fabrics with sheen, glass and brass and plastic and reflective surfaces. Like some exotic creature from a newly invented or reimagined forest, she shunned everything made of wood.

Later, when a bit of money was allocated for the purchase of an object for our house, she chose whatever was featured in the photographs in the Look of the Future sections of her magazines. She was partial to fancy upholstery and huge mirrors and tables with glass tops perched on metal bases.

Pink was her favorite color, followed closely by red, then black. Sometimes she worked all three into one ensemble. With pink, she seemed to have no favorite shade in particular—anything pink would do fine.

My brother and I were experiencing our own decorating frenzy for the first time. Oh, the joy of opening a can of paint bought solely for me to use in my room. Daddy said we could move things around the way we wanted and we could even put up pictures.

Leslie Ray's decor was a twin bed with an old bedspread and an old wooden bedside stand with a radio on it. Everything in his room was plain. He liked things neat and clean and symmetrical. He made his bed the minute he got out of it. He kept funny books hidden anywhere he thought Daddy wouldn't find them. I knew the hiding places, but would feel odd, even now, if I thumbed through any of them without asking him first. He craved privacy. What was his was sacred.

I said to Ruby, "And here's my room," as if this was a normal room in a normal girl's house, but inside I was shouting, I HAVE MY OWN ROOM! And that's my own chenille bedspread. Do you see that it's mostly still nubby, and the only places where the chenille is worn through you can't even see because I have hidden them on the far side and pushed the bed up against the wall?

I painted my iron bedstead myself. Daddy said I should've taken the rust off first with the sandpaper he gave me, else the paint will peel, but if it peels, I'll just paint it again, because I have plenty of paint and THIS IS MY OWN ROOM.

There, I told her, is the desk and chair I love. Both have been painted many colors in the past and Daddy said I should also sand them down, but I didn't want to wait. I can sit at that desk with my notebooks, I explained to Ruby, and write myself into and out of the lives I plan to live.

"What do you write about?"

Sometimes I wrote the truth, but mostly not. I'd rather imagine how it could be. For instance, I told her, I'm trying to describe this house exactly as it is, but also say how it feels to me, which may be different.

The first and biggest bedroom opened off the front room and that's where Daddy and Mother slept. The parsonage didn't have a big Southern-style front porch. Ours was a little thing with two steps up to it. You could cover the whole span of it in two more steps to the screen door and then you'd be in the front room. When somebody knocked on the door late at night or very early in the morning, which happened more often than you might think at a preacher's house, Daddy got up and closed the door to the bedroom to let Mother sleep.

The kitchen, in the center of the house, was by far the biggest room.

Off the kitchen, a small hallway led to our bedrooms, and in that hallway we could crank the handle on the phone on the wall to reach Sarah, the town operator, or hover near someone else's conversation to eavesdrop without being seen.

On the back porch, the house tour was complete. This was my favorite part, because a washing machine summed up our new lives. We'd never had one before. Mother or Daddy started a load of wash during the day, then after school Leslie Ray and I ran the heavy, soaked garments through the wringer, and depending on whose turn it was, one of us gathered the cloth bag that held wooden clothespins (it had a strap that slung over a shoulder) and trudged outside to hang the wet clothes to dry. Whichever one of us didn't do the hanging would be required to bring in the clothes and fold them.

On the floor next to the washing machine, resting side by side, were three pairs of old, overused shoes, Daddy's, then Leslie's, then mine, ready to respond at a moment's notice to our next call out to the garden.

Daddy's weather instruments were mounted on the wall.

Ruby said, "My Daddy can tell the weather by how he feels."

"Mine too, but he likes to check these to see if they agree with him."

It was silly how excited I was to learn about another thing my new friend and I had in common. We had weather-watching Daddies who grew up needing to know about such things in order to work the farms that kept their families alive.

Each night when I turned off the lamp on my bedside table, I knew this house in this town would be just fine for a few more years. After that I would be taking off anyway for my new life near Gene Autry's Melody Ranch in California.

It was the happiest we'd ever been except for time spent at Gramma's house, but one morning at the breakfast table with Daddy changed all that. He lowered the newspaper he was reading.

"Nita Faye, I don't want you playing with Ruby anymore."

I was shocked. Ruby was always polite to my parents, never forgot her yessirs and yessums.

"Why?"

"Her people are not believers. I heard they don't go to any church."

"Because they travel around so much."

"I could think different about it, maybe, even if they were Baptists, but they don't belong to any church."

"Because they *travel!*"

"A person's got to be in church on the Sabbath. There's churches everywhere. Ruby's Daddy coulda found one."

Leslie Ray kicked me under the table, not to shut me up but the opposite. He was coaching me. He wanted me to talk back, or jump up and leave, or any of the other ways he'd been expressing himself lately. I couldn't. I didn't have the courage to be the reason Daddy was disappointed again.

Ever since we came home from California, Leslie and I had asked him so many questions about why he believed the way he did and he grew weary, but he never raised his voice. He quoted scripture. He related personal anecdotes about how his love for Jesus made his life complete. He always ended by saying how it grieved him that his children failed to see the light. After every talk he got up and left to go pray for us.

I wouldn't pitch a hissy fit but I also wouldn't give up my first and only best friend.

"I don't see what's different about us. When you were little your family picked cotton. We travel all the time. Well her family picks crops and travels."

"It's how people *believe* that makes the difference. Ruby's Daddy needs to get right with God and then we'll see about it."

"How do you know what he believes?"

"He's a drinker. A man oughten to be getting drunk."

"Uncle Leonard drinks all the time."

"I'm praying for him too."

He got up to leave, turned around, and said, "Girl, you're gettin' just as pigheaded as your brother."

Leslie and I brought audacity home from California with us. We didn't agree that everybody needed to believe the same. We talked about it a lot, about how you could like people even when you knew they were sinners. We liked Gramma K and she was one. If Ruby was one too, she'd still be top of my list of people I'd lie and risk punishment for.

We stopped telling our parents about new acquaintances, stopped bringing friends home, and made excuses about why we couldn't have them over to our house. We met a boy at school whose family had a television set and we snuck over to his house with his parents' permission, but without telling them we were breaking Daddy's rules. It was risky business. It was a very small town, and we were the children of The Joneses, who were already the subject of much speculation.

Chapter 10

Sister Fern Won't Go to Town

Murfreesboro, Arkansas, 1952

She was sending out tapes again. I didn't know if Daddy knew about it and I wasn't going to tell him. It's not good to be the messenger who carries information that an adult doesn't want to acknowledge.

She gave her tapes to me to take to the post office in town and she didn't say to keep it a secret from him, but my guess was she hadn't brought it up yet. It wouldn't be a secret for long, but it wasn't going to come from me. She didn't drive, and she didn't like walking, so her need to send out packages involved Leslie or me.

I walked to town carrying a package from Mother and waited while the postmaster weighed it. He took his time, long enough, I knew, to memorize the name and city of the recipient. By the time I left Courthouse Square and headed down Church Street on the way home, several other people in town would already know that the new Pentecostal preacher's wife was corresponding with Jimmie Davis, the former governor of Louisiana, who was also the famous singer of "You Are My Sunshine."

I wouldn't tell on her about the tapes she sent to Governor Davis but somebody else would, in a way meant to sound oblique, whispered by small-town gossips who thought they were clever enough to ease Reverend Jones into adding something to their story. They didn't know who they were dealing with. Daddy had been a preacher for much of his young life and was already a veteran among gossips. He even played with them a bit, egging people on.

Somebody in town would say, "I saw your girl over at the post office yesterday, Reverend," or "That boy of yours, did I see him at the barbershop Saturday?" Then they'd pass the time of day and it would be Daddy who worked the subject back around to where he wanted it, so that by the time he got home, he was up to date on every place his children had been and every word we had said in town, and who in town was and wasn't saved.

Mother quit going to the dime store herself. She said it was because the one time she bought face powder in a shade she considered exactly like her own skin color, and therefore not a cosmetic enhancement but merely an effort to correct a shiny nose and forehead, someone from our new, the-Lord-loves-a-bare-faced-Christian congregation had spread the word that Sister Jones was wearing makeup.

I walked as slowly as possible for a while, in order to stretch out the trip, then skipped for a while in celebration of freedom from hanging the wash on the line, and because of the unadulterated joy of going to town by myself.

This wasn't a day when I carried tapes for Mother. This day I was on a regular errand with nothing to hide. Still, when I heard the car slow just behind me, and saw it was ours, my first thought was Daddy had somehow sussed out the history of my previous missions and decided to check on it himself, which meant he'd ask me a bunch of questions in order to hear me say something he might already know about Mother's tapes.

He rolled up alongside me on the road, driving the green Pontiac the Anthony family from church helped us buy. It was the first new car we'd ever owned. It was a beauty, with sculpted covers that dipped over the back wheels. When you looked at it from a certain angle, here came a ship out of water, floating to a stop on a dirt road.

Daddy's white shirtsleeves were rolled down and his tie was hitched up close so I knew he was on a pastoring call.

"Where you headed, Nita Faye?"

"Town."

"How come?"

"For Mother. She said to."

"What're you after?"

"I am going after . . ."

I pulled the wadded-up shopping list from the pocket of my dress and read it out loud to impress him with the importance of my mission.

"I'm going after some Coty face powder and a sewing machine bobbin and a spool of pink, number 50 extra-strong thread."

"Uh-huh. What shade of powder?"

He either didn't believe me or he was playing a game with me, and if he could trap me in a fib, it wouldn't be the first time. Daddy was always checking up on us after school, making sure we completed our assigned duties, seeing to it that we weren't anyplace we weren't supposed to be.

He thought he'd caught me messing with the truth.

"What shade?"

"Rachel Number One."

He said, "Last week when I went after it, they told me they were out."

I was ready. "They just got some in today. Mother called up."

Daddy often brought home her powder and her women's magazines and even her feminine hygiene products, without a hint of embarrassment. He knew all her specifics and could have tripped me up on the powder availability had the facts not been on my side.

Face powder was a curious purchase, Leslie Ray and I decided, for a woman who promised to swear off adornment of any kind. We speculated about just what was and wasn't makeup. Mother gave up lipstick and fingernail polish for Daddy but she wouldn't give up Coty face powder or Vaseline or her eyelash curler. Her brows and lashes were dark enough anyway, but she used a tiny, stiff-bristled Maybelline brush dipped into the Vaseline jar just to make sure. She rubbed Vaseline into her curls and slicked it onto her lips too, and she powdered off the shine on her face with Coty.

She spent a lot of time on her fingernails. She owned a manicure set that folded up into a pouch for travel, and when it was unfolded, each section contained a specific implement for filing, shaping, buffing, and polishing, plus a chalky pencil to whiten underneath her nails. I watched her moisten the tip of the pencil on her tongue and apply it to her fingernails several times a week, then she'd hold out a hand and wiggle her fingers, admiring the perfect ovals.

We didn't begrudge her the powdering and slicking and buffing, but in our picayune moods, it did seem it was at the very least, skittering right along the boundary of vanity, which Daddy's sermons declared a sin.

Daddy didn't seem inclined to move the Pontiac along. I talked fast.

"And she said I can bring home some candy for me and Leslie Ray and some cashews for her. And if the cashews aren't fresh—"

"Bridge Mix," he said.

Completing the written portion of the interrogation, I folded the note carefully, treating it as an important document, further establishing the authenticity of the mission, and put it back into my pocket. I was so close to escaping an afternoon of chores, if I could only ditch him, but he hadn't moved away yet.

"Did yore Mama give you enough money for all that?"

"Nossir. She said to charge it."

He opened the car door, got out, and reached into his billfold.

"Here. You pay for it. I don't want you charging."

"But Mother said tell them it's for her and it'll be fine."

"People will be saying the Joneses charge things. I don't want people saying that."

I took the money and pushed it into the pocket with the shopping list. He got back into the car.

Leaning out the window, he said, "Why don't you get in and I'll carry you to town?"

"Nossir. I like to walk."

I also liked to make the trip take a long time so I didn't have to go back home and hang up wet clothes.

"How are you supposed to answer me?"

He wasn't upset, he was always teaching.

"I *said* nossir."

"Nossir, *what?*"

"Nossir, much obliged."

"That's the time. You hurry up, you hear? I don't want you fooling around in town all day."

"Yessir. I'll hurry up."

I started walking with him coasting alongside for a while before he pulled away. I wasn't going to hurry up if I could help it. If it really meant that much to him, he would double back through Courthouse Square later on to see if he'd catch me hanging around. Sometimes he would. If the need for escape was great enough on a given day, I'd risk getting caught just to stay out of the house. Leslie Ray was braver. He took the risk every time, got caught plenty, and did it again.

In front of the post office, Postmaster Dillard stood chatting with passersby. He called me over.

"Nita Faye, tell your mama she can save on her postage if she'll wrap things different. I'll show her how."

Having the postmaster in town advising the preacher's wife about how to send something to a former governor wasn't a conversation I was eager to have. Mother was already under pressure from Daddy to appear more like a pastor's wife and that fit perfectly with our own plan to stay put. We hoped she would quit putting her songs on tape and mailing them around. We hoped she would adjust to this part of her life and downplay the entertainer part. Anything we could do to help her blend in while at the same time slowing down her singing and songwriting career would be more along the lines of what we wanted to accomplish.

"Much obliged, Mister Dillard. I doubt she'll be mailing anymore."

Our congregation bragged about their handsome preacher with his beautiful wife, and if she was known to be participating in something other than church business, it would give people a chance to talk about us even more. We were pretty sure no other pastor's wife in town was communicating with Governor Jimmie Davis.

When it was just Leslie Ray and I with her, she left us to our chores while she played piano in the front room or painted at an easel over in a corner or retreated to the bedroom. She told us without prompting when she was sad or lonely for her mama or worried about money or pondering how to get her songs heard. She wasn't curious about how we spent our time as long as we left her alone except when she needed something. We were slippery when it was just her at home, taking any opportunity to ease out the door.

We hadn't spent much time in places where we mixed with the same people every day and saw them again and again. We were greedy for every sight and sound. We reported our findings to each other, speculating about other people the same way they talked about us. We believed all the rumors we heard about our new town, that folks said there was a secret card game in the back room at the hardware store where people placed bets and drank liquor, that Doctor Duncan turned down an offer to run a big hospital in Nashville because he liked the people here so much, and that our local branch of the Anthony family was as rich as just about anybody in Arkansas.

At the dime store, I gathered my thread and the round box of Coty with the fat powder puffs printed on it, then got the attention of the counter girl so she could bring the candy scoop over. She was the only help in the store and some people were taking forever at the cash register. She rolled her eyes at me to let me know she was running out of patience with them.

She called out, "Hey Nita Faye. Be right there."

"Hey, Earla Dean. No rush."

Earla Dean wasn't named that way because her daddy wanted a boy and got a girl instead. They already had a couple of Earls in her family. People around here named their kids whatever they felt like, no matter which sex they were, so Earla Dean got that name because evidently her family couldn't get enough Earls.

She joined me at the candy counter.

"I thought I'd never get shed of them."

Each kind of treat on the other side of the glass had its own bin, with small white bags and larger white bags stacked on top of the counter for carrying them home. She picked up the metal scoop to measure out the contents of each bag.

"Dime's worth of candy corn, please."

Into the white bag it went, onto the small scale on top of the counter, and knowing it was for Leslie Ray and because they went to junior high together and she had a crush on him, she tossed in half a scoop extra and handed the bag to me.

"Dime's worth of Bridge Mix."

For me she put in just the regular amount.

"Dime's worth of cashews if they're fresh. Mother says they have a funny smell if they're not. She can tell."

I unzipped my purse. It was a change purse made of equal parts bright yellow and bright purple heavy cloth. Around the bottom was a border of pansies, each tiny blossom fully realized through intricate stitching. A dangling yellow pansy adorned the zipper pull. The inside was lined with satin, a fancy flourish that no amount of dirty coins could ever diminish in my eyes. It had recently arrived in the mail from California, representing both Gramma K's skills and my own independence. It was a special piece to carry on a trip to town alone.

It was Leslie Ray's turn to handle the laundry after school. He would plop a load of wash into a basket, then onto the clothesline, the same load of wash that as I left was awaiting a trip through the hand wringer. Leslie would have to finish that part.

Earla Dean pointed to my purse.

"Where'd you get that pretty thing?"

"My Gramma K made it."

"Can I see it?"

I handed it over.

"Look at this flower!"

She touched the crocheted pansy on the zipper pull.

"I wish I had me one like this."

Since she always gave extra candy to Leslie Ray, I wondered if I asked Gramma K to make Earla Dean a purse like mine, would I be the recipient of more Bridge Mix? How many times would that bargain hold? What was the relative value of a purse with crocheted pansies measured against extra scoops of candy? While I considered whether to strike that bargain, the tinkle of the bell over the screen door announced the arrival of another customer.

Miss Ruth's Beauty Shoppe was next door and she filled in her slow times by checking up on what people bought at the dime store. She approached the candy counter.

"Your mama sure does love her cashews."

"Hey Miss Ruth."

"Hey Nita Faye. When're you gonna let me give you a permanent wave?"

"No thank you. I don't want a permanent wave. I want me some bangs though."

"Well why don't you come on over and I'll cut you some right now. Get that hair up out of your face."

Some people will say anything to kids. Because we were onstage often, there were lots of questions everywhere we went.

"Are you twins?"

"Who taught you two to sing?"

"How do you like being a preacher's kid?"

Some of the questions were probably innocent, but not all of them. Some were merely an opening for the adult to add an opinion, and it was often one that did not enhance our self-esteem.

"Where did you two get that red hair?"

Both our parents were dark haired. We didn't look like them, but however we felt about that fact, we were still required to answer every adult politely.

"Our Grandaddy Salisbury."

But by then we had been singled out again, cut away from a herd of other children at a time when we were attempting to vanish. On previous trips to town, Miss Ruth blurted out whatever was on her mind. We were on to her now, but kinder people also did the same thing.

My hair was always under too much pressure. It was at odds with the reality of my daily life, and at no time was it more evident than when I went to town on a hot day. The front part started out pinned up, but by the time I reached my destination, chunks hung down on either side of my face, while a ponytail held up the rest of the mess in back. I wanted to cut it. Daddy's sect forbade hair cutting for women. It was a touchy subject.

"Oh, that's right . . ."

She looked like she was talking to me, but she used a loud voice, which told me she knew what she was doing and wanted to be sure everybody else could hear it.

"You people don't cut your hair. You people are Holiness, aren't you?"

"We're not Holiness. We're Pentecostal."

"Same thing. Holy Rollers."

"No m'am."

I hit the m'am hard and looked straight at her to let her know that I specifically did not mean the form of address as any kind of personal respect.

"It's not the same thing. We're not Holy Rollers."

You could call Daddy a Pentecostal or Evangelical or Full Gospel, but he did not appreciate Holy Roller. Somehow I knew Miss Ruth already knew this when she said, "My sister-in-law over in Fort Smith, she came to your Daddy's church one time and she said it's the same thing. She said everybody was rolling around on the floor down by the altar."

"They are not rolling around. Some people fall out in the Spirit."

"What does that mean 'fall out in the Spirit'?"

"It means when you get the baptism of the Holy Ghost and start to speak in tongues, or you get healed, sometimes the power of the Spirit strikes and you lay back."

And there I went explaining and giving the appearance of defending practices I didn't understand myself. To let them go undefended would have made me seem pathetic and it would have let people know about my own doubts. If I allowed my doubts to be public, I would disappoint Daddy again by speaking out in disagreement with what our parents preached.

I couldn't leave the store soon enough. I wasn't even surprised at Miss Ruth, though I did try sometimes to avoid her because I didn't believe her questions were ever without guile. She wasn't the only one. This was the way a lot of people had of saying they thought what Daddy and Mother believed was objectionable. I guess they knew if they told it to us children, it would eventually be transmitted to the adults at home.

There were details about our denomination's beliefs and Daddy's particularly strict interpretation of them that our new town would soon know about us.

No doctors or dentists or medical care of any kind. Faith healing only.

No movies.

No dancing.

No sporting events at school. (People might be tempted to bet on them.)

No swimsuits. (Mixed bathing is a sin.)

No makeup.

No pants on women.

No jewelry.

No hair cutting for women.

No cussing, drinking, or smoking.

Divorce is a sin.

Sinners must be saved and filled with the Holy Ghost to get into heaven.

New sins could be added to this list at any time.

You could follow all the precepts but you're still not a real Christian until you've had a full-immersion baptism.

My brother and I revealed only limited portions of this list and only in small doses to people we met. We were assured by a teacher once in a school in Texas that she'd be happy to get in touch with our parents about an up-coming event that required suspension of one of these rules. We begged her not to interfere. Some teachers might be genuinely well-meaning, but any contact with our parents added to our discomfort at home, bringing us more sermons from Daddy. Sure enough, she talked to them and we heard from Daddy about it.

"It hurts my heart that my own children are going around telling people at school they question the word of God."

He treated any curiosity we brought home from the outside world as a personal affront. Leslie and I sided with the strangers. We had the same questions they did, but if we talked bad about our parents, we would be pitied, and pitiful was the last thing we wanted to be, so the older we got, the less we revealed about our real lives.

This was the longest time so far we'd spent around unbelievers, except for the stay with Gramma K. Before that, we were always in church or in revivals, and when we went to school for short periods in various towns, we never brought home friends whose people believed something different from what Daddy taught. Now, as we got acquainted, we met people who went to other kinds of churches and people who didn't go to church at all.

It was embarrassing to deal with what outsiders said while our own questions went unanswered at home. What we didn't confide to anyone was that the two of us would be running away as soon as we worked out the how of it, which we hoped would involve living with Gramma K in California.

Miss Ruth was transparent from the start, so when we felt clever enough, she could be a conduit for any information we wanted to pass along in our new town.

I chatted with Earla Dean another minute or two, and when I left, there was Miss Ruth, standing right outside the door, smoking a cigarette. She could take two steps and be at the front door of her own shop, but instead she lit up by the dime store, where she stood puffing and talking with Naomi Flowers, my fifth grade teacher.

"How're you, Nita Faye?"

"Fine Miz Flowers, just fine. Heading home."

I was eager to get to the contents of the candy counter bags. I didn't dare take a bite until I was back home. Daddy said don't chew on the street—it's crude. I started to walk away but Miz Flowers kept talking.

"You must be a real big help for your mama right now. How's she feeling?" She gestured toward my bags.

"She craving cashews again?"

Miss Ruth joined in.

"I craved watermelon. That's all I wanted. Watermelon. In the *winter*." Both women laughed.

Miz Flowers said, "There's no telling, just no telling."

Now the conversation belonged to them and I could move along.

"I better go."

Miz Flowers asked, "Are you and your brother happy about getting a baby?"

"We don't have a baby."

"Not yet. But soon."

It happened so fast I couldn't take it in. People in town knew something about our family we didn't know. Leslie Ray and I were careful to disseminate only information of our choosing, and we knew nothing of cravings or due dates or any details concerning how and when anyone got their babies. Nobody was ever "pregnant," nobody was "expecting," but they somehow got babies. I didn't want to be the last person to find out this was about to happen at my house. I was so shocked, it came out sounding huffy.

"I have to *go*!"

Miss Ruth turned snippy.

"Well *bye* then, Nita Faye."

The two women returned to their own talk and clearly didn't realize they had just sent shockwaves through my life.

At home I dropped my bags on the table and ran to find Leslie Ray.

"Miz Flowers says we're getting a baby."

"*When* did she say?"

"In town just now. She and Miss Ruth both said."

"But *when* did they say a baby will get here?"

"Soon. That's what they said. Just soon."

"Yeah, I knew about it."

"No you didn't. If you'da known, you'da said."

"I don't tell you everything."

"Yes you do."

He didn't know. He began adding up clues.

"She wore those smocks because she's got a baby under there."

I had watched her sew up full smocks with big gathers in front in all different patterns and never once questioned why.

Leslie said, "I asked her why she was wearing those things every day. She said she was covering up her good clothes while she paints."

He was also humiliated, thinking the whole town knew something so personal about our family.

"But she doesn't paint every day. And she's always lying down and she stays in the bedroom all day."

"She always did that. Not just lately."

"She didn't want to go to meetings ever since we got here."

"She never did before either."

He said what both of us thought.

"Gramma shoulda told us."

Our good friend and ally, who spilled all kinds of personal secrets about our parents to us while we were in California, should have said something and not let us get broadsided in our new town like this.

Leslie Ray said, "Maybe they told her not to. Besides, *how's* Gramma gonna tell us?"

"In a letter. She writes to us all the time."

"They read them first."

Those blacked out portions of letters received from California must have been about babies, but why did any of it need to be a secret?

We waited for Daddy to get home, and despite the fact that questions from children were not encouraged, and answers were not always forthcoming, we were going to ask. The minute we heard him at the back door, we seated ourselves at the kitchen table where he'd have to pass by.

"You two get your work done already?"

He took off his cream-colored preacher Stetson and put it on a peg just outside the kitchen door.

"Yessir. Nita Faye went to town."

"I saw her on the road."

"I hung out the wash."

"It's just about dry. Bring it in before dark, son, you hear?"

"Yessir."

Now he was at the kitchen sink, washing his hands.

"Nita Faye, you help fold."

I wasn't willing to wait for Leslie Ray to work whatever diplomacy he had in mind to get us some answers. We had obviously been tricked by our parents, been treated like we didn't have good sense, and been confronted with embarrassing information.

Our ignorance of reproductive details was monumental. Our lack of knowledge about how babies came into the world was profound. Sex was not only sinful, but babies were also steeped in mysteries that generally involved doctors. Our family did not use doctors.

"Miz Flowers and Miss Ruth said we're getting a baby."

"They said that?"

"Yessir. Today. In town. I told them we're not."

He pulled out a chair.

"Matter of fact, we are. We are gettin' us a little baby."

Leslie asked, "When is our Baby coming?"

"A few weeks now. Nita Faye, go see if your Mama's sleeping then come on back here and seddown."

I ran fast and reported back.

"She's asleep."

"All right then. Your Mama's gonna need a lot of help when The Baby comes. I want you two to come straight home from school every day to help out, you hear?"

Was he going to skip right over the important parts?

I asked, "Who will bring our Baby?"

"Some women from the church will be here when it's time."

"Thelma says Doctor Duncan brings all the babies in town and I said we don't go to doctors."

"We don't need Doctor Duncan. We have plenty of good church people to help."

Leslie said, "And we'll be here too."

"Naw, son, you and your sister are going over to the Cokers' when it's time. Sister Coker will be right here with your Mama. I'll call you up when our Baby gets here."

He stood to leave. He was done. We would have to figure out the rest of it ourselves.

Daddy went into their bedroom.

I asked Leslie, "Are you glad about The Baby?"

"As long as it doesn't follow me around like you do."

"I do not follow you around."

"Yes you do."

"Do you care if it's a boy or a girl?"

"Nope. Don't care."

"I don't see how Mother is going to take care of a baby. She sleeps while we're at school."

"Maybe she won't sleep as much when The Baby's here."

Then he said, "I'll tell you why I'm glad. Because when The Baby comes, we can't travel anymore. Babies have a lot of stuff. There won't be room in the car—"

"And we'll get to stay home!"

"Yep. We won't be evangelists again, ever."

Chapter 11

We Got Us a Baby

Murfreesboro, Arkansas, 1952. New Population: 1,076.

Daddy crunched into the gravel driveway out front and called to us as he rushed inside.

"Y'all go on over to the Cokers' now."

He said he'd call as soon as he had news. "It's her time" was a phrase we did know and we figured this must be it.

Sister Coker hugged us at her door.

"Now don't worry a bit. Your Mother has been through this before and she'll be fine."

It hadn't occurred to us to worry. We just wanted to see who our Baby would be. Sister Coker left to go over to our house to help with the birth while Leslie Ray and I ate supper with her family.

It was barely daylight the next morning when Daddy called to say we could go home and meet our new sister, but we had to be quiet because Mother was very weak and was resting in the bedroom. We ran all the way through the snake field. The Baby already had her eyes open wide. We circled the bassinet Daddy had tucked her into in the front room, looking at her from every angle, memorizing eyelashes and miniature arched eyebrows just like Mother's, a forehead just like Daddy's, and the amount of fingers and toes a baby needs, and the way her mouth curved up at the corners. She was perfectly formed.

We were in love with our Baby from the start. At first Daddy said since she was only a few hours old, we probably shouldn't hold her yet, but then he gave in and let each of us sit on the couch while he put her into our arms.

When we got to school, we knew the party line had been busy since everyone knew about our new Baby. We were congratulated all day. Our friends asked when they could come home with us to see her. Daddy said he'd make up a schedule so each one of us could bring someone home, but only for a few minutes at a time.

That first day of our Baby's life, we walked by Doctor Duncan's house on the way home from school. He tended to his flowers out there whenever he had a break from doctoring.

"How 'do Miss Jones." He gave me his usual bow and a smile. "You on your way home?"

"Yessir."

"Would you like some flowers?"

"Nossir, I have to hurry up and get home."

He handed a bunch to me anyway.

"For your mama. She might like them."

"Much obliged."

"You helping your mama out?"

"Yessir. We'll be helping her every day."

"That's real good. She can rest up with you two in charge of things."

That first afternoon, with Daddy out on a pastor call, we were supposed to watch The Baby in the front room so Mother could sleep. I snuck into their bedroom, wanting to see Mother and find out what a person looked like after a baby and what it meant when Daddy said she was weak.

The room was dark and Mother was asleep, propped up on a bunch of pillows. Her eyes were sunken, with deep smudges under them, and her cheekbones, which normally curved over a heart-shaped face, seemed now to jut out at a new angle. Her skin was an unnatural color. I thought she was dead. I started to cry and then it got worse until of course that woke her up. She opened her eyes and tried to smile at me. I had no idea until that moment how fierce the craving for a mother could be.

Sister Coker said to Daddy, "You best send for her mama."

"She's already on the train. She'll be in Little Rock soon."

He said to us, "You two need to take care of your Mother when I can't be home. Gramma K will be here soon."

After he left, I said to Leslie, "I'm not going in that room again."

"I don't want to either."

But we had to go in there, had to tiptoe in and out because their bedroom was where all The Baby's things were kept, in a chest of drawers Daddy filled just before she arrived. Church people assembled the crib and brought it in. It was the only piece of new furniture our family had ever owned, but so far the bassinet in the front room was where we cared for her.

One day when I had to go into their room, there were small and odd bottles on a table by the bed, dark brown bottles I'd never seen before. I was sure they hadn't been there the first day. I asked Leslie Ray what he thought was in those bottles, and he said we'll find out when Gramma K gets here.

Daddy drove to the train station in Little Rock and brought back a clenched-up version of our California Gramma. Her forehead frowned, the sides of her face had lines I didn't remember, and her lips were pushed together tight. I wondered if she'd been like that all the way from Union Station in Los Angeles to the train depot in Little Rock. If so, she would surely be letting out some steam soon because she looked about to explode. She could erupt at the least little thing and she was also capable of carrying on for days. Mother was the same way. You didn't want to rile either one, and if you accidently hit on a touchy subject, you'd wish you hadn't. We hadn't yet determined what Gramma was so riled up about, but her face told us that obviously it had something to do with this unexpected visit and we'd find out soon enough.

Leslie Ray carried Gramma's suitcases into my room. She shooed me in there after him and shut the door and started in, spitting out the words.

"She's got no business having another baby in her condition. No business whatsoever."

"What condition?"

The door opened. Daddy stood there looking like a bull about to charge. We knew that look meant hush up, but Leslie wasn't so easily silenced anymore. He ignored the warning and persisted.

"What condition?"

"We'll talk about it later," Gramma said, meaning when your Daddy is not around, though he knows full well how I feel about certain matters and he knows I will say anything to you two that I feel like saying.

There wasn't much Daddy could do about Gramma K's interference. Mother wanted her mother, so she was here. As soon as Daddy left us alone with Gramma, details would be forthcoming.

It was anemia, she said later. It was serious, diagnosed by the doctor back in El Dorado when Mother was a girl.

We asked, what does a person with anemia look like? Act like?

Like your Mother looks right now after the Baby, Gramma said, and she was supposed to get it treated but she didn't because she married your Daddy and now they don't believe in doctors.

Gramma took over our house. Daddy let her. She cooked and tended to Mother and The Baby, and when Daddy offered to do things, she said no, you go on about your business, which didn't seem to upset him a bit.

Church people immediately adopted our Baby as their own. The Women's Missionary Council made baby blankets and quilts with thousands of tiny stitches. They chose pink and jonquil colored flannel and sewed it into soft gowns, and they prepared The Baby for her attendance at future church services by trimming the smallest dresses I'd ever seen with embroidery and crocheted edgings.

These women who looked after their own husbands and families, kept clean houses, and cooked three meals a day, and worked in the garden too, also produced exquisite handwork, and with their investment of time, they rendered the start of a new life profound.

Their work was so delicate, it was Cinderella's ball gown. In the movie,

Disney creatures brought Cinderella's dress to life, all of it removed from reality, with fantasy embellishments drifting into place. That's how beautiful our Baby's new wardrobe was.

Churchwomen came over to bring food and stayed to talk with Gramma K, who appeared in the kitchen in full makeup and flashy jewelry and her California clothes. Sister Coker was the voice for all the other churchwomen, and she enjoyed a special relationship with Mother. Nothing Mother did or said seemed to bother her, and vice versa. Sister Coker assured Gramma the Jones baby would want for nothing.

In our church, babies were dedicated, but not sprinkled. The water was saved for later. By age twelve, which was considered the age of reason, there would be full-immersion baptizing in a nearby creek. There was talk of the women making a special dress for the dedication. Gramma got her dander up.

"I believe I'm capable of making what my grandbaby will wear."

Sister Coker, experienced with the opinions of strong women, put on her most reasonable tone.

"Oh Miz Kalbaugh, we thought with all you have to do . . ."

"Yes, I *am* busy with my daughter and these two . . ."

We two sat on straight-backed chairs against the kitchen wall, unwilling to risk missing a word of these conversations. Everyone present knew my brother and I had been cooking for ourselves for a while and handling all of The Baby's diaper changes and bottles and laundry and then fixing whatever Mother felt like she could eat, but Gramma was in charge now. She continued.

". . . So I guess we could put our heads together and come up with something—"

"Oh having your help will be such a blessing!"

Sister Coker beamed as if she had all the time in the world and nothing would give her greater pleasure than to come over to our house and soothe the two high-strung women in residence.

Daddy would say the prayers of dedication over his infant, and Mother, when she got well enough, would stand in front of the congregation holding our Baby the way it had been done forever.

Sister Booty said, "Maybe we should wait on the dedication until Sister Fern feels better and let her decide about the dress. Lord knows she's so artistic, she might already have something in mind."

Sister Anthony mentioned to Gramma, one seamstress to another, the particular way so many of Mother's dresses were cut on the bias and how they flattered her figure, and based on the murmurs from these sewing women and their smiles of assent, I guessed that cutting on the bias was a compliment.

Sister Fern and Zula K, two women who made all their own clothes, were alike in their ability but different in their approach. Gramma K treated her big old filing cabinet full of dress patterns like a sacred space. When she finished cutting out yard goods, she carefully refolded the patterns and filed them away. Her precision was part of her tailoring business.

Mother, a member of the Disney magic floating creations school of sewing, cut without patterns. She hovered over her precious yardage and quickly snipped the outline of her dream.

If Mother sewed something wrong, she ripped out her stitches with her mouth set, leading one to wonder why she didn't just give in and plan things first. Her vision for her own look was her only guide as she cut through slinky jersey and created blouses with billowing poet sleeves which she wore with full skirts, gathered tightly at the waist with belts in various colors.

Somehow I couldn't imagine a suitable baby dedication dress resulting from either Mother's or Gramma's specific styles. For the sake of the photographs that would live in our scrapbooks forever, I hoped the churchwomen would prevail.

Mother sent word out from the bedroom that she would be happy for the church's assistance with the dedication dress. She did have a preference. She wanted the dress made of dotted swiss, the softest they could find, on a pastel colored background. If the yard goods store had only the stiffer kind of dotted swiss, would the women please soak it in Ivory Snow first to soften it? And could they make a little petticoat of lawn to wear underneath, and trim it with grosgrain ribbon to match the dotted swiss? No sooner were her wishes expressed than the women were on their way to turning them into reality.

Chapter 12

Daddy and the Doctor

Leslie Ray and I were stuck in the front pew in church that Sunday, exiled from our friends who got to sit farther back. We were up close because of recent misbehavior, which could be any one of a number of events unbecoming of a preacher's kids like talking in church or passing notes written on paper smuggled in the pages of a Bible. We never figured out how Daddy conducted a worship service and watched us so closely in our preferred seats all the way in the back row.

Gramma went home to California, but only a few months later, she turned around and came back for an extended stay. She didn't go to church. Instead she took off downtown to have coffee and donuts with Miss Ruth. Gramma said she would return to California "as soon as your Mother's color's better, because Jim will be missing me."

We guessed Uncle Jim hadn't minded all that much. After spending months with the two of them, it was easy to picture Uncle Jim and Pedro puttering around the house in Glendale, sharing their morning ritual. You could hear it from the next room, Uncle Jim whistling, stopping to remark about something to Pedro, toasting his bread once, twice, turning it into a dark plank, then scrape, scrape, scraping off only selected dark bits, then spreading it with peanut butter, carrying it over to the breakfast nook, and clicking on the little radio that waited on the table. Just the two of them.

Mother was singing again. She sat behind the pulpit up on the platform that Sunday. We were in charge of The Baby, who was asleep on the pew on a blanket spread between Leslie and me. Daddy finished his sermon and was winding down the service, about to lead the congregation in the altar call song.

"Let's turn to page four oh two, 'Let the Lower Lights Be Burning.'"

During the time it takes for a churchgoer to locate the song in the hymnal, not because they didn't know it, but because sometimes Brother Jones would ask for the third verse and many hadn't memorized that one, in that pause of a few seconds, when the only thing to be heard was the rustling of pages turning, into that silence, The Baby fell with a sickening thud.

The congregation suspended their search for page 402 and immediately looked in our direction, as if every one of them had identified the sound a baby makes when she falls. The sound was magnified, amplified through the building, or maybe that was just our memory of it. There was no crying. It seemed like there should have been crying, but there was silence.

Someone in the back shouted, "The Baby fell!"

Brother Booty jumped up and headed toward us.

"Somebody get Doctor Duncan!"

Daddy stayed up on the platform and said to Leslie and me, "Y'all take The Baby home. I'll be there directly."

Brother Booty disagreed with Daddy, standing by the altar, looking him right in the eye.

"Best wait for the doctor."

We turned to Mother, who seemed stuck in place.

Daddy said, "Honey, you go on home with them."

She stepped down from the platform, didn't look at us or anyone else, and zombie-marched right out the side door of the church.

Daddy said to Leslie Ray, with more force this time, "Son, do what I say. Pick up The Baby and take her on home."

Leslie carried The Baby and I dragged her blanket along and a buzz of conversation followed us out the door.

At the parsonage, Leslie Ray put the blanket on the couch and laid The Baby there. Her eyes were still closed.

I said, "She was sleeping right by us."

Mother acted calm like The Baby was just taking a nap and hadn't fallen on the floor.

"Looks like she's gonna have a big ol' bruise. Leslie Ray, put her in her crib."

"Can't we keep her out here on the couch and watch her?"

The back porch screen door slammed. Daddy went straight to the couch and knelt by The Baby.

"How's my girl? Here, give that baby to her Daddy."

He picked her up and walked with her, talking to her.

"Can you hear Daddy? Wake up now. Wake up and give Daddy a smile."

Mother asked, "What about Brother Booty? What'd you say to him? He's the one always calling the doctor."

"I asked him to think on it and pray on it before calling anybody. Some of them have been going to the doctor all along in spite of what the Bible says. Maybe the Lord's testing our faith with our own Baby. Maybe Daddy's little girl is going to help us teach them the power of divine healing."

Gramma K rushed in. She heard in town that Reverend Jones's baby had fallen. She marched right over to Daddy.

"Raymond, I am asking you to do the right thing for this baby."

"Zula, you know how we believe."

Someone knocked at the front door. Mother peeked out through the lace curtain at the long window where people could clearly see you peeking, and once they'd seen you, you couldn't pretend they didn't.

"Raymond, it's Doctor Duncan!"

Leslie ran to the window on the other side.

"Yep. I see his car."

Daddy put The Baby back on the couch.

"You two go on into the kitchen now."

"How come, Daddy?"

"Boy, don't ask me questions. You and your sister go on with your Gramma."

Daddy opened the front door, but not very far.

We heard Doctor Duncan's voice.

"How 'do, Reverend."

We didn't close the kitchen door and we made no effort to hide. We stood in the doorway, watching. Leslie was in front.

I asked, "Can you see anything?"

"He's got his doctor case in his hand! And he's pushing the door open."

"I hope he's gonna make Daddy let him see The Baby."

Leslie said, "He can't make Daddy do anything."

Daddy's tone was already past chilly and moving right along to frigid.

"Doctor, what brings you here?"

"I was around the corner checking on a neighbor. Thought I'd stop and see how your wife's doing."

"Thank you kindly, Doctor, but my wife's not up to company today. She's fine. We are all mighty grateful for your help that night."

I whispered to Leslie, "What help? What night? What does he mean?"

The only night we could think of when Mother might have needed help was the night our Baby was born. But we were all born at home with church-women to help.

"Is Miz Jones taking the tonic I left for her? It's very important. She needs to build up her blood. You be sure she takes it like I told her."

Mother backed as far away from them as she could get, working on disappearing while the two men discussed her.

Leslie Ray said to Gramma and me, "Doctor Duncan gave Mother medicine!"

Daddy hadn't warmed up any when he spoke.

"She's been taking it easy and we're seeing to it she eats right. She'll be fine, Doctor. I'm sure she was just run down before she went into labor."

It was now confirmed that Doctor Duncan was at our house the night our Baby came. Before we could accept the enormity of that, he had more to say.

"We almost lost her, Reverend. We can't take chances with her condition."

"Sorry I can't ask you in, Doctor, but we've just finished a church service and we've got to get started on our dinner."

Leslie whispered, "He's coming in anyway! Daddy doesn't want him to but he is!"

The doctor walked right past Daddy and over to Mother, just like a welcome guest.

"How 'do, Miz Jones. Oh, there's my little girl. I sure deliver pretty babies, don't I?"

Having a doctor in the house was so unusual, we missed the word "deliver" at first.

He chuckled at his own Doctor humor while he moved over to the couch.

"Now don't you be stingy with her. I love to hold my babies."

Leslie was blocking the kitchen doorway and announcing everything.

"He's picking her up."

"Let me see!"

"He's holding The Baby!"

We both squeezed into the same doorway, Gramma right behind us, none of us willing to miss a second of this. The Baby's eyelids seemed to be trying to open. First they came up in slow motion, a tiny little slit, then closed again, and then slowly she blinked. That was her only movement so far.

"What's this on her forehead? Looks like a big bump. Now how'd that come to be there, right on the front like that?"

Leslie whispered, "He knows! He knows she fell. Somebody told him."

"Brother Booty?"

Leslie said, "Gramma was it you? Did you call the doctor?"

"No, I didn't. I was in town with Ruth and somebody said The Baby fell and she gave me a ride home."

Doctor Duncan was plainly aware of our presence a few feet away. He had picked up our Baby and was cradling her like this was just a friendly visit.

"Where are those redheads? Those two are pistols. They say hey to me every morning on their way to school. Leslie Ray, you in there?"

Leslie marched right out and sounded as confident and calm as if it was an everyday thing for the town doctor to be in the faith-healing preacher's front room holding the preacher's baby.

"Yessir, Doctor Duncan. I was out in the kitchen helping Gramma start dinner."

He was not. Where did he get the guts to tell big fibs like that?

"I hear you're taking piano from Miss Sue. You playing in her recital next Saturday?"

"Yessir. *Humoresque*. It's hard but I like it."

"I'll be there. Miss Sue never lets me miss a recital. Nita Faye, how are you doin'?"

"Fine, Doctor Duncan, just fine. I wrote some words to *Humoresque*."

Leslie objected, "*Humoresque* doesn't have any words."

"It does now because I wrote some."

While my brother and I completed one of our normal exchanges, Gramma smoldered in plain view in the kitchen doorway.

Doctor Duncan asked the two of us, "Is The Baby trying to roll over?"

Mother started to speak, but we answered before she could. We spent more time with The Baby than she did. We answered nossir, we haven't seen her do that yet. We knew everything about her and how smart she was and how she was learning things much sooner than other babies, and still we had evidently failed in our duty to care for her this time. It wasn't for lack of trying. What if she was capable of more wiggling than we knew? Then maybe she shouldn't have been sleeping on a pew and maybe we should have been holding her and maybe her falling was our fault.

Doctor Duncan kept talking to us but was looking at The Baby.

"You helping your Mama with The Baby after school?"

Leslie said, "I do."

I said, "We both do."

Daddy had had enough of the unexpected, uninvited, unwelcome chitchat. He was wound up, we could tell, but he kept a barely civil tone.

"Run on now, kids, and start some cornbread. Doctor, good to see you. We'd best be fixin' our dinner. We're all hungry and we've got to get ready for church tonight."

He put his arm around Mother's waist.

"My wife needs her rest."

The doctor ignored Daddy, sat right down on the couch, put The Baby down and listened with his stethoscope. This was the closest we had ever been to medical equipment of any kind. We watched as he checked her little arms and legs and fingers and gently pushed up one of her droopy little eyelids, and it stayed open! Then the other eyelid came up. After one long silent stare, both eyes fully open, they stayed open and the doctor smiled.

"Aren't you the cutest thing? Seems like you just got here and you're getting so big already."

He turned to Daddy and Mother.

"She's starting to come around now, but she may have a concussion. I want you to watch her closely and call me if she vomits or cries a lot or sleeps too much or if there's any change."

To Mother, he added, "You take care of yourself, Miz Jones. We don't want any more of those episodes."

"Those episodes." "That night." "Labor." "Tonic." "Her condition." All the words together telling a story we hadn't heard before. My brother and I might as well have been kicked across the room, that was how shocked and then angry and then hurt we were. We retreated.

Leslie said, "Daddy called the doctor for Mother, but he didn't call that time my stomach hurt so bad."

"He didn't call the doctor when my tonsils swole up."

Doctor Duncan picked up his bag and moved to the front door.

"Reverend, you need to watch this little one closely. Promise me you'll call if there's any change."

"No, Doctor, I won't promise you that. I put my faith in the healing power of the Lord."

"I'm a man of faith myself, Reverend, been a Methodist all my life and a Doctor for a long time. I don't think the Lord has any disrespect for my efforts."

"We just believe different, Doctor."

"You're quite a persuasive young man, Reverend. I hear they're going to put you up for president of the County Ministerial Alliance."

"There's some talk. I'd be honored if it happens."

"You'd be the first Pentecostal they ever elected." The Doctor's tone became a pointed thing with sharp edges. "Answer me this, Reverend, if that baby dies and people ask you about it, would you say—"

"It's the Lord's will. The Lord's will, Doctor, that's what I'm called to preach."

He closed the door.

Leslie wouldn't let it rest. He kept bringing up to Daddy what Doctor Duncan said about the night our Baby was born, and each time he brought it up, Daddy equivocated, deflected, changed the subject, then finally and firmly told Leslie there were some things he would learn about "in due time." What Daddy never did was admit it was him, that he was the one who called the Doctor that night to help his wife.

To say that the day The Baby fell was a turning point would be to understate its impact. From that Sunday forward there was no going back to earlier childhood notions when we carried a seed of hope that things might change, that the course of our lives could possibly alter enough to lead us to a place where parents took care of their children when they were sick.

The wall between us and them fell into place with a resounding thud, solid as a block of concrete reinforced with steel and strong enough to last a lifetime.

Chapter 13

The Other Babies

Gramma's visit made our lives much more enjoyable. Leslie and I shared many of her opinions. The three of us whispered together. She cooked our favorite foods every day, though our kitchen was spare compared to hers and our weary stove wasn't even a distant cousin to the giant in her California kitchen.

With Gramma in town Daddy had more time for pastoring. He could stay out most of the day making his sick calls instead of stopping by the house several times to check on Mother, something he did even before we got our Baby. Gramma and Daddy eased back into their banter over cooking and vegetable growing. After supper Daddy spent the rest of the evening with Mother listening to the radio in their room.

Gramma didn't like churches in general and she especially didn't like ours. She and Daddy never mentioned it during the week, but each Sunday morning Daddy asked, "Zula, you coming?" Gramma always responded, "Raymond, you know I'm not."

When we got home from church, we found a nice dinner spread on the table, but Gramma was gone off somewhere. One rumor had her in the back room of the hardware store, that same spot where card games took place, and though we never knew for sure whether she was participating, we were proud she might be. If she was, she'd be the only woman there.

Gramma and Miss Ruth smoked cigarettes over at the beauty shop. They may have even had some wine in there. I tried to avoid Miss Ruth when Gramma was in town because Daddy would ask me later what I saw or heard, and I knew Miss Ruth would be talking about Gramma and whatever misdeeds the two of them were up to.

Mother spent more time in her bedroom and less time at church events, but she remained faithful about Sunday mornings, singing one of her "specials" while deacons took up the offering. When the noise of coins clinking on coins in the offering plates indicated few paper bills were donated, Mother shook things loose with a spiritual.

While Daddy and Mother took a nap after church, Leslie and I took care of The Baby. Sometimes Gramma wandered in and we pulled out scrapbooks and photo albums. Looking through them was a favorite pastime, especially when somebody other than our parents told the stories behind the pictures.

Mother chronicled everything in those albums, every revival stop, every newspaper story, every handbill or publicity photo used in campaigns. Then there were volumes of family pictures. This woman we believed to be unsentimental treated her albums as treasures and added new material often, trimming the pasted-in mementos with fancy photo corners.

The books were so detailed and Mother's handwriting so elaborate, they made our everyday comings and goings seem adventurous. Before we could read, we'd memorized every page. We knew which book had the picture of Leslie sitting on a pony in El Dorado, Arkansas, when a man with a camera walked up and down the streets, leading his pony, carrying his equipment, stopping to knock on doors to ask if anyone wanted a picture taken for a quarter. We knew which book had the picture of Mother and Daddy so young and cuddly, and which books contained images of more distant relatives.

There was a book devoted to our two dead babies. Two more Joneses had arrived after I was born, and both went to heaven very soon. Centered on one page was a large photograph of Baby Fern in her coffin, which was lined with pleated white satin. Embroidery spelled out "Our Darling" on a plaque inside the top.

It didn't seem strange to have a picture of our dead sister at her funeral. Everyone in the family talked about both babies, Dolores Fern and Raymond Wayne. Mother and Daddy never discouraged it, and if she was around when the baby book was open, Mother joined in, taking out a handkerchief which she needed to use until we closed the book and put it away again.

As we looked at the funeral pictures, Leslie said, as he always did, "Baby Fern. Rest her soul." I repeated "rest her soul." Custom dictated that all our deceased be remembered out loud whenever their names came up.

Gramma asked, "What does your Daddy say about how Baby Fern died?"

I said, "God took her up to heaven to be with Him."

Leslie added, "Because when a soul departs, it's the Lord's will. The Lord decides."

Gramma had managed to make it through the Sunday The Baby fell without bringing the house down on top of us, but she was ill equipped for stifling her opinions for long, so if you sat there awhile, you were bound to learn more.

"Your Daddy loves his babies when they're little. Carries them around. Sings to them."

Leslie said, "He carries our Baby around."

I asked, "Did he carry us around like that when we were little?"

"He sure did. Your Mother, now you hand her a baby and she acts surprised, like she doesn't know what to do with it. I never saw her pick up a baby except when there was nobody else to do it, or once in a while to have pictures made."

This may or may not have been accurate. As we got older, we knew it wasn't wise to take everything Gramma K said about her daughter as absolute, and then the same was true about what Mother said about Gramma. We were constantly weighing where the real facts might reside.

The pictures in our albums were mostly in black and white so we liked to have the colors added with detailed explanations, some we'd heard many times but never tired of.

"Was Baby Fern's hair like Mother and Daddy's?"

"No. Red like yours. Dark, dark auburn, darker than you two. Skin like your Mother."

When we saw this picture of Baby Fern we always remarked about how dark her hair looked, just so we could get Mother or Daddy or Gramma to assure us Baby Fern was a redhead, which somehow made us proud, that we had red hair in common with this beautiful creature.

"Your Daddy carried Baby Fern around night after night when she took sick."

We'd heard parts of this story, some of it told by our parents, but a completely different version came from Gramma this time. It might have been because we were older, or on account of the Sunday The Baby fell, or just because she wasn't good at keeping her emotions tamped down for long.

"It was 1944 in El Dorado. Baby Fern had been sick for weeks. I came to help because your Mama was expecting another baby and she was very weak." This time, Gramma added, "Your Mama's got no business having so many babies, and her hemorrhaging every time."

"What's hemorrhaging?"

"Bleeding too much."

"Is it dangerous?"

"It sure is, especially delivering a baby at home without a doctor. I warned Raymond every time, but they still had all of you at home with some churchwoman in to help."

She continued, "One night while I was there with your Mother waiting for the new baby to come—"

Both Leslie and I knew about our brother, and we said in unison, "Baby Wayne, rest his soul."

"Baby Fern screamed out in the night, like she was in agony. Some said it was the infantile paralysis, but we don't know, because your Daddy never took her to the doctor."

Leslie asked, "What did he do?"

"He took her over to the church instead, wrapped her up in a blanket and laid that baby on the altar and had the whole church pray for her. I begged him to get a doctor. He wouldn't. Baby Fern died the same day your new little brother was born."

"Where were we?"

"Leslie Ray, we told you to take Nita Faye and go outside and you two sat out there on the curb."

He said, "I remember that house was way up off the ground and the steps were steep."

Leslie Ray claimed to remember a bit of Baby Fern's life, the part our parents told us about how pretty she was and how she would try to go to Daddy when he came home. She was an early walker, they said, but she plopped down on the floor and got up again laughing every time. Gramma continued, and this next part of the story contained information our parents had left out.

"Baby Fern died while the new baby was being born. Exactly the same time. That churchwoman was in there with your Mother and your Daddy was walking the floor, praying over his sick baby. But it was too late. I could see she was gone, and I told him so. Anybody could see that. I kept saying, 'Raymond, the baby is gone.' He didn't hear me"

Gramma's voice got so soft, we had to lean close.

"I said it again. 'Raymond, the baby has crossed over now,' and he said NO!"

Gramma's voice broke every time she told any part of this story for years to come, and she never tried to hide it. She took out her own handkerchief.

"I said, yes, Raymond, she's gone. I kept telling him, here, Raymond, let me hold Baby Fern, but he wouldn't. I said give me the baby now and he said no, no, no."

"Then, what happened?"

"It was a Sunday and we had to call the people at the funeral home who come to your house when someone dies, and it took a while for them to get to us."

Leslie asked, "What did Mother do?"

"I asked that churchwoman not to tell your Mother. She was so weak and she didn't know Baby Fern was gone, but the woman walked right in there to their bedroom and said, 'Oh Sister Jones, I am so sorry about Baby Fern passing.'"

Leslie said, "I saw them take Baby Fern away. A man walked down the steps, carrying a basket with a blanket in it. That was her, right?"

"Yes, he took the baby away. Your Mama couldn't do anything but cry over her little girl. She'd lost so much blood, she couldn't even get out of bed to go to the funeral. She told me exactly how she wanted Baby Fern dressed, because we would take pictures at the funeral for her. I called up the man who owned the best store in town, and when he found out it was the preacher's little girl, he said he would go open the store up and I should come and pick out whatever we wanted and show it to your Mama to see if it was right."

In the picture, Baby Fern wore the beautiful dress Gramma K and Mother chose. She looked like a doll that closes its eyes when it sleeps.

"When we got home from the funeral, I packed my suitcase. I couldn't stay any longer in that little house in El Dorado. Walls thin as paper and so much pain. I heard them talking late into the night. Your Mother and her pitiful squalling you could hear all over the house. She said, 'My baby,' and he said, 'We have to keep trusting the Lord.' She said, 'My baby is dead,' and he said, 'She's with Him now in heaven.' Your Mother cried and cried all day and all night. One night she hollered out, 'I want her HERE, Raymond. I don't believe the Lord needs to take little babies just when they're learning how to walk.'"

I had to go get a handkerchief myself while Leslie wiped his face on his sleeve.

He asked, "Then what did Daddy do?"

"He kept telling your Mother everything was meant to work out that way. It's the Lord's will."

Gramma moved to the story about the next baby.

"Raymond Wayne died soon after I got back to California. We never did find out what he died from, but I know they never took him to a doctor either. After that, I hated their religion, and I told your Daddy so. Know what he said? He said I might be the one going to hell for not trusting in the healing power of the Lord. I tell you what, *I'm* not the one going to hell. *I'm* not the one with two dead babies."

Leslie said, "But you don't hate Daddy now."

"I don't hate him anymore. I hate his religion."

I asked, "Are you the one who called Doctor Duncan when The Baby fell? Tell the truth. Did you do it?"

"I did not. I'm not sure who did. Could've been anybody."

Leslie said, "Mother says it was probably Brother Booty."

"I wouldn't be surprised. Your Daddy knows not everybody agrees with him. Preachers can teach what they want to about faith healing, but they're not going to get everybody else to go along with it. People believe all kinds of different ways in the same church."

I added, "One woman in our church wears makeup and sleeveless dresses. Sister Janway has a bathing suit."

Gramma said, "Maybe your Mama went to see the doctor herself and didn't tell your Daddy. She had medicine in there, in their room, the kind that comes from a doctor and your Daddy didn't try to hide it."

Gramma had snooped enough to wonder at the mystery we noticed when our Baby was born. Did Daddy think we wouldn't see the medicine? Harder to believe was the possibility of Mother keeping such a big secret from him, that she might still be seeing Doctor Duncan on her own. Sending tapes of her songs out, that was one thing, but visiting a doctor?

Knowing now about the dead babies, learning a doctor was available to Mother but not to us, Leslie and I whispered between us our assurances to each other that Gramma would liberate us. She did not. We assumed because we'd stayed with her in the past and because she knew medical care was not available to us, she would find a way to get us to come live with her in California. She did not.

Nobody was coming to save us from what happened with our other babies. This became a more and more frightening possibility. Gramma had done us no favors telling us about our dead sister and brother and then leaving us alone with our imagination.

Chapter 14

Raymond's Doll Baby

Daddy came in from picking up the special food Mother wanted. This time it was barbecue from the deep pit place at the edge of town. The rest of the family ate supper earlier but Mother wasn't hungry then. He glanced around, and not seeing her, he rushed to their bedroom.

"You're lying down?"

In a small voice she expressed surprise.

"I don't know what happened. I was picking up around the house a little and all of a sudden . . ."

Her voice took on the upward tilt at the end of a sentence that children use to convey a first-time experience.

"All of a sudden I had to sit down."

Neither of them acknowledged the frequency with which this event occurred, the fainting or the near-to-it. Both of them treated each episode as if it was new.

"Honey, you stay right here and rest. I'll fix up a nice tray for you."

Even after Doctor Duncan's visit, after Mother's condition being discussed openly and with Gramma filling us in about it, Daddy seemed to assume first that another day in bed was due only to one of her headaches. When he wasn't around, Mother talked openly with Gramma about how she felt, and the more days Mother was pale and stayed in bed, the madder Gramma got.

In the parsonage, if you wanted to tell a secret, you'd be just as well off telling it standing out in the front yard as trying to whisper it inside. I'm not insulting the parsonage because I loved everything about it, but sometimes you did have to hear things you'd just as soon not hear. With Gramma K and Mother, you didn't have to go to the trouble of eavesdropping because they talked to each other the same way no matter who came into the room.

Mother said she felt well enough to paint, and we helped her set up the easel by a window, laying newspapers under everything to catch the spatters. Gramma's daughter was molded in her own image. Both of them were adroit at opening a conversation with a question intended to incite. Sometimes, though, a listener never found out what provoked them. Everyone would be calm and then in the next minute one of them snapped.

The Visiting Queen of Incendiary entered and spoke to The Princess.

"What's *this* you're painting?"

"It's part of a mural we're fixing to put up behind the pulpit. I'm painting scenes about the crucifixion. Right here is Jesus in the Garden of Gethsemane, reaching up for—"

"*This* is what he's got you doing now?"

"Mother, just stop it. You're not interested in the work we're trying to do here."

"No, I really *am* interested, Fern. I am interested in knowing how you can persuade me that you're happy, looking like this . . ."

"Looking like what? What's wrong with the way I look?"

Gramma hesitated a moment, and it was clear she meant Mother's skin color, which had recently gone from pale to pale yellow, and that was what Gramma was looking at but that's not what she said.

"That dress. Where'd you get a thing like that?"

"I made it."

"Is that one of those little wash dresses your church ladies wear?"

"I made it out of yard goods I got on sale. I like a print once in a while."

When she was feeling more herself, The Princess usually began by shooting back comments worthy of a pretender to the throne, but she departed from their script once in a while and dissolved into shoulder-shaking floods of tears.

By the time Mother said the part about how she liked the dress she'd made, anyone could tell she was wavering, that she was about to cry, that her appearance mattered a great deal to her, and if you were familiar with their habits, you would also know that Gramma K knew all of that when she started.

"Quit picking at me, Mother. You just keep on . . ."

"*Picking* at you? Look at you, dressed like some old woman, because your husband tells you that's your place. Trying to play like a preacher's wife. You know how you look? Do you? I'll tell you. You look *plain*."

"Mother, you are just plain *mean*."

"Where's the jewelry I sent you? Is jewelry still a sin, because I saw some of your good churchwomen with brooches on?"

Gramma K had been through the list of dos and don'ts for a pastor's wife often enough to know the wearing of jewelry was discouraged. Hearing her line of questioning from the next room, without seeing Mother's face, you could tell it was going to take some doing to fix what had already gone wrong with this visit, and maybe it couldn't be fixed at all. Was Gramma taking on her daughter's life again, after all these years, because Mother was easier to intimidate than Daddy?

"What harm would it do you to put on a little color? Even a string of pearls?"

"It's important to Raymond."

"You've got no business out here painting pictures for him and running over to that church building so soon after you *nearly died* giving birth to that baby. He ought to be making sure you stay home."

"I'm the one who wants to go sing my songs in church, Mother. The Lord is using my music to help bring in souls. Raymond takes good care of me. You're all the way out in California. You don't know what goes on here every day. You don't know what all he does for me."

"I know what you need. What you need is a husband who doesn't try to turn you into somebody else. You give me nothing but back talk about growing up poor. Yes you *do* still talk against me. I know you do. Then you go off with a man who says he's got a calling to preach in some little town. Why doesn't anybody around here get a calling to see to your health and take care of those kids in there?"

"I want you to hush, Mother. You're making me sad."

"What's sad is everything he's asked you to change. How does it feel going without makeup and giving up your picture shows? How is any of that gonna send you to heaven? You could have done anything, if you hadn't married a poor preacher."

"I love him."

"Love's not enough. Never has been. When a woman gives up too much, she's borrowing trouble. You keep borrowing trouble, and I promise you, one day the payment comes due."

"You're jealous, Mother. Because I have a good man. He loves me and he cares about me and he always will and you have never had anybody who cared about you like that."

"Don't you miss singing the songs you used to sing? And dancing? Don't you miss dancing?"

"It seems like every time you come visit, you make me cry. Is that what you mean to do, Mother? Make me cry? Because that is what you do. Every time."

The next sound, a predictable finish to the conversation, was the bedroom door closing. Mother would be in there for hours with the rest of us taking care of The Baby and Daddy going back and forth between the kitchen and the bedroom, checking on her.

The next day we took Gramma to the train station in Little Rock. Abrupt departures were not unusual after one of their episodes. We were once wakened in the middle of the night during a visit to California and told to get your things, we're leaving right now.

Chapter 15

In the Garden

Behind the parsonage, past the backyard and the weeping willow, our garden sprang forth, Reverend Jones's agri-painting spread out in rows of different colors. Daddy's years of living on farms taught him everything he needed to know about planting and tending and harvesting, and he was determined we would also learn to grow and cook what we needed. This was the first time we'd had space for growing and we used every inch of it.

Gardening meant time spent with Daddy and we were always seeking more of his attention. He was teaching us survival skills, when to plant and when to harvest and how to cook what we grew. He circled back from time to time repeating lessons until he declared us capable. When that happened, we blossomed in the glow of his "That'll do fine. Just fine."

Our vegetable patch was enclosed on three sides by a chicken wire fence with climbing vines already moving up it and a row of marigolds around the base. Daddy said marigolds shoo away unwanted pests. The fourth side, closest to the house, had a picket fence with a gate. Adjacent to the garden was a shed where Daddy kept our tools.

When he called us to come work in the garden, we raced to the back porch to put on our gardening shoes, which were last year's school shoes. Daddy didn't own casual shoes either. He gardened in his oldest hard-soled church shoes and pulled galoshes over them. We went straight to the shed to pick our implements.

"Nita Faye, that hoe's too big for you. Get that little hoe over yonder. Easy now. Lessee, maybe we'll give you this trowel instead. Son, did you feed your rabbits?"

Even when completing the assigned chore was more a future plan than an actual fact, Leslie answered the same way every time the question came up.

"Yessir."

Daddy took the trowel from me, knelt down, and demonstrated.

"Turn the dirt over real gentle. Don't slice into things."

I laid the trowel aside and tried barely sticking my fingers in the dirt.

"You gotta work with *intention*, girl, like this."

He reached around under there and brought up the sweetest tiny potatoes in one swoop. Then he turned his attention to Leslie.

"How about the chickens?"

"Fed 'em."

"Son, tell me, what were you thinking, letting those pigeons out on Sunday?"

"I wanted to see if they'd come home. See if they're homing pigeons."

"You know where your pigeons went, don't you? They flew straight over the congregation while church was letting out." Daddy was trying not to laugh. "The whole situation coulda been avoided if you'da been in Sunday School class where you belong."

I said, "He hates Sunday School. Leslie Ray's a heathen."

"Shut up, Nita Faye."

Daddy responded, "Leslie Ray, you know better'n that. I don't want to hear 'shut up' come out of your mouth."

"Yessir."

I pressed the advantage, with a proper degree of self-righteousness.

"Yeah, Leslie Ray, stop talking to me like that."

We weren't allowed to yell at each other or hit each other, and though my brother and I got along just fine, we slung around some language to make a point. We called each other the strongest names we could think of that wouldn't be prohibited, often appropriating Daddy's language describing sinners.

Daddy kept hoeing. When he was in the garden, nothing bothered him much so he responded with only vague reproach.

"Nita Faye, you can quit being contentious."

"Yessir."

One day I called Leslie Ray an idiot which was evidently a word too far.

Daddy heard, stopped, and said, "Don't call your brother an idiot. He is not an idiot."

"Well he's stupid then."

Daddy considered for a second.

"He might *act* stupid once in a while but an idiot can't help himself."

(In Daddy's voice, "Your brother is not a idiot. . . . A idiot cain't hep hisseff.")

"Idiot" was a word reserved for those among us who were not quite right mentally. Daddy couldn't abide an expression that might impugn.

"Son, you know what those pigeons did right on top of the congregation, don't you?"

He burst out laughing and we joined in and had to stop digging, we were laughing so hard.

"You shoulda seen Sister Anthony! You better hope they come home a different way next time!"

He strode up and down the rows, a satisfied man plucking a weed, tapping a cantaloupe.

"Leslie Ray, bring in some-a them green onions. That row over yonder's about right. Nita Faye, you're not doin' so good with those potatoes."

"Daddy, can we have new potatoes and creamed peas and cornbread for dinner?"

"We can if you don't chop those poor little things all to pieces."

He started to whistle, then he hummed, then he winked at me and started singing "Back in the Saddle Again."

I sang too.

Leslie Ray started in, the way he always did.

"That's Nita Faye's *boyfriend's* song. She loooooves Gene Autry."

"Yes I do. I'm gonna marry Gene Autry and sing on the radio with him and move to California and live right by Gramma K."

Daddy said, "Well now, Nita Faye, you can't marry Gene Autry."

"Yeah, because when you grow up he'll be too old to marry you by then."

Daddy kept collecting vegetables, putting them into the basket we used so the dirt could shake out before we took them into the kitchen.

He was serious when he said, "Naw—'cause I'm not sure he's right with the Lord. Don't matter if a man's famous. He's not goin' to heaven unless he gets down on his knees and gets saved first."

"Uh-huh! I bet he's saved!"

"Well he's not usin' his voice to sing the Lord's music out in public like he ought to. The Lord gives you a gift like that, you got to use it only for him."

Mother opened the screen door and called to us.

"Leslie Ray. Nita Faye. One of you come change The Baby."

Leslie said to me, "You do it."

"Nuh-uh. I did it last time."

"Did not. I did."

"Leslie Ray, you're a heathen *and* you're mendacious."

"Now where'd you get that word?" Daddy asked.

"Your sermon."

"Before you go calling your brother something, you ought to find out what it means."

"Yeah, just shut up, Nita Faye."

"Boy, didn't I just *tell* you? I don't want to *hear* 'shut up' again."

"Well *hush* then, Nita Faye. Quit calling me names."

Daddy said, "Well, girl, we are waitin' on you to tell us. What does 'mendacious' mean?"

"I don't know. What?"

"Look it up."

"Can't look it up. Don't know how to spell it."

"Ah, now your Mama, she's the speller in the family. You get her to help you look it up. Go ask her."

"I don't want to go in there. She'll make me change a dirty diaper."

Leslie Ray asked, "Why can't Mother change diapers herself? How come we have to?"

"Your Mama has got her hands full. She is *tryin'* to write a new song."

Leslie said, "Or maybe she's just reading a magazine and doesn't feel like it."

"What did you say, boy? You better not be sassing, you hear me?"

"Yessir."

"Any more back talk outta either one of you and you won't get dessert. I'm fixin' to go in there and sweet-talk Mama-gal into making us a raisin pie."

He picked up the basket full of beautiful baby potatoes and headed to the back steps, where he took off his galoshes and went whistling into the kitchen.

Chapter 16

Hey Good Lookin'

Fans wrote to us, and while we were out on the road, radio stations forwarded the mail to general delivery, or our mail would go to a pastor we knew, and we'd stop and pick it up when we passed through. Mother wrote back to every letter that included an address. She read some out loud.

People asked why she didn't make records. She wanted to. Fellow evangelists and gospel singers were selling their own records, boxes full of 78s too heavy to lift, but we didn't have money for the pressing.

A few quartets got famous enough that selling their 78s generated considerable income. They drove the same roads we drove, only now they pulled trailers filled with boxes of records. Eventually famous quartets traveled in their own buses, old and reconditioned, but still a luxury.

We didn't have a trailer, and even when we were still out on the road, Mother's dream was hampered by more than our lack of resources. Only "race stations," as they were called then, played women with her sound, and their stars were Sister Rosetta and Mahalia, who were Black. Even if Mother could make a record, what radio station would play it?

In Murfreesboro we let her be whenever she was in the front room with her guitar or at the piano. Either way, we tried not to disrupt whatever she was doing. We were taught respect for people who were creating things. She played a chord, wrote down something, hummed, sang a few words, and did it again. She remained completely engrossed, strumming her guitar then leaning over the notebook on the coffee table, her cloud of curls obscuring her face. She didn't take notice when we came home, or when we took The Baby out of her crib and changed her diaper, or later when we returned to get The Baby to make her a bottle.

Daddy hung his hat on the hook on the back porch, took off his preacher coat, loosened his tie, and went into the room where Mother was singing.

There are some people who say we cannot tell
Strum.
Whether we are saved or whether all is well
She wrote on the pad.

Daddy moved her notebook over a little and sat down on the coffee table, facing her.

"How's it coming, Sugar?"

"I think this is my best one yet. You know how I usually write songs for my own voice? Well honey, *everybody* can sing this one!"

"I like the name. You still callin' it 'I Was There When It Happened'?"

"Oh I wouldn't change the title. The Lord sends me my titles first. Then I put the songs to them. Someday, Raymond, one of my songs is gonna sell so many records, we'll have a pink Cadillac. And I'll wear a mink stole to the DJ Convention in Nashville every year."

He reached over and took her guitar from her and started strumming.

"You sure are pretty when you're writing songs, Mrs. Jones."

"Raymond, you go on now. I want to finish this."

He didn't leave. Instead he sang to her the first part of Hank Williams's "Hey Good Lookin'" all the time watching her, waiting for the smile he knew would be along soon.

She gave him the smile and he stopped singing.

"You remember that bathing suit you had, the one I liked? You still got that?"

"Oh honey, I threw that old thing out. Got no use for it now."

"What if we wanna go swimmin'?"

"Raymond! I can't put on a bathing suit. Somebody from church might see me."

"I know where there's a creek. Never seen another soul there. Water's nice and cool, big trees all around."

"My bathing suit's gone, Sugar. It makes me sad sometimes but you know you said a Christian woman can't be showing her bare skin."

"I've got a picture of you in that bathing suit, swimming down by your Mama's house in El Dorado. Remember that day?"

"No you don't! Show it to me."

"Here it is. In my billfold. Carried it with me ever since."

He joined her on the couch and had his arm around her. She put her face up close to his.

"Honey, do you think I'm still that pretty—without makeup?"

"You're my big ol' walkin' talkin' Doll Baby. That's just what you look like. A big ol' baby doll with Doll Baby curls and great big Doll Baby eyes."

He picked up the guitar and was getting ready to sing again but Leslie Ray poked his head in the door.

"Daddy, what do you want from the garden for supper?"

Daddy handed her guitar back to Mother.

"Mama-gal, I gotta get outside or these young'uns will have everything dug up."

My brother and I viewed her new songs and her musical dreams with apprehension. She could perform for a crowd of hundreds at Singings. Add in revival tours and all the people under the big tent every night. Add in radio listeners. The combination created the widest exposure possible for her at that point in her career, and any time that was going on, it meant the two of us not having a home.

On the other hand, on Daddy's watch, a Sunday congregation when we pastored might be anywhere from fifty to two hundred people. Not many of our churches could hold more than that. His dream was just the right size for us.

Chapter 17

I Was There When It Happened

The return address on the letter said "Governor Jimmie Davis." That wasn't a big surprise since Mother sent tapes of her songs to many people, including the Singing Governor, and once in a while she got a response. Letters arrived with return addresses from Acuff-Rose Music or RCA Victor saying, "None of these suit our artists, but please keep sending your new songs." Sometimes a letter was blunt: "We don't have a market for the songs you write."

She saved every letter, sure that one day she'd remind everyone how she kept trying until she succeeded, an outcome no one except Mother seemed certain of. What she really wanted was to sing her own songs, record them in a studio with great musicians, and have them released on a famous label with her name as both composer and artist.

Daddy said, "Sugar, there's mail for you out here," and he laid it on the kitchen table. She didn't come running. She'd been making tapes and sending them out for a while now. We all drifted away until we heard her shout.

"Governor Davis wants to record my song!"

Daddy asked to see the letter. He read it out loud. It was true. Governor Jimmie Davis wanted to record "I Was There When It Happened." Anything the Governor recorded would receive lots of airplay.

There was a paragraph near the bottom saying Governor Davis would also like to publish the song. He was offering to buy the song from Mother, price to be determined.

None of us except Mother knew anything about music publishing. She heard from studio musicians that Jimmie Davis was credited with writing "You Are My Sunshine," but in fact he may have bought it from someone and put his name on it. Even Daddy's favorite, Hank Williams, was rumored to have bought some of the famous songs he was credited with writing. Nothing dishonest about it, they said. Many singers wanted to own the music they recorded. There was money to be made from the records, of course, but also from publishing rights.

The letter was typed on formal stationery, and it had a phone number on it and a P.S. in handwriting from Governor Davis saying how much he liked the song and how he would love to hear from her about it soon.

Mother stood in the hall at the wall phone, rang for Sarah, and gave her the Baton Rouge number. We heard her talking to somebody on the other end. Heard her give her name. Heard her say the name of the song. Heard what seemed like friendly chit-chat with the Governor, then she said, "No, the Lord sends me my songs. I can't sell them."

We waited through another silence.

"Half, then."

She hung up. She would let the Governor put his name on her song as the cowriter. Before we could ask her why, she told us.

"He wouldn't record it at all unless he could own half of it."

Chapter 18

Musical Pie Lady

The Homecoming in Little Rock was where Sister Fern planned to be ever since the invitation to perform arrived at the parsonage, but we figured when Daddy said no this time he really meant we wouldn't be going.

Mother's new relationship with Governor Davis, his praise for her music, their frequent phone conversations, all affected what would happen next in our family. We watched with dread as she worked to change Daddy's absolute no to we'll see to here we are in the car again.

It started off with Daddy saying, "We need to stay home and tend to our church." Singing out of town on a Saturday, he reminded her, wasn't part of what a pastor's family did. The whole family ought to be busy preparing for the Lord's Day. If they accepted this invitation, everyone's duties would need to be completed late at night after we came back from Little Rock. We would postpone sweeping the church, filling communion cups, checking each pew for the proper spacing of hymnals and Bibles and paper fans, setting up chairs in Sunday School rooms, clearing and resetting the wooden reader board hanging in front that showed which hymns we would sing, laying out the plastic numbers for a deacon to slide into the slot telling how many attended church and the amount of the offering collected, polishing the family's shoes, ironing church clothes, and whatever else Daddy determined needed doing before Sunday morning.

First Mother cried over his no. Then came hours of silent retreat with her floating around the house in a pink peignoir. During this period she spoke only a few words, and when we asked her a question, she looked right through us with her huge gray eyes, and a vague phrase issued forth from her lower register, down where the blues originated. We were carrying on conversations with her ghost. She whispered, "Oh, I don't know," or "Go ask your Daddy," and floated away again, dissolving into herself like cotton candy does when you touch it.

Mother owned several sets of gowns with matching negligees in sheer fabrics that she sewed herself. She made them in red, pink, and black, and she changed into them at just about the time Daddy was going to bed. Since they slept at different times, she slipped into the bedroom early in the evening to tell him goodnight. Hers must have been an effective ploy, since it resulted in moving Mother from the Saturday Sabbath preparation to the place she would rather be. When Daddy finally acquiesced, she regained her energy, and by the time she stood onstage to sing, no one could have guessed she'd nearly died in childbirth months before.

We started our trip in the same old way, with us in the back seat, them in the front. Mother would be keyed up, practically vibrating by the time we arrived in Little Rock, furrowing her pretty forehead all the way there, worrying about how the humidity would affect the elaborate meringue of curly hair piled high and the slippery bobby pins required to hold it up. Daddy was skilled at diversion. When she got jittery in the car, he started conversations that included compliments about her.

This event in Little Rock would include dinner, and safe subjects were always food and music. Daddy wondered what we'd be having to eat. One of us started talking about favorite church food and everyone added to the list.

"That cake in Memphis. That was *some* cake."

"That pecan pie, the one we liked so much, was that Sister Culbreth in Galveston?"

"No, Sister Culbreth made those little risin' biscuits."

"I'm thinking about the buttermilk pie in Odessa. Who made that buttermilk pie that was so creamy?"

That would be Daddy wondering about buttermilk pie. To Daddy's mind, anything made with buttermilk or anything dipped in buttermilk would turn out just fine. When he couldn't get to sleep and wrestled into the night with a problem, he hunted down a piece of cornbread, crumbled it into a tall, cold glass of buttermilk, and ate it with a spoon, and if his stomach still questioned his decisions in the morning, he'd do that same thing again at breakfast time.

Any mention of pie started Daddy off on his favorite pie story. Telling it again was him writing another love note to his Big Ol' Doll Baby.

"You want to know the best pie maker in the whole world?"

We knew her identity but we never interrupted.

"That's your Mama-gal settin' right here next to me."

There was a pause while he either reached across the front seat to touch her cheek, or made like he was going to tickle her in the ribs, or else he took his eyes off the road for a beat too long to let her know with a look that she still had it as far as he was concerned. She loved it.

"*Raymond!* You pay attention to the road, now."

He resumed his familiar pie lady tale. He was such an accomplished storyteller, you could stop him at any point and he'd pick up the thread without dropping a stitch. He was a smooth yarn-spinner who could turn the car sharply to dodge a rabbit in the road, let out a "Wooooeeee!" and pound the steering wheel to congratulate himself on his maneuver, and still pick up his story.

"I don't know if we'da ever finished building that church in Americus if it hadn't of been for your Mama knowing how to make the best pies in the world and helping us raise money."

One of us generally said "uh-huh" about there. No sense being rude.

"She taught every woman in church how to make her piecrust and she had 'em all over to the parsonage rolling out dough and stirring up filling 'til I swan, I don't know how many hundreds of pies they sold! And do you know how much they sold them for—mind you there was a war on then—do you know?"

This was our part.

The back seat answered in unison, "A dollar apiece."

"That's right. A dollar apiece and people in Georgia they'll tell you they never tasted a piecrust tender as your mama's, and her raisin filling, well there's people that'll ask you to this day how to make that raisin pie. Every time we see them. Every time."

Daddy seldom pronounced the word "every." Most often he said "ever," and the last part of a sentence was sometimes repeated, in pleasant affirmation that yes sir and yes m'am, *ever time*, that is exactly what happened.

He was teasing Mother about how he guessed there wouldn't be any pies here today nearly as good as hers. He glanced to see how she was taking it in, and we all knew this time he wasn't just retelling the story to say I love you, but now he especially needed his wife to participate with the women in the new church like she used to do in Georgia when they were brand new pastors, back when she baked pies to help build a church.

Different tactics might soon be necessary. Daddy's supplication alone wouldn't likely persuade her. My brother and I had already observed with some alarm her lack of interest in the details of our new town and especially church activities. Her absence from typical pastor's wife functions was the subject of whispers. Add in this new excitement about her song being recorded and our alert level increased to critical. It seemed we two were a bit ahead of Daddy in realizing the enormity of the approaching tide, but we had Gramma K as a coach.

Mother could have seamlessly performed the role of pastor's wife if she wanted to. If she chose to demonstrate her mastery of the role, she would have you believing.

"Sister Whitmire, aren't you precious to remember us with this fresh okra! Brother Jones will be tickled. We'll fry it up tonight. I would *love* to invite you in, but The Baby's just waking up from her nap."

Daddy said how happy he was that some members of our own church would also be making the hundred-mile trip to Little Rock, proud that their new pastor and his wife were famous enough to be performing there. What our church members didn't yet know was that the pastor's wife felt her real ministry was writing songs and performing.

It was going to be harder, if not impossible, for him to interest Mother in fundraising, or even chatting on the front porch with a church lady, when she had become completely immersed in making music and when the larger world of music makers was paying serious attention to what she did.

We heard the yearning in his voice as he told his pie story. I guess pies were as safe a topic as any if what he wanted to do was avoid another subject entirely.

Delivering a little religion to the masses at events like the Homecoming in Little Rock was Daddy's specialty. He always wove in some testifying. In the middle of a song, he'd shout out, "Let me hear you say AMEN!"

If the response wasn't loud enough, he kept going until amens bounced off the walls. Everyone in the auditorium seemed excited, even the worldly ones who hadn't declared Jesus as their Personal Savior. Leslie and I didn't join in. We'd rather have been walking barefoot down a dirt road going anywhere away from here, but we were obviously the exceptions.

Word had spread about their appearance. Fans who listened to them on Kousin Karl's radio show were there. People who'd only heard them and were now seeing them in person for the first time nudged each other and talked about how good-looking Daddy and Mother were and how flirty they were together.

Kousin Karl took the mic and began his own version of call and response.

"Y'all ready for some fine, fine music?"

Applause. Some answered back.

"What's that? I can't hear you."

"Yesssssss" and foot stomping and applause until Karl introduced the first act, then another and another until just before dinner it was Sister Fern's turn to sing.

He always said nice things about Mother. From the start, years back when they met at a radio station, he believed she should be a star. His introduction today was even more laudatory, and when he said Jimmie Davis would be recording a song she wrote, the applause reached new levels. These people were big fans of the Singing Governor. His imprimatur mattered.

As always, Daddy played rhythm guitar behind her, weaving in and out of the lineup of other players onstage, all the time watching her. On the way home, he would turn back into Pastor Jones but up there on the stage he was a schoolboy with a crush.

In the back seat there were several noticeable differences. After all the years of changing Betsy McCall's clothes on the road, the practice provided no comfort this time. Leslie Ray didn't even try. He left his sketchbook at home. There would be no diversions for him, no voluntary conversation, only the back of his head as he turned to stare out the car window. Sitting next to me now was my brother, the back seat storm cloud.

Chapter 19

His Eye Is on the Sparrow

Changes in music were moving fast. Our congregation was getting used to how Sister Fern sang and to the visiting Saturday night musicians who dropped in to play of a Sunday morning. The music they made was exactly the way Mother had been doing it all our lives, but to the rest of the town, the sound coming out of the little Pentecostal church wasn't like any church music they'd ever heard.

Sister Fern rocked before anyone heard of Elvis and Patsy Cline and Jerry Lee Lewis and others who ventured over into the rockabilly sound. Mother knew the value of her currency. She cleverly adjusted her striving to suit the constraints of a preacher's wife. She was good-looking and talented, and since her teen days she'd relied on both to get along. She pushed the limits of how much of her figure she could display, how much could be deemed acceptable to a congregation, and once she discovered rayon and jersey, she made all her clothes from those fabrics, so her skirts moved everyplace she moved. She was seldom seen in anything made of cotton, even in the heat of Southern summers. The cut of her clothes showed off her bottom-half assets to full advantage while sweetheart necklines, stopping just above the provocative divide, did the rest.

She was self-conscious about her occasional bouts of jaundice and avoided wearing anything with tones of yellow or green or gold. When she was feeling her best, her skin was remarkable, complemented by her favorite colors.

Up there on the platform, the pastor's wife put on a good show. While Daddy believed the music was merely one way to reach sinners and get their attention before the sermon, Mother felt her job description was a bit different. Any message the Good Lord wanted to send through her would best be addressed in song. She didn't include packing or loading or unloading the car for trips in her list of Fern's chores. After everything was set up, she emerged from the car or she sauntered out of a backstage area to take her place in front of a warm microphone.

Leslie Ray and I knew that many people came to our revivals and church services and Singings just to get a closer look at this couple who interacted onstage as if nobody else was watching. It was a free picture show without anybody needing to enter a forbidden movie theatre.

In church when he brought her up to sing one of her specials he lingered a moment, looking right into her eyes, saying "Come on up here, honey," taking her hand, referring to her as "my sweetheart" or "the best wife a man could have" or "his gift from God." The way he praised her in public was exactly the way he treated her at home. Their devotion was the truth.

However, by the time we moved into the parsonage, our parents' individual opinions about music in the ministry had begun to shift in different directions. Daddy sang a hillbilly high tenor and favored his tried and true standards, "I'll Fly Away" and "I Don't Care What the World May Do." As soon as Mother heard Stuart Hamblen's "It Is No Secret," a new inspirational song, she adapted it to her style, giving it a different interpretation. Her rendition in church leaned way over toward music that was popular on the radio.

Her version of Red Foley's "Peace in the Valley" was a favorite, one that audiences asked for often. She also took songs that'd been around awhile, "How Great Thou Art" and "His Eye Is on the Sparrow," and rearranged them to even greater dramatic heights, so by the time she was winding up for the big finish, listeners were on their feet, raising their hands in praise and shouting out. Our Sunday morning church services at the all-white Pentecostal church sounded like the Black church across town.

My new, my only, my now-and-forever best friend, Ruby, told me after school that some of her people from another town heard about Brother Ray and Sister Fern's music and how they're on the radio in Little Rock. I said it's true. Ruby said maybe she'd come see them sing one day. I didn't encourage it. It was my small rebellion against Daddy's rule that church attendance was a crucial quality in a friend. I didn't agree with him and I certainly didn't plan for Ruby to have to earn my friendship when, in fact, I was in awe of her.

One Sunday, Ruby walked into our church and stood by the back door, not taking a seat, looking straight up at the platform where my parents were. Leslie Ray saw her and nudged me and I got up and went back there with her. Of course Daddy saw all of this. He must have thought she was finally seeing the light.

But in fact she whispered that she was leaving. Her family was outside in the truck ready to go. On the first day she arrived at the fifth grade classroom, she said she'd have to go when a crop came in somewhere that her family could harvest, but I put that out of mind because as long as she was in town, I had a best friend. She was so smart, she had no difficulty completing the same work as students who went to school every day.

When she said she was leaving, right then, during our Sunday morning worship service, I refused to believe it. I had to go outside and see for myself. We stood by the truck where her family waited.

We hugged, and though we both knew she wouldn't have an address for a while, we promised to write each other as soon as we could. She climbed back up into the bed of the truck, and her Daddy began to move away. I yelled at Ruby. She pounded on the window of the cab and he stopped. I shouted at him.

"Wait! Please wait. I'll be right back."

Ruby jumped out and spoke to her Daddy where he sat behind the wheel. She nodded okay and I took off running as fast as I could back to the parsonage.

In his mirror, Ruby's Daddy saw me returning and started up the motor again. Ruby was in the back with her brothers and sisters. I handed her my Betsy Wetsy doll and she clutched it tight, then we waved until she was out of sight.

Chapter 20

Goodbye Again

"I can't believe they're taking my kids away from me."

"Don't cry, Sister Coker," I said. "I'll go bring in the eggs for you."

"You gotta find somebody else to do the churning now," Leslie said. He was capable of witnessing a river of tears from his Mother without reacting, but when Sister Coker started crying he was shaken and took a step away so we wouldn't see.

"Leslie Ray, you come hug my neck. And take care of your sisters, you hear? Nita Faye, you carry this sack for the trip. It's some of my biscuits with ham like y'all like and there's pie in there. And where's my baby? You tell your Daddy he better not drive off 'til he brings The Baby over here to say goodbye."

We headed back across the field, running with the paper bag from Sister Coker's house to deliver her message to Daddy.

Though Gramma K was out in California, her voice came in clear as day, defending her prediction.

Here, Hotshots. Here's another sack. You better take some of these new potatoes and onions and peas from your garden. And some of those flowers out by the fence, and some mint from the bush by the back door. It'll be a long time before you have a garden again. You won't be in one place long enough to grow anything, unless they have another baby and have to slow down for a minute.

Of course we were aware of discussions between our parents about leaving the pastorate so The Joneses could be evangelists again. There were incessant talks, back and forth, which they made no effort to hide, with Mother saying her calling to music was every bit as sacred as Daddy's calling to pastor, and with neither of them ever saying a word about what another move might mean for Leslie and me.

Faith versus ambition. Same old story. The pattern of our lives. We'd let ourselves believe it could change. Settling down, going to school every day, growing through experience, spending time with people who didn't share our parents' beliefs, every one of these advances would be lost as soon as we drove off again.

The two of us were forever changed by our time in that parsonage. We knew a doctor. We knew some people get to keep whatever they own. We treasured personal possessions by then and not because ours were valuable but because they were part of our personalities. All this knowledge made the goodbye more painful. We couldn't erase the people we had become and we didn't want to try. The people we were now had even stronger objections to the life our parents planned. This move plunged us back into our default positions, me sad and Leslie Ray mad.

How could they keep leaving everything? It wasn't a normal way to live. Gramma K said they once owned a home and drove a new car. Daddy worked at a regular job, but before we met them they'd already taken their vow to live through church work, existing on whatever income that provided. They both became ordained in their sect and made lifelong commitments, which included living with uncomfortably scant means.

In the first parsonage I remembered, in Americus, Georgia, everything was donated to us, furniture, clothes, food, everything. When we left there we left it all behind. I was four and Leslie was six. The first possession I loved passionately was there. It was a small red rocking chair made for me by a church member. I rocked in that chair every day while Leslie Ray went off to first grade, moving it closer and closer to the front door as I waited for him to come home from school and tell me stories.

As we prepared to leave Georgia, Daddy and I trudged up a flight of stairs to the apartment of the family who would now take possession of my red chair. I cried going up, cried coming down, and tripped and fell down those stairs, and I still carry the indentation in my forehead where a cut that should have been treated with stitches was treated with prayer.

As we left Murfreesboro, the plan they worked out for traveling with a baby was to leave one of us, Leslie Ray or me, in an apartment in Texarkana with a relative or some believer from a nearby church, then they said they'd return and exchange that one for the other.

The one on the road would be responsible for The Baby's care. The one on the road was also away from school and mailed homework back. The worst part of this arrangement for us was being separated from each other.

Though we'd long since divided ourselves into us versus them, we considered The Baby neutral territory. We were so involved in her upbringing that when the traveling one returned home, it was with many tales about the new things The Baby knew how to do. Under this arrangement, not only was one of us missing the other, but the one at home also missed being with The Baby.

It was 1953, and there we were, saying goodbye again. As we packed up for the revival circuit, we didn't know it would be two years before we'd have a home.

Chapter 21

Harmony in the Car

I didn't read music but I could sing a harmony part, so Daddy devised ways of teaching us the songs and parts we needed to know, songs we would sing at the next stop. It was easier for him to start off with a favorite song from the radio, then ease us into a hymn in the same key.

We headed toward a revival in Amarillo, the first since leaving Murfreesboro. We were now three in the back seat, but after this stop we'd leave one in Texarkana, initiating the new plan. Daddy and Leslie were expert car loaders. They used every inch, building our supplies up until our heads nearly touched the top of the car and leveling off the seat with quilts over everything. Leslie Ray and I took turns stretching our legs while The Baby bounced around on top of us.

Daddy said, "We need to practice. We're almost there. Sugar, sing your part."

"I don't feel like singing, Raymond. You do it."

"Nita Faye. I'm gonna sing your Mama's part and you sing higher than me."

I'll keep rolling along

Daddy loved the Sons of the Pioneers. We all did. "Tumbling Tumbleweeds" was one of theirs. He also taught us parts using the songs of Hank Williams or The Harmonizing Four.

"Now you sing the next part with me."

Deep in my heart is a song

Daddy glanced back where Leslie Ray was looking out the window, just like Mother was doing in the front seat.

"Leslie Ray, why don't you sing with us?"

"I don't want to sing. I told you that."

"Boy, why are you so pigheaded? I never once sassed my Daddy like you do, never back-talked him one day of my life. You ask your Paw Paw Jones if I *ever* did. He'll tell you."

I said, "I don't want to sing either. I don't like singing the high part. Why can't Mother sing the high part?"

"Your Mama's voice is lower than yours. You got to sing over her like I said. Everybody in Amarillo's wantin' to hear you and your Mama sing 'Jesus and Me.' You like that one."

"No I don't."

"Well now you're actin' just like your brother. Girl, what am I gonna do with you? Lord, oh Lord, why did you give me such ungrateful children? Come on now."

I'll keep rolling along
Deep in my heart is a song
Here on the range I belong
Drifting along with the tumbling tumbleweeds

"You hear that note we started on, Nita Faye? That's gonna be the first note of "What a Friend." You got it? Whaaaat . . ."

I started on that note.

"Whaaaaaat . . ."

"That's right. You stay on the lead right there and I'll take your harmony so you can hear what it sounds like. You ready?"

What a friend we have in Jesus
All our sins and grief to bear
What a privilege to carry
Everything to God in prayer

I held back on the next part, unsure whether I was lead or harmony, then without even turning away from the window, Leslie Ray sang.

Oh what peace we often forfeit

Daddy stopped singing. I stopped singing. Leslie sang.

Oh what needless pain we bear

Then Mother added another part, and the two of them, the two who were barely civil to each other, sang.

All because we do not carry
Everything to God in prayer

Daddy said, "I hear you back there, son."

It was a good kind of quiet in the car for a minute.

Long stretches of Route 66 through the Deep South offered nothing to look at except tumbleweeds, giant puffs of them rolling free on the highway or stuck to a fence. Daddy played a game with them. A huge tumbleweed clump was minding its own business somewhere in Texas, and as we got closer it loomed about half a car in size. The motion of our big old sedan invited it to dance. It floated up and plopped on the windshield, covering the view. Leslie Ray told Daddy he better stop but Daddy said watch this. Instead of stopping and freeing the thing, his game was to keep driving and speed up then brake quickly, trying to get it to release itself. Man against nature. It wasn't safe, but not much about car travel was back then.

Mother glanced at us in the back seat, flashing a naughty smile, she sang.

I hate to see the evenin' sun go down
Sure hate to see the evenin' sun go down

Cause my man of mine, he done left this town
Leslie and I jumped in.
Feelin' tomorrow like I feel today
Daddy laughed.

"Now all y'all are gonna be in trouble . . ."

Mother said, "Raymond! There's a Dairy Queen. I want me a Co-Cola with crushed ice." To all of us or none of us, she said, "Don't you just love crushed ice? Makes a Coke taste twice as good."

I said, "I want Orange Crush."

Leslie Ray said, "Can I have a snow cone?"

Daddy stopped.

"I reckon. Mama-gal, see what you started?"

He got out of the car and went up to the window to order. Mother opened her door and stretched her legs out.

"Look at your Daddy over there. Isn't he the cutest thing?"

Leslie Ray said, "I don't see what's so cute."

I said, "You think Daddy's *cute?*"

"I sure do. So did all the other girls. When I met your Daddy, he was dating his boss's daughter, Margaret, the richest girl in El Dorado. I fixed that right quick. I let him chase me awhile, but I liked him from the start."

Leslie Ray recited the next line.

". . . and then he took you to a dance."

"That's right. Your Daddy and I, we could really dance!"

My brother said, "That's what Gramma K said."

"What did she say? Tell me what else she said about dancing."

"I don't remember."

"Yes you do, Leslie Ray. What did your grandmother say about me and your Daddy?"

I said, "I wish we could see you and Daddy dance."

I had made a wrong choice. Her answer was chilly.

"You know we don't dance anymore. Dancing's a sin. Leslie Ray, go help your Daddy carry those Cokes, and ask him to get me a chocolate-dipped ice cream too."

Back on the road, everyone was quiet for a long time, even The Baby, who took one messy bite of Mother's ice cream, then climbed back over the seat and curled up to sleep between us.

Daddy asked, "What should we sing?"

He meant sing for pleasure, the songs we sang in private, the ones that weren't church music.

I named a favorite.

"Home."

I also had a favorite version of the hit. Mine was the Mills Brothers.

Mother liked the way Nat King Cole sang it, and Leslie Ray wasn't listening to hits lately, but he still absorbed every song, as kids who live with a soundtrack underscoring their lives eventually will. Each of us was attached to our radios in the last parsonage. They were old and well used by previous owners but they were ours for a while, an unbelievable luxury. Leslie kept his by his bed, I kept mine on top of my chest of drawers, Daddy used the one on the kitchen table, and Mother appropriated the big old console in the front room. We all stayed close to our radios as much of the time as we could.

Daddy said, "Okay, Nita Faye. Start off."

When shadows fall and trees whisper day is ending . . .

I poked Leslie Ray, and though he'd said he wouldn't sing anymore, he meant just not with them. He picked up the melody and I switched to harmony.

My thoughts are ever wending . . . Home

Daddy started to whistle the next part.

Mother sang.

When crickets call, my heart is forever yearning
Once more to be returning . . . Home

I thought Leslie would drop out when Mother dropped in, but he didn't and the four of us joined, with everyone adjusting parts.

When the hills conceal the setting sun

Daddy tossed in a bird-trill whistle right there.

Stars begin to twinkle one by one
Night covers all, and though fortune may forsake me
My dreams will ever take me . . . Home

Chapter 22

Tents

Our gospel caravan was fueled by Hershey bars and snow cones, Co-Cola and Dr. Pepper, Moon Pies from every gas station, Royal Crown Cola on the road to Oklahoma, Peanut Patties in Georgia, Orange Crush in Mississippi, biscuits and grits in Arkansas, tamales in El Paso, po' boys in Louisiana, and baloney sandwiches all over the place.

We stopped to refuel at small country stores with one gas pump outside and a screen door with an Orange Crush metal plate serving as a handle. Leslie and I wandered around inside wishing for much more than we had money for. We ordered baloney from a big log sliced at the counter. Store-bought bread was a treat we had only on the road. We slathered it with Miracle Whip or pimento cheese or Underwood Deviled Ham. We split open and laid flat little canned Vienna sausages, pressing them onto the bread.

We stayed in motor courts with kitchenettes, and we had favorite stops where proprietors knew us and offered a clergy discount. Our car was so laden, I wondered what other guests thought when we pulled in. We may have resembled the Joads carrying guitars out of the Dust Bowl, but in fact we were a bona fide gospel wagon train crisscrossing Southern states with both musical and edible provisions onboard.

Daddy cooked most of our meals in his deep cast-iron skillet. Kitchenettes were stocked with plates and glasses, hot plates and usually a couple of pots, but gastronomical limitations dissolved when Daddy unpacked his skillet and additional seasonings. The first night in town he'd make gravy over bread or rice or potatoes. Rice and potatoes were plentiful and cheap, and we ate a lot of them.

Daddy invented one of our favorite meals and named it corned beef stew. It featured a can of corned beef chopped up fine, onions, and whatever quantity of potatoes fit the biggest pot. He covered it with water, added salt and pepper and his own seasonings and cooked it until everything was tender and the flavors came together. It turned into much more than those simple ingredients and it was even better reheated the next day. Just before ladling out the stew, he heated some lard and fried hot-water cornbread in his skillet.

Our motor court meals were supplemented, complemented, and enhanced to a great degree by church cooks. Wherever we went, church folks brought special dishes for us to enjoy back in our room.

Revivals were a complex business, and Mother and Daddy did a surprisingly efficient job of running things from the car or our home base, the rented apartment in Texarkana, from kitchen tables on the road or the guest rooms of sponsoring pastors.

Mother carried publicity materials wherever we went. We had regular family photo sittings, with the chosen photos turned into woodcuts for printing. She kept a selection in different sizes to be used for newspapers, handbills, and posters. These photos were also featured on postcards she sent in advance and thank-yous she sent after we left. We mailed out Christmas cards from "The Joneses" for years featuring the two of them and the two of us.

Mother charmed committees and pastors and newspaper reporters and radio hosts and even the crop dusters who flew to drop handbills for us. Local businesses were happy to put her posters in storefronts. She wrote personal notes in her fancy handwriting on her good stationery and sent them to leading citizens in towns we'd be visiting. From the road, she stayed in touch with everyone important to our work.

It was competitive out there on The Glory Road. Publicity campaigns now featured novelties. Brother Ogden, a handsome and talented painter, demonstrated his skills during a worship service, completing an entire picture while his wife played accordion. Mother may have had a bit of a crush on Brother Ogden, and for several days before the Ogdens left a region, when we had just pulled in for our revival, he helped her learn to sketch quickly with artist's chalks. This was one thing she tried that she wasn't good at. The quality of her pictures didn't seem to matter though, since it was enough that this pretty lady stood up there by that easel.

Ads for revival campaigns sometimes took up a whole page in the local newspaper. This required Mother or Daddy working in advance with the churches who would sponsor our spectacle, in order to secure funds for the advance publicity. Word of mouth among performers steered us away from uncooperative pastors who didn't do their part with promotion. Churches from miles around combined to support revivals in the hopes of winning new members.

Everybody was looking for something different from this latest revival tour. Sister Fern would sing her songs for bigger crowds and she'd be invited to sing at every radio station on our route. Brother Ray sought to save lost souls. What the crowds wanted was acknowledgement of guilt for their Saturday night ways, redemption to get them to Sunday morning, great music, stem-winding sermons, and stardust from the attractive out-of-towners.

While our family unpacked outside Amarillo, Daddy went off to meet with the ministers of the region and the construction crew and the electricians and the people who rented us folding chairs and, finally, the roustabouts, strong men who earned their keep as soon as the trucks carrying the tent and equipment rolled up to the edge of the field.

They would lay the tent sections flat on the ground, push them up with big tent poles, and stretch the guy-wires tight. Before departing on tent day, they taught deacons and other volunteers how to work the flaps, some flaps up, some down, employing a specific choreography intended to outsmart the weather.

The last time we stopped in Amarillo for a revival in 1950, we ended up waiting outside of town for a few days. Because of a missed communication, we learned too late that Oral Roberts was on his way too. Daddy said we'd begin our revival in Brother Daly's church and move it out to our tent after Brother Roberts left. No evangelists in the field wanted to carry on in the face of the enormous impact of an Oral Roberts campaign. Daddy also regularly checked campaign schedules for Brother Billy Graham and Brother Rex Humbard who were by then evangelical stars, using tents that held thousands more people than ours did.

Brother Roberts must have changed his schedule somewhere along the way and all we could do was wait until his trucks drove out of town. Daddy insisted we should go to a service under his tent and hear his powerful testimony. As soon as Brother Roberts began to talk about his own salvation, weaving in a fascinating life story about a poor little farm boy who was told one day at school to "go home and put on your *good* clothes," a storm rolled in bringing powerful gusts of wind, the fearsome enemy of huge tents.

In the aisle next to Daddy, a center pole came loose from its moorings and swung wildly back and forth, knocking people down. Daddy grabbed the pole with some other men and yelled at us to get out from under the tent. Slogging and snaking through mud, we found our way to the car parked out in the field. Daddy joined us and we were on our way back to the motor court as emergency vehicles raced toward the tent.

The next day's papers were filled with stories of injuries and of Brother Roberts staying right there as long as they'd let him to pray over people. Brother Roberts said he had the gift of healing in one of his hands. I forget which, right or left, but he preached about it that night, and while Daddy read us the newspaper stories about him staying to pray over people, Leslie said he must have tired out that healing hand during just that one night. Daddy said that he, personally, had not been given the gift of healing, but "I believe God is the great healer, and if he wants to work through Brother Roberts like that, well bless him."

Three years later, after Brother Roberts was moving on to greater and greater acclaim, here we were back in Amarillo. There was no overlapping with Oral Roberts this time. His tents now held ten thousand people and he was planning a television show.

Daddy supervised every detail of our tent going up. Leslie Ray and I could go along with him all day if we wanted to, over to a church office, to a midday dinner in a cafe with local backers, and then out to the field, where sponsoring ministers floated around the site to watch Reverend Raymond Jones, the charismatic evangelist, wielding a hammer and driving tent stakes into the ground alongside the crew. We'd seen and heard all the details many times, but we went along to get out of watching The Baby and to remove ourselves from the case of nerves that struck Sister Fern Jones before just about every performance.

Our first stop was in Brother Daly's office in a building next to his prosperous church. It felt sumptuous because some of the chairs were upholstered and not hard-back chairs donated from a church member's dining room set. Two preachers were already there. They greeted Daddy and took off their jackets and got down to business. Leslie Ray and I occupied ourselves with the books we carried everywhere. The real fun for us was outside of town where all the equipment gathered, and we'd get there as soon as this meeting was done.

Brother Franks pastored a church in Oklahoma, and we had held several revivals for him there. He was in Amarillo this time to go through all the steps involved in putting together our larger tent revival, since he'd be hosting us soon. Tall and skinny, even taller and skinnier than Daddy, and old enough to be Daddy's parent, his demeanor was dignified, even elegant, but Daddy brought out the silliness in Brother Franks. These two loved each other.

Brother Daly was on the rise in religious circles. He was smooth and pin-striped and in charge, and though he was short, his hair got bigger and bigger every time we saw him, so we had to squint to see if he'd actually grown a couple of inches. He was a picture of a famous person with perfect teeth. He held your hand a second longer than he had to, so you felt special as soon as he looked your way.

Brother Franks started off, of course, inquiring about the condition of the roads. Brother Daly joined in, and for a while the three of them discussed nothing except which were the best routes from there to here.

Brother Franks asked Leslie and me how're you two doing, and Daddy answered for us, teasing.

"Oh 'bout the same. Everybody's hollering, wanting to stop for something every other mile."

The three men chuckled.

Brother Daly said, "We're looking forward to hearing some of Sister Jones's new songs. She still writing?"

"Yes, and you'd better start calling her Sister Fern from here on in."

"Sorry, I forgot."

More chuckling. Everybody in the room had known a high-strung woman at some time or other.

Daddy said, "She's got a bunch of new songs and she's painting again too. She's gonna make a picture right in front of the congregation one night and auction it off at the end of the meeting."

"Praise God!" Brother Franks said, then asked Leslie and I, "Are you kids still singing?"

I said, "I am but Leslie Ray won't."

Brother Daly said to Daddy, as if we two weren't right there, "Some young'uns are just hardheaded. My biggest girl's like that."

Well, well. Maybe Margaret Daly's older sister was on the same path as my older brother, but I still hadn't forgiven Margaret for putting religious restrictions on our friendship years ago. Former friendship.

Brother Franks and Daddy murmured their sympathy to each other about stubborn children, then Brother Daly moved to the business at hand.

"We sent in an article to the *Pentecostal Evangel*, put in some of those new pictures Sister Jones . . . Sister *Fern* . . . sent us."

"Somebody showed us a copy. Much obliged."

"And they're interested in another story after the revival's over. They're starting to print numbers, how many got saved, how many baptisms, church attendance before and after the revival, that kind of thing."

Brother Franks said, "Keeping track of revivals now, are they? Well, we've got the evangelists right here that can draw a crowd! We got some young'uns putting handbills out. Did anybody find out about the airplane?"

Brother Daly said, "Got one crop duster from a few miles over. He'll drop some handbills when he's done spraying. We printed up enough to cover three towns so far. After we see how the crowds are, how the offerings are going, we can drop some more, farther out if we need to."

Brother Franks and Daddy both said "Amen!"

"Everybody's looking forward to hearing The Joneses on the air." Brother Daly seemed to want the other men in the room to know what he was capable of arranging. "Y'all will be booked on every station within a couple hundred miles."

Daddy's tone never changed. If he ever noticed somebody bragging on something, he didn't let on.

"Well, we're sure ready to sing, and I'll be proud to see the *Evangel* write us up. We'll ask the Almighty to send us some big numbers to talk about!"

Brother Daly asked, "How did you want to handle the baptisms this time, Brother Jones?" He turned to Brother Franks. "That's something you need to plan on for your revival. Last time we used the baptistery here at Amarillo First Assembly."

Daddy said, "Brother Daly, I say let's give them too *many* people to baptize indoors! Let's get so many filled with the Holy Ghost there'll be a line a mile long out by the creek."

Brother Franks joined in.

"That's right! Let's have a baptism that lasts 'til suppertime. How many healing nights are we planning?"

"I like to have healings on Tuesdays and Thursdays," Daddy said. "And spread the word about which nights, so people can come from a ways out. Now we need us some space for the people praying through."

Uh-huh, uh-huh, the other two preachers mulled this for a minute.

Then Brother Franks said, "I know your altar calls get people down on their knees. We want to be sure we've got enough room down front at the railing."

"I have a question about that," Brother Daly said. "We had us an evangelist through here. I won't say his name out loud, God bless him, but he reached people with his altar call. As soon as 'Softly and Tenderly' started up, people were out of their seats and they'd be laid out down there, praying through, waiting on the Holy Ghost, and he'd ease out the back, and up and leave. Straight over to eat at the diner."

Daddy answered both concerns.

"When we get over to the site, we'll be sure to get us an altar rail long enough to handle a crowd. Brother Daly, I know some preachers, they give all they've got and they let down right after, but I'm not like that. I'll stay down there with every one of them, 'til the last soul has prayed through, if it takes all night. Course I'll need some of you to help with the laying on of hands. My wife—now she may have to go back to the room."

Both preachers nodded. Mother was known by most in the field to have some kind of mysterious condition. Since nobody on the road knew exactly what it was, some referred to it as "a delicate disposition."

Daddy was ready to wrap this up. He would always rather be in action.

"What's going on out there? We got us a tent yet?"

"Trucks were due in a couple hours ago," Brother Daly said. "Same company we used last time out of Dallas. We rented folding chairs from all the funeral parlors and the Elks and the Masons this time, so we won't run short."

Daddy agreed.

"Cheaper than bringing in extra from out of town."

Brother Daly wasn't quite finished.

"*My* church paid for the tent."

Daddy and Brother Franks didn't respond and Brother Franks stood and put his coat back on, so maybe it wasn't what it sounded like.

"Sister Franks wants us to have supper together as soon as you get settled in over at the motor court. She's looking forward to having y'all staying with us when you get to Oklahoma."

"I'll check with Fern and see. She's been real tired lately. Traveling takes it out of her. We might need to wait on that supper 'til later."

"We'll ask the Lord to give her strength. I sure look forward to hearing her sing. Voice like an angel."

Brother Daly said, "I don't mind saying—gives me chill bumps! Pretty as a picture too."

Daddy moved all of us toward the door.

"I don't know about you, but I'm ready to go put up a tent!"

Chapter 23

Revivals

Our caravan drove on, not always in a logical sequence and definitely not in a straight line. We were booked on specific dates in specific regions which didn't always connect neatly, so we backtracked on and off Route 66.

Houston

An old woman under the tent said, "Nita Faye, I heard you sing and I want to tell you you're a good girl, devoting your talent to the Lord."

Nobody except Leslie knew my plan was to finish out this last revival campaign before telling Daddy and Mother I wouldn't sing on the road anymore. A big challenge for me was making it through the rest of our stops without committing some kind of ungracious behavior in front of people. Since I'd made up my mind, it was difficult to behave otherwise.

The woman continued, "I want to give you something. Maybe your family can come over for supper while you're here."

These invitations came often. At every stop we became acquainted with lonely people who attended services every night, not to get saved, but just for the company. Often Daddy said no, the family was too tired from the late nights, but this time, because she lived in a suite at the Shamrock Hotel, a place we wanted to visit, we begged and he said yes.

In her upholstered, old-lady, treasure-filled bedroom, she opened the doors to a chifforobe and removed a jewelry box.

"Close your eyes, Nita Faye."

She fastened a necklace around my neck. It was large and heavy. Everything below my chin began to sparkle. This piece was obviously meant to be worn by a substantial woman or a woman of substance.

She said to Daddy and Mother, what a blessing, this child singing like she does, and then she hugged me.

In the car Leslie stared at the thing around my neck.

"That's ugly."

"I know it."

I unclasped it and handed it to Mother. Except for the woman believing her big old necklace was an appropriate gift for a child, everything else about the visit to the Shamrock Hotel was a story I liked and planned to keep re-telling. When we left Houston, Mother put the necklace, resting in its velvet case, in her suitcase.

I said, "Let's give it to Gramma K. She'll love it." Mother said Gramma K would not appreciate this dear woman's heart and love for the Lord. Daddy said that the necklace was valuable, the stones in it were real, and it was given to us for our service in God's work. So we would sell it and use the money for that. Mother was disappointed. Though their religion prevented her from wearing such adornment, the girl inside her was still attracted to it. There would be no further discussion. The necklace was treated as tithes.

The contradiction between the donations we received when we pastored, which were tithes of meat and dairy, versus jewelry from a wealthy woman we met at a revival summed up the contrasting dreams of our two parents, one of them content with whatever the Lord provided, and the other always in search of options.

El Paso

Mother loved tamales. Daddy loved Spanish guitars. El Paso was an excellent place for both. Our motor court was a village in a half circle. Each cabin had a stoop with its own steps. All the front doors were heavy and all were different colors, once bright but now sun-bleached into softer and beautifully faded versions of themselves. Leslie and I spent as much time as possible outside, fascinated by the comings and goings of our fellow travelers.

Revival tent crewmen pointed Daddy to neighborhoods with homemade tamales, and late at night after revival services, the three of us went out chasing tamale carts. Mother and The Baby stayed at the motor court while Leslie and Daddy and I got a closer look at El Paso by night, following the ding ding ding of food cart bells. We took home bags filled with them, the best we'd ever had.

Daddy asked local musicians to teach him songs in Spanish. We were off one night a week in El Paso, and on those nights Daddy and two or three guitarists sat outside on the steps while he learned to play and sing "Maria Elena." By the time we left El Paso, he also performed a credible version, in Spanish, of "Nosotros."

Daddy loved the language and vowed to learn to speak it better. He began the quest at that revival stop in El Paso and continued it all his life. His accent turned "si, senorita" into "see seen-yer-eeter," "see" with two syllables of course.

Texarkana

We looped back to Texarkana where we unpacked in our apartment on Pecan

Street. Mother updated her scrapbooks, and we spent a few weeks holding revivals on the Arkansas side of town at Brother McGaugh's church, then we went over to the Texas side to Brother Prince's church.

Our denomination was diverging, with preachers like Brother Prince urging his congregations to seek medical care, and preachers like Brother McGaugh and Daddy still teaching faith healing only. Wherever we were when one of us was sick, Brother McGaugh was the first person Daddy called to start a prayer chain.

In Texarkana, there were two states and two interpretations of the Word, but both invited Mother to sing and Daddy to preach.

Tulsa, Oklahoma, and St. Louis, Missouri

As we packed for the Oklahoma and St. Louis stops, Daddy announced Leslie Ray would be staying in Texarkana. At age fourteen, they felt he was old enough to be alone, and since Brother and Sister McGaugh lived within bicycling distance from our apartment, he could always go over to their parsonage if he wanted to.

I was angry. My brother gained his freedom partly by fighting, and I hadn't yet found that to be a workable option for me. Mother and Leslie Ray disagreed on just about everything and it made Daddy tired. It was carved in stone that Daddy would never take a side other than hers, and since she and Leslie had similar temperaments, the two of them set off multiple eruptions.

Leslie and I hadn't counted on how much we would miss each other. As we drove away, headed for Tulsa with The Baby occupying Leslie's usual space in the back seat, my brother stood on the sidewalk in front of the apartment house, looking exactly the way I felt. When we came back home from that first trip without him, he ran to the car to help Daddy unload, but also to pick up The Baby and see what new things she'd learned. After everything was calm, he and I sat on the front porch.

I asked, "What did you do while we were gone?"

"Went to school."

"Did you go to church?"

"No."

"What else did you do?"

"I made pimento cheese. I eat it every day on light bread."

"Lucky! Where'd you get light bread?"

"I did some work for Brother McGaugh and he paid me. Sister McGaugh showed me how to make the best pimento cheese."

"Better than Gramma K's?"

"Mine is better."

If I hadn't missed him so much, I'd have been even more jealous that he got to eat store-bought bread whenever he wanted.

He said, "It's in the icebox. I'll make you some."

Back on the porch, sandwiches in hand, bag of chips between us, we made it through that first separation and our center still held.

Columbus and Americus, Georgia

In Georgia The Joneses were celebrated as returning heroes. After we stopped in Columbus to sing on the radio, we went on to Americus. It became clear the denomination, at a national level, viewed Daddy as one of their most successful pioneering pastors.

Everywhere we went in Americus, stories were told about how during the war Daddy got a farmer to mortgage a crop to buy lumber for the new church, but there was no lumber to purchase so Daddy used the money to buy an old hotel and deconstruct it, turning the woodpile into a church building.

There were few able-bodied men of our denomination left at home during the war. Preachers were exempt from military service so Daddy became part of the construction crew. He rallied a group from the Black community who were ready and willing and worked alongside them every day, shirt sleeves rolled up, while believers from all the other churches in town fed them.

Mother organized bakers to help sell pies to pay for the building. She was told about dust storms that, when you forgot and left a window open, would deposit a layer of red dirt over everything. It only took losing one batch of pies during rationing to remember to close up the house before setting pies out on a counter to cool.

Since little else was being built in Americus during that time, watching the construction was a favorite pastime. Visitors stopped by to see the progress and often stayed to work. One frequent visitor was a peanut farmer from Plains, just a few minutes away. Brother Earl Carter came into Americus to do business and made a habit of stopping by. Daddy said Brother Carter was a fine man and a Baptist too, which was the next best thing to being Pentecostal. A man's religion counted in Daddy's assessment of his character.

By the time we rolled away from that trip to Georgia, I knew more about the history of Daddy and his calling. Mother's calling had become clear even sooner, of course. We had just left pastoring for her.

The McGaughs put Leslie on a bus in Texarkana so he could join us in Jackson, Mississippi, for the start of another revival campaign. From Mississippi, we would head down to Louisiana's bayou country. Leslie wasn't unhappy about his temporary loss of independence since we'd soon be spending time with one of our favorite people, Brother Janway.

Jackson, Vicksburg, Hattiesburg, Pascagoula, Biloxi, and Gulfport, Mississippi

Mississippi was a blur of tents and churches and motor courts and radio stations and auditoriums and empty storefronts and old warehouses big enough to hold hundreds of chairs and lights and sound systems.

Chapter 24

Down on the Bayou

Westbank of New Orleans, Louisiana: Westwego, Marrero, Gretna, Metairie, Algiers, Lafitte, Des Allemands

Cecil Janway had a heart full of love for all children. He and his wife, Ollie, were obviously sent from heaven to soothe the souls of two young and weary Jones travelers.

Brother Janway was one of the most popular evangelists and pastors in our movement. A musical firebrand like Fern, he was also a calm presence in his home like Daddy. Brother Janway and Sister Fern were going at a similar pace, moving church music into widening circles of influence. The two of them got along swimmingly and so did Daddy and Sister Ollie Janway. The Janways' home was the only place we visited where our parents' first names were used. When they were together, the four of them became Cecil and Ollie, Ray and Fern.

Brother Janway always had time for Leslie and me. With one of his own little ones slung on his hip, he moved around the kitchen, putting together excellent meals. He prided himself on learning to cook the specialties of each region so we ate quantities of stuffed, soft-shell crabs and anything that could be made with shrimp and crawfish. Rice accompanied everything down on the bayou.

He let us chop and mince and sauté alongside him, regaling us with outlandish stories, stopping to tease, to pat a head. Unaccustomed as we were to overt displays of affection, we were big-eyed with gratitude for the attention. On a sticky Louisiana summer day, Leslie went out fishing with some local boys. After a while, the screen door slammed and my brother practically danced into the kitchen.

Brother Janway said, "Leslie Ray, you better have plenty of crabs in that bucket."

"Look at these! Soon as we dropped our strings in the water, all these crabs were grabbing onto them!"

"Didn't I tell you? You put some fatback on a string, you'll be beatin' 'em off with a stick."

"James took me down the canal on his pirogue, but I can't hardly understand a word he says."

"He probably can't understand you much either. What's he sayin' to you?"

"Sounds like 'tee fee' and 'tee bo.'"

"James is talkin' Cajun. 'Ti beau' is a boy and 'ti fille' is a pretty girl. I reckon you'll pick *that* up quick enough."

I was surprised when Leslie dove right into a subject we never discussed with anyone except Gramma K.

"Brother Janway, do you take your kids to doctors?"

"Yes I do. Sister Janway and I pray for them too, and we get a church prayer chain going."

"We go to the same kind of church, so why doesn't Daddy believe in doctors?"

"I tell you what, it's a complicated situation right now. The District's leaving it up to preachers to teach how they believe, so when your daddy teaches faith healing and then he backs it up with scripture and his own congregation agrees with him, the District is satisfied."

"So you preach scripture but you still go to doctors?"

"Different interpretations. There's room for that in the Word."

"What's your interpretation?"

"That God is the Great Physician and doctors are also healers. Every time I take somebody to a doctor, I pray that the doctors will be guided by God."

"I don't believe in faith healing. We ought to get to go to the doctor when we're sick."

"Son, you have to treat your family's beliefs with respect. That's about the most important job you've got, right after serving the Lord."

"Your family's different. Sister Janway takes care of your kids. She's not like my mother."

"Now don't you go speaking ill of your mother. Your mother is called to a music ministry and she's had some trials of her own."

"If I ever wanted to be a preacher, I wouldn't have kids."

"Oh you'll likely change your mind when the time comes. Son, you've got a gift for fixing things. You could be a mechanic or even an engineer."

"That's not what I'm going to be."

"The Almighty will let you know what you can do for the Kingdom and I expect you'll heed the call when it comes. You can do the Lord's work wherever you are. Sister Janway says half my church work gets done right here in this kitchen." He raised his voice toward the kitchen door. "Who's gonna help me cook red beans and rice?"

Daddy answered the call.

"Is that you hollerin', Cecil? Give me an apron. Where's a sharp knife?"

Daddy found a knife that suited him.

"How many onions do you want in this skillet?"

"Wait a minute. I'm doing it different now. This is bayou country, my friend. Crumble up some sausage first."

"You got three kinds of sausage here."

"That's right. We'll use all of them, mild and medium and hot. You blend all those together, that's Cajun!"

"Which one do you like best."

Brother Janway gave the question serious consideration.

"I'm gonna have to say andouille. Course I like any good sausage, but you take andouille, it goes in just about anything."

Brother Janway kept a piano in his kitchen, and he'd lay down his spoon, slide onto the piano stool, and play a song. We'd never been in a house with a kitchen piano, but if anybody would have one, it'd be Brother Janway.

"Y'all come on over here and sing this with me."

He started off on "Jambalaya."

Leslie and I sang while Daddy sizzled away. He kept stirring but he sang with us. He never let a Hank Williams tune go by.

Brother Janway's kitchen piano playing was even wilder than his outside performances. He pounded the keys using hands and elbows, all the time bouncing around on the bench and winking at us. Once in a while he jumped up then sat down again without messing up the rhythm. Then he'd stand up, kick the bench away, and lean way over to play the last notes.

We'd only recently learned how his music inspired nonbelievers too. When he was a teenager and his family preached in a little church in Ferriday, Louisiana, Cecil Janway took up the piano to help out in church, and some cousins from nearby came to hear the teenaged evangelist play. Jimmy Swaggart and Jerry Lee Lewis and Mickey Gilley gave him some of the credit for their style.

That was one way he and Mother were alike. They simply heard music a different way, which encouraged Saturday night performers to find common ground with the Sunday people. Both of them believed Jesus loves a good beat. Brother Janway slid off the piano bench and resumed cooking with Daddy.

"Raymond, the congregation down here loves you and Fern. You're already honorary Cajuns. There's something the District asked me to talk to you about."

Brother Janway had recently decided that, though he loved pastoring, he also wanted to be part of growing the denomination. He led a church in Westwego but his other duties took him to many churches. He coordinated our appearances and set up a revival venue for us in an empty shrimp processing plant. Evening services during heat and humidity smelled exactly the way you imagine. My brother and I crossed the Mississippi with him, running errands over and back, over and back on ferries and the Huey P. Long Bridge.

It was a different world from where we began in Arkansas, different from any other state we visited.

"We're needing a church in Bogalusa, he said to Daddy. Every time we have a revival, the crowds get bigger. They're ready for their own pastor."

"Do they have a building?"

Daddy often said the most trying part about pastoring was the business part, building churches, keeping properties in good repair, making sure the congregation's pledges to the building fund were paid on time.

"No they don't. But they've got believers ready to give the land for one. That's why we thought of you. You've had success building and—"

"Cecil, let me stop you right there. I'm too tired to build another church. Worrying all the time about meeting the monthly notes. I don't think I've got another building campaign in me."

"Looks to me like you're tireder of traveling around."

"You know I am. I feel like the Lord's calling me to preach in one place, build up a congregation, teach people to be strong in their faith. That takes time, though, and Fern . . ."

"I know people who can make it easier this time. The Quaves own a lot of land up there. Wouldn't surprise me if they might be persuaded to provide a home too. Not a parsonage, I mean some land and a home of your own that you and Fern would own. Bogalusa's just across Lake Pontchartrain. Not far. We can trade pulpits once in a while, preach for each other, like we used to in Arkansas."

"Fern's music is getting more popular all the time. All she wants to do is sing. You know that song she wrote in Murfreesboro—'I Was There When It Happened'?"

"Good song. Governor Davis sang it with The Sunshine Boys in New Orleans a while back."

"He's talking about recording it. The Governor's got a publishing company too and she feels like if they get some sheet music, get more people singing her songs, she'll be closer to getting her own recording contract."

"You've got nothing to worry about, Raymond. She's not going anywhere. She never wants to sing a note without you standing right there."

"I don't believe I could get Fern to move into a parsonage again."

"What I said was, it wouldn't *be* a parsonage. It'll be a home of your own, land donated, plus building costs. The Quaves would do that to get you two to minister there. Got that sausage cooked down some? Throw in those onions. Some garlic. Ready for some beans."

Daddy and Brother Janway moved seamlessly from talk of career matters to a pot of beans to Hank Williams songs to fishing spots and circled back again.

Daddy said, "I like to mash some beans up when they're cooked, put 'em back in the pot. Thickens the gravy up nice."

"Listen Arkansas boy, you're in Louisiana now. That's for pintos. I'm not mashing up my red beans."

He stirred everything around, lifted a big spoonful of broth from the pot and tasted.

"This'll do fine."

Mother came and got us. She wanted us to go in the front room and hear a record she and Sister Janway just bought. All of us in that house listened faithfully to *Hit Parade* every week, but Mother said no, this is a new recording, it hasn't been on yet. She played Elvis's "That's All Right Mama" and asked all of us what we thought.

Brother Janway tapped a foot. Daddy grinned and said uh huh, uh huh. Sister Janway said play it again. We listened several times to Elvis singing the song which was new to us, but Mother said it was recorded a long time ago by a Black man and played on some of the stations she listened to. She already knew the words. It really wasn't that much different from how Cecil Janway and Sister Fern sounded when they cut loose together in front of a big crowd.

I said I like it fine. Leslie Ray said it's okay, it's not my kind of music. Daddy reminded Leslie to be nice because Elvis is the same denomination as us.

"He came up in the Tupelo church."

Brother Janway said, "Sweet little congregation. Do you know the pastor?"

Daddy did know the Tupelo pastor and was also in touch with the pastor of Elvis's church in Memphis. They were all part of the same faith group, and their musical paths wove them together through the quartets who participated in all the gospel Singings where Elvis was a frequent visitor.

"Brother Smith says Elvis is a good boy. Been coming to church with his mama and daddy for a long time, since he was little, and wanting to play the guitar. Brother Smith taught him all the chords he knew."

"Well now he's left there and I wonder if he's still a churchgoer."

"Yes he is. The Memphis church. One of the Blackwoods said something about seeing him there at all-night Singings."

"Well. Long as he's still faithful."

Daddy nodded, proud to offer a glowing report of this young Christian man.

"Doesn't smoke or drink or cuss. Treats his mama right."

Daddy had his own standards, no matter how much musical talent one displayed.

Leslie said, "I know somebody who's friends with him and he says Elvis drinks Jax beer every chance he gets."

I doubted my brother had heard any such thing. I didn't doubt though that Leslie and his friends participated in trying out some of those things themselves and that he said what he did only to pique Daddy. It didn't work. Daddy had his mind made up.

"Brother Smith says he's a good boy."

Chapter 25

Junior and Them

Through Brother Janway's genial patronage, Leslie and I met families named Thibideaux, straight out of Hank Williams's "Jambalaya." James taught Leslie new cuss words in a Cajun patois and I made the acquaintance of Rita Pleasance (Play-zahnz) at Sunday School.

During revivals, evangelists never competed with local churches on Sunday mornings, so our family attended Sunday worship at Brother Janway's church. The Baby was in the nursery and Leslie and I were required to attend Sunday School classes. It was my good fortune to find Rita there, as bored as I was. She took me home to meet her family and opened a window onto her Cajun view.

Rita's daddy owned a shrimp packing operation and she took me out on a canal in one of their pirogues. She did the poling, pushing off, and turning us around expertly in shallow waters.

Down on the bayou, the crawling and flying things seemed much bigger than the ones I'd met previously. There were chiggers and ticks and fat mosquitoes and giant red ants and snakes. Cottonmouth water moccasins floated alarmingly close to us near the banks of the canals. In other parts of the South, we were accustomed to rattlesnakes who liked to hide. Several had been known to rattle from Paw Paw's woodpiles on our way to the outhouse, but these bayou moccasins didn't even try to cover up or warn anybody. They floated right there in plain sight while we docked.

Rita said there were gators in Bayou Gauche, and you could go out at dark and shine a flashlight in the swamp and the alligators' eyes would be red, looking at you while you looked at them. I told Leslie what she said and he was raring to go.

I spent the night at Rita's house and though I understood no more than a few words of the conversation at the supper table, we declared ourselves new best friends. We talked about how much we would miss each other when my family returned to Texarkana.

Then came a reprieve. Brother Janway announced on a Sunday morning that The Joneses would be holding a revival in Bogalusa, and everyone from all the Westbank churches ought to make a point of going over there to support these tent evangelists. Rita asked her parents and they promised they'd bring her.

Daddy agreed to help Brother Janway assess prospects for building up a congregation there. We would begin with a revival lasting several weeks. I wasn't there when Daddy told Mother, but my brother and I imagined Daddy may have presented this extension of our time in bayou country as a way of gaining a financial cushion before returning to Texarkana to regroup and plan our next tour.

Daddy was so good at pioneering churches, our denomination was always asking him to build churches where there were none and to travel to churches where membership flagged. When the invitations came, in formal letters of request written on the denomination's stationery, Daddy mentioned them to Mother: "They're talking about a new church in Fort Smith" and "Gulfport needs a new church."

We heard her respond, saying the same thing in different words each time, distilled into how reluctant she was to pastor again, and then each time he whistled his way into his next task without seeming to be upset about it.

Between Daddy and Brother Janway, the topic of Bogalusa kept coming up, and whenever we heard about it, they were talking only about holding a tent revival outside of town. Though Daddy may have presented this detour to Mother as a favor and a way to help the District, we knew what we'd heard that day in the kitchen and what Brother Janway had offered.

Bogalusa, Louisiana, 1955

Mother was singing in the car, leading the back seat to believe Daddy hadn't mentioned anything about staying in Bogalusa. Leslie and I both spent a lot more time looking out the window in silence. There was no need anymore to rehearse our family's songs. I knew my part and Leslie wasn't singing anything.

The formula for pioneering a new church included X number of people turning out under the revival tent, Daddy learning who the leaders were and meeting with them over breakfasts and lunches in the local cafes, X number of people answering questions about what kind of church the locals presently attended, X amount of tithing church attendees might commit to, X number of pledges or cosigners to secure a construction loan, and when the sum of these Xs was favorable in Daddy's opinion, Brother Janway and the District would determine whether to follow his recommendation. If the decision was to build, it would be Daddy talking to the bankers, keeping the balance sheets, adjusting work schedules, and maintaining cash flow to pay laborers. All these things we knew from our own past and the kitchen chatting and stirring sessions.

We packed up in Westwego and cruised across the Pontchartrain Causeway, headed to whatever accommodations awaited us in Bogalusa. That first day, while Mother unpacked at the motor court, the field where the tent would be was already buzzing. Trucks arrived filled with people who drove out to watch the tent go up. Children stayed home from school to see it. A circle of onlookers surrounded the proceedings all day.

Daddy and Mother always conferred about how everything would look, the sign out in front, the cross behind the podium, the altar, and Daddy had specific measurements he was comfortable with for the platform. Several steps were needed and a ramp was built for loading sound equipment and a piano. A generator was concealed behind a tent flap. Our car became our own backstage area. Every night, Leslie and I carried music and instruments and helped set up.

At the end of a revival service, if the altar was still packed with sinners late into the night, we were allowed to sleep under the tent, way in the back, curled up over two or three chairs, or when our revival was inside churches, the last pews were fine for sleeping. As we got older, we retreated to the car.

No matter how late Daddy got to bed, even on the road, he still rose early. The farmer in him woke him up, he said, so we also got up with him, partly to keep The Baby quiet so Mother could sleep, but mostly because it was still our favorite ritual, greeting the dawn with Daddy.

Bogalusa wasn't a large town, but successful tent revivals didn't require proximity to prosperous cities. Often our tents were pitched out in the country near the confluence of several towns, where plenty of parking was available. Distance and road conditions didn't deter attendees. A tent revival with good music and fiery preaching was worth the drive.

Rain or shine, by late afternoon long before the service began, fields filled up with carloads and truckloads of families eating the food they packed for their trip. During setup, crowds were already milling about even before Daddy made his last stop on the platform to check the sound. No matter how many times the sound system was checked in the afternoon, he always made one last check as the seats filled.

Our family had begun working the evangelistic field in small tents that held just a few hundred people, then we gradually expanded into tents that seated three thousand. That was as big as Daddy was comfortable with. That was the largest religious event he was willing to produce.

During a revival service, Leslie Ray and I were required to remain visible in the front row. That was also where the eldest and the lamest attendees were. Daddy invited all sinners to come forward to the altar down in front, and in the case of people who were unable to move, there were volunteers, deacons and elders from nearby churches, who assisted them.

"Kneel if you're able," Daddy said. It seemed to us Jesus could have healed all the sick people right there where they sat instead of bringing forth a line of strong men to half carry them to the altar.

Mother's clothes remained a consideration and the subject of much discussion. There was all that humidity in this part of the country, and she was a woman with naturally curly hair performing in front of thousands during a period when curls were not in vogue. Her hair was a confection when we arrived, but none of her hairstyles were destined to last. Though she pinned and clipped and slicked down her hair with Vaseline, still she battled nature every time she went outside.

At the site that morning, Brother Janway had arrived from Westwego and joined Daddy and the crew, rolling up their sleeves to provide whatever assistance was needed. A long fancy car pulled up. It was Brother Daly.

"Raymond! Cecil! You get over here and hug my neck!"

Daddy jumped off the edge of the platform and joined them. Leslie Ray did too, all of them circling that vehicle and admiring every little detail.

I struck up a conversation with a girl about my age who'd just arrived with her family. Her mother brought food for the workers and put it on the sawhorse table the workmen used. The girl said her people were all Baptists, but their pastor told them it would be all right to go hear the Pentecostals, as long as they were back in their own pews Sunday morning.

Daddy asked Brother Janway about the carpenter. Every large revival required lumber and someone who knew how to make things.

"That's him over yonder. He's the one built the platform and he'll be finishing up everything else."

The best part of going to the tent site and meeting local crews was learning about favorite cafes and nearby attractions we might get to visit, and most important, finding out if any of the workers had kids around our age, because if they did, and if they were believers, sometimes we were allowed to spend a night at their homes instead of the motor court.

Brother Janway said, "We built us a bigger cross this time. Gonna paint it white. Wait'll you see it when we shine that light on it from the back of the tent. This one'll really stand out!"

Daddy said, "Wait. Let's don't paint it. Leave it natural."

A man with a hammer said, "I agree. Natural."

Daddy asked him, "How 'bout a couple extra nails on this end right here?" He pointed to one edge of the platform. "Don't want my wife tripping."

The man didn't make a move to comply. He was a very large Black man with arms like the ads on the backs of the funny books Leslie read when he was little. They promised if you bought enough of this product, you would get muscles so big you could kick sand in the face of a bully at the beach.

"Reverend, are you a carpenter? Because I am. If you want to do any fixing up yourself"—he held out the hammer—"you go right on ahead."

He said it with a smile and a friendly tone and Daddy gave him one of his genuine delighted-to-meet-you grins in return. They shook hands.

"I'm Reverend Jones. Please call me Ray."

This was common practice among ministers, indicating whether or not an honorific was preferred, and if so, which one. Daddy assumed this man was not a member of a congregation that might attend our revival. No Black people ever attended our revivals. Unless this man was part of our sect, no title was expected and a first name would suffice.

"How 'do. You can call me Junior. You in charge here?"

"I'm the preacher at this revival."

"I'll call you Rev."

"That'll be fine, just fine. Junior . . . ?"

"Jackson. Junior Jackson."

Brother Daly joined them and the four men continued the detailed checklist.

Daddy asked Brother Janway, "You got us some people working the flaps tonight? Sky's mighty dark."

"Got volunteers standing by. They'll open every other flap if they need to. Keep it cool in there 'til we have to close 'em."

Daddy looked up, gauging the clouds.

"I reckon we'll just have to let the mosquitoes and lightnin' bugs in with the sinners."

Junior said, "That's right. If we close those flaps and a good wind comes up, y'all will all be lifted up to heaven way ahead of schedule!"

All three preachers took a minute to appreciate the humor.

"That's right!"

"You said it, my brother!"

Junior set out tapping in a few extra nails, then smoothing down edges of the boards on the platform. The next day a truck would roll up and unload a piano. Junior would guide them up the ramp. Daddy would direct them to place it at a specific angle so the crowd could see Sister Fern (and Brother Janway who was bound to play a couple of numbers) and also so the music makers could see the crowd.

A bunch of kids, including us two Joneses, sprinkled sawdust on the ground under the tent. When we heard the putt putt putt of a small plane, we looked up and handbills floated down from the sky. The plane completed a quick maneuver and circled around us.

Brother Janway looked up and said, "Well now he's just showing out."

Daddy picked up a handbill off the ground.

"Fern's gonna like the way you laid this out, with the new pictures. God bless that crop duster, flying in weather like this."

Brother Daly, looking up at the receding plane, asked, "Who'd you get?"

"Got us Leon again."

"He still drinkin'?"

"Some people's just born backsliders I reckon. Leon's got saved for just about every preacher we've had through here. Lasts a couple of weeks, then he's back to the joints."

Daddy said, "I hope he *flies* sober."

"Tell you what, I'm not willing to personally test that out for myself, long as he keeps his hooch away from the tent."

Daddy said, "We got hundreds of folks due in here. I expect this'll be the time somebody'll show up with a truckload of drunks. Junior, would you watch the entrance for us, keep an eye out for anybody with hooch?"

"Naw, Rev, that ain't a job I'm willing to undertake. I'm not telling a bunch of likkered-up white boys where they can and can't be going."

"I take your point. We'll get somebody else to do it."

The finishing touch for the long wooden altar came from a church-woman. She emerged from the field with a folded-up bundle and draped an altar cloth over the fresh wood. It was quite plain except for huge, unusually colored crocheted crosses dangling from each end. Leslie Ray elbowed me.

"Looks like Gramma K or Aunt Birdie made it."

We knew when we described this piece of workmanship to Mother, she would appreciate the story and get the giggles. No offense directed at the good woman from a nearby church, just a reminder of our own grandmother's handwork which we had kept hidden for years.

Gramma K had an awful eye for color. Whatever yarn was on sale, that's what she used. Her crocheting was less shocking because she took requests and we could choose our own color combinations. The only reason I received delicate pansies in yellow and lavender on my change purses and handker-chiefs was because I lied and told her they were the only two colors I liked. That wasn't as mean as it sounds. I'd seen her yarn and thread supplies, and of everything on offer, these were the closest to something I would actually use. She was sure to ask, every time she saw us, if we were using that so-and-so she made for us recently. We stored away her surprise gifts that kept arriving in the mail until we were expecting her for a visit.

The Louisiana churchwoman took a step back to look at her work, then adjusted the crosses again so they were un-miss-able, and moved away with-out a word.

Daddy called after her, "Thank you, Sister!"

Our revivals were always booked for a minimum of two weeks, but when crowds were good and offerings were large enough for us to live on and enough also to get us to the next stop, we held over. If we didn't have another place we needed to be, we could stay in one region for weeks. In Bogalusa, our motor court was paid by the denomination, the crowds kept coming, and offerings were good enough, so it looked like we wouldn't get back to our Texarkana apartment anytime soon.

Daddy said we could get a ride into town and explore. One thing we learned was no matter where you went in Bogalusa, a pervasive smell followed, thicker than air. A paper mill town smells a certain way, even out at the edges. When we pulled into our motor court and the lady handed us our key, she said, "Y'all will get used to it. I don't hardly notice it anymore."

We asked Junior about the paper mill. How do they turn logs into paper? We wanted to see them make paper. He said no, best stay away from there, and he told a story about an awful thing that happened.

"Don't y'all think about sneaking in under that fence. People die in there."

"How?"

"One I knew personally. He was a drinker. We don't know what he was doing over there that night. He crawled under a fence and got in there where the equipment is."

"What kind of equipment?"

"There's one takes the bark off a tree, a whole tree, all at once."

"How does it do that?"

"Big blades, going around all day and all night. A truck pulls up and unloads the logs and those blades'll skin the hide right off. Course somebody ought to be there to see nobody gets too close. People say they still don't know where the mill worker on duty went that night, how come he walked away and left that motor running, with nobody keeping watch."

"No! He didn't!"

"Yes he did. Chopped up a man. Chopped him to pieces. I'm not saying I saw it happen, I'm just telling what I heard. Blind drunk and got tore to pieces on that saw. That's what they say."

Powerful stories, powerfully told tend to last. We accepted Junior's version of the debarking blades and how that poor man died and years later we still shuddered about it.

Junior knew we were fidgeting at the end of our short tether, shuffling back and forth between small quarters and the tent every night, so he and his wife invited us to their home. Daddy took us over there, to Richardson Town, where all the Black folks lived, and we sat on the front porch.

Junior and Marge's son, Wordell, was about my age but so small when we first met him, and the contrast between him and Junior so surprising, that we kept looking back and forth between the two of them. Junior treated Wordell like he wasn't small at all, like he could move mountains. We were in awe of how much respect was shown to a child.

Wordell was on the quiet side, not nearly as outgoing as Junior or Marge, but gracious to two strange kids. He brought out bottles of Nehi Grape Soda for us. Marge asked Daddy if he wanted coffee.

Junior said, "Naw. Rev's waitin' on some sweet tea."

Marge handed Daddy a jar of iced tea and sat down on the porch.

"I'll be glad to help out Miz Jones with The Baby so y'all don't have to be taking her to that tent every night."

Daddy said much obliged and he was sure his wife would appreciate it.

"Junior can carry me over there to the motor court if they let colored in."

Daddy said, "Junior's got plenty to do. I'll come after you."

She said to her son, "You can go stay with—"

Wordell was offended.

"Momma! I'm big enough to stay by myself!"

Indeed my brother and I had stayed by ourselves when we were much younger than Wordell. After some harmonica playing from Junior and some singing and some neighbors stopping by to join us on Junior's porch, they picked a time when Daddy would come back for Marge.

Daddy said Junior didn't trust white people much, with good reason. The whole area was a cauldron that Black people could fall into and disappear without a trace. A short drive away, Emmett Till, a boy about Wordell's age, was lynched.

Wordell was so skinny and so quiet, it was impossible to think anyone could consider him a threat, but logic wasn't a primary concern during those times and Daddy said it was good for Junior to keep Wordell close. After the Emmett Till story received national attention, reporters swarmed the region and stayed to report on the activities of the Klan in Bogalusa.

A reporter from a big city newspaper came out to our tent because he was a fan of Southern gospel music, but then he lasted through the whole long service and stayed around to shake hands with Mother and Daddy.

We were getting into the car to leave and he stood there in the parking field, talking to Daddy. He'd been out to Brother Billy Graham's tent meeting in Oklahoma City, he said, and he thought what Daddy and Mother were doing with church music would be successful in big cities.

Daddy thanked him for coming, thanked him for his opinions, and politely said he wasn't interested in anything different from what they were doing already. Daddy said there were plenty of souls to worry about in this part of the country, and nice to meet you and please come see us anytime.

On the way back to the motor court, Mother said, "Honey, maybe we *should* think about what he said, maybe get out from under the tents, into more auditoriums and such."

"Doll Baby, did you see how many came down to pray during altar call tonight? It was you singing 'Have Thine Own Way' that moved them out of their seats. That's God working through you, and that's blessing enough right there."

"Thank you, honey. I'm planning to change some of my altar call songs though. I was intending to sing 'Just As I Am' but Brother Graham uses that and I don't want to look like I'm copying him now."

"Whatever you pick will be sanctified, Sugar. How about 'Pass Me Not'?"
She hummed, then sang.

Pass me not oh gentle Savior
Hear my humble cry
While on others Thou art calling
Do not pass me by

Daddy paid close attention. If he wasn't driving, he'd close his eyes and murmur a "yes Lord," but he kept driving and said, "Or this one. You sing this so good."

He began singing "I Surrender All."

All to Jesus I surrender
All to Him I freely give
I will ever love and trust Him
In His presence daily live

In spite of the musical interlude, Mother wasn't distracted. She said, "Brother Graham *does* get so many conversions."

Chapter 26

Brother Daly's Gold-Plated Hallelujah

Junior checked on the revival tent every couple of days, walking around the site, tugging, hammering, adjusting, then one day as he was putting his tools in the back of his pickup he said he'd be gone awhile. We asked, where to?

"New Orleans to work some for Reverend Daly."

Brother Janway was at the site that day. He came over from Westwego a couple of times a week and went fishing with Daddy and Leslie. Sometimes he stayed all day, took us all out to a cafe for supper, then left after the night-time service.

He asked Junior, "What're you building?"

"Some old auditorium downtown. End of Canal Street. Daly's turning it into a tabernacle. He just signed papers on it."

Brother Janway was surprised.

"The office didn't say anything to me about it."

Junior said, "It's going to be nondenominational."

Daddy was also shocked that Brother Daly was stepping outside church boundaries.

"He's turning an old building into a church?"

"Different from one of your churches. He wants a big altar down in front, bigger'n you people use. Tall and fancy like the Catholics have."

Brother Janway was amused.

"Uh-huh. Oh yes he *would* want it tall."

Some gentle teasing about how Brother Daly was not blessed in the height department went back and forth while Junior pulled a roll of paper from his truck and spread it out.

"See here. Here's his platform."

Daddy said, "That *is* big!"

"It's where the pulpit's going too."

Brother Janway asked, "And he's gonna preach from way up there?"

By then, Daddy and Junior had caught his tone. Junior laughed.

"Whole lot of steps he can use to get up there."

Daddy moved in closer.

"What's that there in the back?"

"It's a studio. See, here. We're puttin' a television camera right in front of that glass."

Leslie joined us.

"Who's got a television camera?"

"Brother Daly." I pointed to the plans. "Come look at this. Brother Daly's new church."

Junior corrected me.

"Tabernacle. He's calling it a tabernacle."

Daddy asked, "What's he need a television camera for?"

Leslie said, "He's putting his church service on television?"

Daddy was shocked.

"Y'all are putting a television camera *inside* a church service?"

"Way in the back. Up on a riser I'm fixing to build. I'll set the camera there and bolt it down and point it at the altar and all they have to do is turn it on."

By now a few preachers had television programs, and it shouldn't have surprised us to learn Brother Daly would be the first one in our group to start one. As he moved all around the South, Brother Daly's churches kept getting bigger and bigger and his personal style evolved. By the time his tabernacle took shape in New Orleans, he was a wavy-haired, Brylcreemed, double-breasted Pentecostal star with a handsome profile and a lot of ambition.

"Brother Daly says shut-ins will be able to worship the same as if they was right there in the pew."

Daddy said, "I reckon it'll be a long time before a poor shut-in widow woman will be buying herself a television set. Nobody asked me, but I've got some—"

Junior and Brother Janway looked at each other. They knew what was coming.

Brother Janway said, "Opinions? Go on ahead, Raymond."

"In the first place, I worry about television all by itself and now you're about to mix up television with religion?"

"Quartets are singing on television," Brother Janway observed.

"Rev, everybody don't feel the same as you. There's a mess of folks don't agree with you at all," Junior said. "Them that can afford it, they love their television."

Brother Janway, who usually remained above every fray, continued.

"Raymond, Brother Daly might be able to help more people. Folks who don't get out to church anyway."

"He said they can mail in their requests and he'll pray for 'em right there in front of the camera," Junior added.

"They're gonna get their healing through the camera? Nossir. No siree. Looking at a television set and waiting for your healing's not the same as a laying on of hands. I'm willing to trust the Lord for my healing. Find me somebody anointed and start praying. Cecil, you're not preaching faith healing anymore?"

"Yes I am, but you know I believe doctors are healers too, and some of them are anointed. Got a man in my church with heart trouble. Asked us to pray for him just last week. We prayed and the doctor did his work too, and the man pulled through. Faith *and* doctoring."

The conversation had veered into tricky territory, the place where Pentecostal ministers were striking out in different directions. Junior interrupted an uncomfortable situation, saying he'd be taking off, and everybody hugged him and he left.

When the tabernacle opened, even before they had all the finishing touches in place, an invitation came for Sister Fern to sing. It would be their first big televised event, and instead of opening on a Sunday for a church service, Brother Daly elected to host a big Singing, pulling in performers from all over the South. By now everyone knew how Daddy felt about the cameras, but we also knew how he felt about Mother, and since she didn't drive, he'd take her there. We headed out across the Pontchartrain Causeway on our first visit to Brother Daly's extravaganza.

In the afternoon, Mother practiced with the band while Leslie and I drifted up and down Canal Street. We got back just before it was time for the music to start and we heard Daddy behind us.

"Karl, you ol' backslider, get over here and hug my neck!"

Daddy called to Brother Janway, "Cecil, you know Karl?"

"Don't believe so."

"Karl's the one who started putting inspirational songs at the end of all his radio programs"

"Kousin Karl! Well, I'll be. We've been hearing about you all over the place."

Karl was getting famous in rockabilly circles and country circles and Southern gospel circles, and rumors said he might be going to California soon to host his own television program.

Daddy asked, "You here to see the Stuckey Brothers? They're something, aren't they?"

"Well yeah, I sure do want to hear them and The Revelators, and your wife. Where's Fern?"

"Back there working on her hair. You going to MC tonight?"

"I sure am. Then tomorrow I'll be doing a radio show right here in New Orleans. I'm hoping Fern can stop by the station and sing. You too, of course. Y'all come do a couple of numbers."

"She'll want to take you up on that. You've given us so much publicity, you're starting to sound like a *believer*."

"C'mon, Ray, you're not gonna get me with that one. No sir, you know better'n that. I'm not a churchgoer. I'm here for the music."

Karl took his place up front, the camera was pointed at him, and speakers all over the huge hall boomed with his radio voice now going out over television sets too. As the band started up a blues-rockabilly-country-gospel rhythm, Karl introduced shut-ins and believers and sinners and anybody who had a television set to the sound of 1950s church music.

A huge choir wore black robes with shiny gold stoles down the front while they sang and swayed. A band with musicians from all over the city, including some from New Orleans's French Quarter, filled a separate platform of their own that was built up on a different level and seemed to float near the main stage.

There was a mix of music past and present and future. Microphones and lights sprouted from every surface. Into this big and boisterous, rambunctious and rollicking, unrestrained party, Mother stepped, assisted up to the high platform by the music director, snapping her fingers, keeping time with the band, turning around to beam at the choir, acknowledging the musicians. She started off with a song she'd just written.

Welllll, He keeps me day by day
He answers when I pray
And He will surely do the same for you
Just can't catch up with my praises to the Lord
His blessings never ever are a few
He keeps me day by day
He answers when I pray
And He will surely do the same for you

The choir sang a chorus, clapping and moving around. A guitarist took off on a solo, then a fiddler did the same.

Keeps me busy countin' my blessings
Keeps me busy busy busy thanking the Lord
Well you know my Lord has been so good to me
He picked me up and He saved my soul
And He set my spirit free
Keeps me busy countin' my blessings
Keeps me busy busy busy thanking the Lord

Brother Daly jumped over to a mic and hollered, "Cecil Janway, you get on up here!"

Brother Janway slid onto the piano bench and laid out his own testimony, flat laid it out way down to the end of the keyboard using his whole body, then he jumped off the bench, motioned for the other player to return, stepped down from the high platform to wild cheers, and ambled on back to take up his place by Daddy, as if nothing big had happened, as if this overgrown boy with the remarkable charisma could turn that sound on anytime, anywhere, first thing in the morning in his kitchen, even before coffee, and he *could*. We'd seen him do it.

My brother and I were allowed to stand back there too, where instead of the camera Junior had described, one they'd planned to mount in a fixed position, this fancy camera moved back and forth and the man working it seemed to know everything about it. This was no basic piece of church equipment operated by volunteers. It was serious and professional transmitting.

Somehow Brother Daly managed to bring together enough funds and skilled personnel to open his new place at top speed. This, alone, was new to those of us who worked out in the field, or occasionally pastored small churches where one week the preacher told the deacons there was a serious need for pew repairs, then over the next few months, very slowly, funds were accumulated to accomplish small goals.

With the opening of Brother Daly's gospel emporium, many preachers' visions were likely to expand. We never saw what the Singing looked like that night as it came through television sets in homes, but watching the camera pointed toward Southern gospel singing stars, seeing it pointed toward Mother, everything changed.

The next decision was a subject Leslie Ray and I speculated about many times through the years. What made them do it? How did he convince her? Was it the prospect of owning a home of their own? A plot of land, plus building and decorating costs, would be given, given outright, by the wealthy Cajun families who wanted a Pentecostal church to the Joneses. Or was it the call of the enormous tabernacle in New Orleans with its cameras and the potential to reach thousands at one time with one song?

Mother was often sad about the home they left behind, the only home they ever owned, the cottage in El Dorado, Arkansas. Fear of poverty followed her through all the small parsonages we'd occupied so far, and she vowed she would defeat it. Whatever the story behind the next step, a couple of weeks after the New Orleans Singing, Daddy said we were moving to Bogalusa. He would do there what he did other places, raise money and build a new church.

Leslie would be in the tenth grade at Bogalusa High School and I'd be in the eighth at Junior High, but before we packed up our Texarkana apartment, Mother wanted to go see Gramma K in California. Daddy said fine, and we could stop in Bossier City on the way and visit his people too.

Fern and Ray in the 1940s.

MERRY CHRISTMAS AND A HAPPY NEW YEAR

The four of us in Columbus, Georgia, in 1945 in a publicity photo for the family radio show, *The Joneses Sing*. This Christmas card was sent to listeners who wrote in. New ones were taken every year for revival publicity.

Leslie Ray and Nita Faye, ages six and four. We're
already gospel gypsies singing with the family.

The Jones kids, Nita Faye, The Baby, and
Leslie Ray, in Murfreesboro, Arkansas, in 1952.

Daddy and The Baby, age
three, in Louisiana in 1955.
We got us a blonde.

HEAR THE JONES'ES

in old fashioned

REVIVAL

Beginning   August   31st, 1947

Services

Each

Night

at

7:45

Rev. R. D. Jones   Mrs. R. D. Jones

Stamps Assembly of God Church
425 Oak street
The Church with a WELCOME

Dynamic Preaching.   Spirited Singing.
Salvation for the Soul.   Healing for the
Body.   Power to Witness.

There will be a special singing the afternoon of
August 31st at 2:00 p.m.   Every one is invited to attend.   There will be many out of town singers,

The Public Invited to Attend.
A. V. HENDRICK, Pastor.

Reverend and Mrs. Raymond Jones set out together, preaching
and singing all over the Deep South in the 1940s.

Consecrated Evangelists Who Are

"Definitely Different"

With a ministry that appeals to the "outsider."

Singing Spiritual Songs "Southern Style"
Making Music That Moves and Inspires
Preaching Pungent, Fiery Messages
Presenting Original Songs and Poems

A Framed Original Painting Given in Every Revival

REV. AND MRS. R. D. JONES
Ministers

BOX 547 - - - TEXARKANA, ARK.

Revivals used novelties to attract attention. Fern's "framed original painting given in every revival" didn't last long because they were awful. In spite of bad paintings, The Joneses' popularity grew all over the Deep South.

ONE WEEK REVIVAL WITH THE JONESES

Every

Night

Special

Singing

It's The

JONESES

Every Night Beginning June 29th
Until July 6th, The Singing Joneses
Want to Sing to You!

BETHEL TABERNACLE
PALM AND BELMONT STREETS

Fern and Ray billed as "The Singing Joneses," doing what they do best and gaining fans.

Nita Faye singing while Daddy plays steel guitar
at an Oklahoma revival in 1953.

Daddy believed he
was called to spread
the Word and build
new churches for
his denomination.
He was good at it.
In 1956, another
church went up in
Bogalusa, Louisiana.

PHENOMENAL GROWTH OF NEW WORK IN LOUISIANA

About nine months ago, Evangelist and Mrs. R. D. Jones from Arkansas, accepted the challenge to secure a District tent and go into the beautiful little town of Bogalusa to pioneer a new work .

On July 21, the first service of the tent revival was conducted and from the very beginning there was no doubt but that the plan of God was to establish a church in that city which had such a large population of Roman Catholics.

Souls were saved and added to the church and a few weeks later the Sunday School was organized with 41 present the first Sunday.

Then came the construction of the church building while the services were being held in homes. With the help of the local people, the Section and the District, construction was soon under way and today, there is a lovely brick building nearing completion.

When completed, the building will have green tinted jalousie windows, a porch effect in the front, blond church furniture, including a blond piano, rubber tile on the floor, carpets covering the platform and around the altar, a nursery, rest rooms and air-conditioning.

Nine months later, when the first opening service was held in the new church building, there were 112 in attendance for Sunday School. A revival is now in progress and the fast growing congregation is aiming for the goal of 200 in Sunday School at the close of the revival.

Radio time has been secured on the local station and for the past several months Rev. and Mrs. Jones have conducted a daily radio program reaching a large audience.

A story praising the growth of the new Bogalusa congregation.

Rev. Jones, "Brother Ray," on the radio.

Mother becoming Sister Fern in Louisiana in 1955. Southern gospel singers paid to make their own records to sell at performances. It took a long time for our family to get enough money together to pay for this many boxes.

Fern and a fan in Nashville in 1959. She signed a Hollywood record contract and got her pink Cadillac and a mink stole for Nashville's DJ Convention. This picture appears to be Fern's happy ending, but it was the beginning of a storm.

THE ORIGINAL
WALLY FOWLER

Anniversary

Edition

Anniversary

Edition

GOSPEL AND SPIRITUAL
ALL-NITE SINGING
CONCERT

1959 MONTH OF NOVEMBER 1959

SOUVENIR PROGRAM

RYMAN AUDITORIUM

Nashville, Tennessee

FRIDAY NOV. 6, 1959

Eleventh Anniversary

7:45 to 8:00—Audience Singing

Prayer—Wally Fowler

Songs

(4) 8:00- 8:15 THE LeFEVRES

(4) 8:15- 8:30 WALLY FOWLER

(4) 8:30- 8:45 BLUE RIDGE QUARTET

(2) 8:45- 8:53 FERN JONES

(4) 8:53- 9:08 BLACKWOOD BROS.

(2) 9:08- 9:15 JOHNSON SISTERS

(4) 9:15- 9:30 CHUCK WAGON GANG

(2) 9:30- 9:37 JENNINGS TRIO

(4) 9:37- 9:52 STATESMEN (Hovie Lister)

(4) 9:52-10:08 SPEER FAMILY

(4) 10:08-10:23 OAKRIDGE QUARTET

(Allow 7 min. Emcee)

10:30 to 11:00 P.M. INTERMISSION—Two concessions in back of auditorium main floor & balcony, serving: Hot Dogs, Cold Coca-Cola, Sandwiches, etc.

NOTE: All songs on broadcast not to exceed 2:00 min.

11:00 p.m. to 12:00 Midnight
BROADCAST RADIO STATION WSM

All Singers On Stage

Sponsored by
B. F. MYERS & SON FURNITURE & APPLIANCE CO.

Goodlettsville, Tenn.

TIME FURNITURE SUPER MARKETS (HOT POINT)

1. WALLY FOWLER
2. LeFEVRES
   (Com.)
3. BLUE RIDGE QUARTET
4. FERN JONES
5. BLACKWOOD BROS.
6. JOHNSON SISTERS
7. CHUCK WAGON GANG
8. JENNINGS TRIO
9. STATESMEN
10. WALLY FOWLER
    (Com.)
11. SPEER FAMILY
12. OAK RIDGE QUARTET
13. LeFEVRES
14. BLUE RIDGE QUARTET
    (Com.)
15. BLACKWOOD BROS.
16. CHUCK WAGON GANG
17. STATESMEN
    (Com.)
18. SPEER FAMILY
19. OAK RIDGE QUARTET
20. WALLY FOWLER
    (Com.)
    Theme
("Looking For A City")

The program from "The Original Wally Fowler All-Nite Singing Concert" on November 6, 1959, at the Ryman Auditorium, home of the Opry. The detail shows the list of performers for the live show and the WSM radio broadcast performance, both featuring Fern.

GOSPEL CONCERTS PRESENTS...

THE SUNSHINE BOYS
from Wheeling, West Va.
Dot recording artists . . .
veteran performers of
19 motion pictures . . .
currently appearing on
the ABC Network show,
"The World's Original
Jamboree" and also
on WSTV-TV.

PLUS

THE SONGFELLOWS
Southern California's greatest gospel music quartet.

FERN JONES
Dot recording star and noted soloist of countless
personal appearances.

. . . in a concert of the finest
in Southern Styled Gospel Music
for the enrichment and
entertainment of all.

FRIDAY
MAY 20
8:00 PM

LONG BEACH MUNICIPAL AUD.

FOR TICKET INFORMATION — FRontier 9-9861
MAIL ORDERS -- Send check or money order, payable to
Gospel Concerts, to 2716 Fisk Lane, Redondo Beach. Include
a self-addressed, stamped envelope. Tickets also available
at Humphreys Music, 130 Pine in Long Beach.

GENERAL ADMISSION   **$1.35**
RESERVED SEATS $1.50 - $1.75 - $2.00

EMCEE — KFOX DISC JOCKEY
HUGH CHERRY

Sister Fern's last performance in 1960 in Long Beach, California.

Gramma K (Zula) and her daughter Fern in Glendale, California, in 1957. Can't live with, can't live without each other.

Uncle Jim with Pedro and one of Pedro's little friends, both of them "mean as the dickens," in California in the 1960s.

The Baby in Glendale, California, in 1957, starting school at age five in dresses made from the same pattern Mother used for me more than a decade earlier.

Leslie and Anita in the 1970s.

Leslie and Anita on a Sunday (after a jazz brunch) going to see his new law offices in the 1980s in Orange County, California.

Anita (Jones) Garner on KBIG Radio, Los Angeles, in the 1980s.

Musical Houses

Chapter 27

Age of Reckoning

By the time we arrived back in Bogalusa after our visits with grandparents in Louisiana and California, my brother was getting away with more sass than I'd ever have guessed would be possible. I couldn't have duplicated his tactics with any success even if I'd tried, because you'd have to swear off caring what anyone thought or what they might do about your behavior, or at the very least, you'd need to make them believe that's how you felt.

I couldn't tell whether Leslie really didn't care anymore or if he was putting on an act to be free from discussions with them. What was certain was that he demonstrated his temper more often and that he provoked Mother most often. His temper was a match for hers.

The Joneses Sing aired live every Saturday morning from WHXY radio studios in the lovely Pine Tree Inn but Leslie no longer had to accompany us anywhere. He proved that being difficult could get you a Saturday morning to yourself. While he did who knows what those days, Mother and Daddy and other singers and musicians and I put on a gospel show. Daddy offered a brief devotional at the end, but mostly we made a lot of music. Sometimes Leslie watched The Baby at home. Sometimes we took her with us to the radio station, but she hadn't yet sung with us.

Here's something Daddy liked to repeat when people asked about his singing children. He never volunteered information about how or why Leslie was no longer part of The Singing Joneses, but he still held on to this old routine whenever someone asked, *all* of you sing? "That's right. All of us. If we had any that couldn't sing, we'd have to send 'em back."

It looked like we'd get to keep The Baby, because boy could she sing. She sang everything she heard. By then she was three and it was time for her to sing a church song on Sunday morning. They stood her on a chair to reach the microphone and Mother played her intro on the piano. The Baby started off in the right key but then veered off in a new direction. Mother kept playing the rehearsed intro and The Baby stuck to her own choice.

She sang, "How Much Is That Doggie in the Window?" perfectly copying Patti Page's radio version, including sound effects. During her "woof woof" dog barks, Mother laughed and played on while Daddy tried hard to maintain his preacher face. The Baby kept singing while Daddy lifted her down from the chair and still she sang while being escorted to the front row to sit between Leslie and me. She'd looked forward to her debut and she was going to have it.

At home she listened to the radio and sang with her favorites. We didn't know yet if she heard harmony parts, but she could stay on her melody just fine while we sang harmony around her on "Tonight You Belong to Me" and "Oh Baby Mine" and "My Happiness."

She learned "Mockin' Bird Hill" from Patti Page, then switched over to Les Paul and Mary Ford. She didn't take a step away from the radio when she heard "The World Is Waiting for the Sunrise" and "How High the Moon." She loved everything they did. So did we. She was obviously not yet disposed to sing only the Lord's music so Daddy waited awhile to try her again in church. Though he'd planned to introduce her on the radio, he was cautious about what might happen there too.

Mother and Gramma K both liked to sew for The Baby, so by the time she was released from nursery care at the back of the church and allowed to sit in a pew, she had many outfits to choose from, which she cared nothing about. Music and her tricycle were what she loved. She rode her tricycle as fast as she could away from us, away from the house, down the street as far as she could go before we caught her.

We were supposed to be watching her at all times in the Southern way, the older ones looking after the younger ones, correcting their missteps, but Leslie and I thought everything she did was funny or cute and we laughed instead of pointing out the error of her ways. We picked her up and carried her home, with her protesting all the way.

After the awful health scare at Paw Paw's house, the hospital, and then the trip to California, Leslie pushed back against everything Daddy taught. In Bogalusa, Daddy told Leslie Ray it was past time for him to be baptized. In our denomination twelve was considered the age of reason, when a young person is required to choose a religious path. Leslie postponed for years.

Young people were meant to show a conversion experience. Getting saved. In some churches, speaking in tongues, evidence of being filled with the Holy Ghost, was expected as proof of one's conversion. Leslie had not experienced either of these.

Full immersion baptism of the convert was required. None of our small churches had baptistries. Instead a dunking in a nearby creek was the practice. Everyone wore white and the congregation waded out from the shore, holding hands ankle deep in the water, forming a circle, and singing "Where He Leads Me I Will Follow" and "Trust and Obey." Then the preacher lowered the new Christian into the water in the name of the Father and the Son and the Holy Ghost.

It appeared Daddy had given up on the first two, conversion and speaking in tongues, so he skipped ahead and concentrated on talking to Leslie about making a declaration of faith through baptism. Leslie said he wasn't going to declare anything, he wasn't sure what he believed, or even *if* he believed. Daddy backed away, turning quiet the way he did when he was upset, and those times were always painful, when he named one of us as being the source of his broken heart. He believed without baptism we would perish in hell. We could see he meant it, but somehow, though his approval would be withheld, the two of us were not willing to lie to him about our doubts.

Leslie said he'd never get saved, never speak in tongues, never get baptized.

"Then you can't enter the Kingdom of Heaven."

"Then I won't."

"Boy, you are breaking my heart."

The more often these conversations occurred, the briefer they became.

"I will pray you under conviction, son."

"That won't work if I don't believe in it."

Eventually the two of them sat in silence.

On Sundays, when all of us were climbing into our spit and polish, Leslie dressed for church, walked in, sat in the back row, then sneaked out. Soon he stopped making even a token appearance, then he moved closer to provoking confrontation. We were having services in the new church even while it was under construction. There was a scaffold on one side that reached all the way to the roof, and during worship one Sunday, my brother climbed up there wearing his suit and tie. When I came out after church, he saw me, whistled, leaned forward, and waved at me. He stayed up there doing I don't know what while the church emptied, with Daddy standing just inside the front door shaking hands with departing churchgoers. Leslie slid forward and back, leaning against the roof, feet braced, so first I could see him and then I couldn't. If Daddy had glanced up, he'd have seen him too. Maybe that was the point.

Though Leslie still responded yessir and yessum when addressed, it was without the properly deferential tone. More frequently, he echoed Mother's tendency to darker moods, to temper, to silences, to drifting away from everyone. It made home a most uncomfortable place, and then it got so much worse.

Each time Daddy went up or down the back steps, he squeezed the leaves on the mint plant by the door. As soon as a rental house was finally available, he filled tubs with plants, scattering them around the barren yard, which looked like it hadn't seen a rake or hoe or shovel in decades.

He said mint will always perk you up. It's easy to grow, it'll thrive for you, but it'll take over if you don't watch it, so he kept it contained and released the fragrance each time he touched a leaf. Every time he smelled it he offered a laudatory comment. "Mighty fine," he'd say, speaking to the mint and to himself. Though he seldom flavored anything with it, he delighted in having mint as a neighbor.

I went down the steps, carrying laundry to hang outside. I inhaled mint, which is how I guessed Daddy had just passed by, probably going inside from the driveway. While I clothespinned our wet wash to the line, the screen door opened again and my brother came out and plopped himself down on the top step. He had Daddy's biggest knife in his hand. He started chunking the huge meat knife into the ground at the foot of the steps. Each time he threw it, he sent it a bit farther away and it made a thunk sound in the dirt. He stayed on the step and kept it up.

Chunking the knife in the ground.

Chunking the knife.

Chunking it.

Chunking it.

With my back to him, I had just realized the chunk-thunk had stopped when the knife whizzed through the air landing a short distance away from me, parallel to where I stood. I started shaking, not from fear but anger. I whirled around and screamed at him.

"What's the matter with you? You could have hit me!"

It didn't occur to me that he was aiming at anybody. I just thought he was being stupid and reckless and was probably angry about something, and then I saw Mother had come outside too and she was much closer to the knife than I was.

He jumped up and ran to me.

"I'm sorry. I didn't see you. I'm sorry."

Mother yelled, "You threw that at *me!*"

He yelled back at her.

"I didn't see *you*, either."

Maybe he didn't. He might not have noticed anything, because when he was in a dark mood, nothing penetrated until the anger subsided. It was the same every time with him and her. That day's episode was one more in a series that escalated, so by the time we moved into the too-small bungalow, their voices were often raised and no house would have been big enough for their outbursts.

The next day Leslie Ray and I talked only briefly about the day before. I was curious about how he could throw the knife and not see who was standing out there. He said he didn't know and I believed him. We didn't have our usual discussion though, wondering what Daddy would say and when he would say it. There was no point speculating about the aftermath anymore because Leslie made it clear he didn't care.

A few days later, something fell and broke on the kitchen floor.

Mother yelled, "Leslie Ray, you did that on purpose. I saw you."

Who knows how the bowl broke? Only the two of them were present at the time. It was inconsequential and certainly not a specific treasure, since we didn't own such. While she accused him of breaking it on purpose, I doubted he would waste his time destroying something as benign as a dish.

I followed Daddy into the kitchen. Leslie was holding tight to Mother's wrist. She didn't give in easily.

With her face right up next to his, she said, "Let go of me, you hear me?"

She pulled and twisted and he didn't let go. Daddy took a step closer to the two of them.

"Let your Mother loose."

Leslie didn't. He spat out his words, looking right at Mother, but talking to Daddy.

"You tell your wife not to ever touch me again. She tried to slap me. Tell her if she ever raises a hand to me, I'll—"

"Son, you leave your Mother be."

Leslie still had hold of her arm.

"It's not right to slap people. She oughten to be slapping anybody."

Daddy put his hand over Leslie's hand, looked him right in the eye, and made a slow ceremony of removing his son's hand from Mother's wrist. He lifted up Leslie's fingers to loosen his grip and Leslie let him.

What happened next wasn't like any other time Mother and Leslie fought and Daddy intervened. The aftermath of this incident didn't end with some form of reprimand. Daddy looked from one of them to the other and said, "What am I going to do with you two?"

We all left the kitchen and headed in separate directions. Daddy didn't say another word to Leslie. No lecture. No talk about how disappointed he was. Daddy put his arm around Mother and the two of them went into their bedroom and shut the door.

Leslie Ray went out the back, letting the door slam. I followed a few steps behind him, but by the time I got there, he was already gone, loping down the road away from our house. I sat on the step for a while waiting for him. I squeezed some mint leaves and they didn't offer any of the solace they provided for Daddy.

Leslie came home after dark, found me in the kitchen warming up food, and said he didn't want any supper and I should go ahead and eat. Daddy came out of the bedroom, made a tray, and took it to Mother. I ate by myself at the kitchen table and went to my room to read. I kept listening for familiar sounds.

Daddy never did go to Leslie Ray's room that night to sit on the bed the way he used to and talk to him about the error of his ways and then assign him extra duties and counsel with him, once again, about how a young Christian man ought to act. We all stayed in our own rooms.

The next day, Daddy said Gramma K was coming on the train. He said it was because Mother was going to sing over at Brother Daly's in New Orleans again, and also Gramma loved New Orleans and wanted to spend some time there.

This visit was a surprise, since we'd been to see her in California a few months before, but Daddy reminded us Gramma was always the one encouraging Mother to sing at bigger places. She hoped Mother would appear on television on a regular basis, and since Brother Daly's services were broadcast, everybody would get what they wanted. Fern would sing on television and Gramma K would be proud. Brother Daly took out ads in the newspapers to say who would be appearing. Mother's name was right up there in big letters.

Leslie and I rode with Daddy to New Orleans to pick up Gramma at the train station and all of us chatted on the way home about Bogalusa. Daddy told Gramma about the Cajun families who broke away from the Catholic church to become Pentecostals and how several members of two prominent families were behind his efforts to put up a new church building.

Gramma wasn't interested in talking about religion, but she did ask about Brother Janway. Did he play piano on television yet? She liked a good show and Cecil Janway put on a good show. She'd known him since he and Daddy were very young evangelists and she had a soft spot for him. She wasn't surprised to hear about Brother Janway moving up through the ranks of the denomination, but she said she sure hoped he wouldn't quit playing piano just because he was going to be a church executive. She also liked to flirt with him.

"Cecil's a charmer. If he wasn't married, I'd be moving back here myself to take up with him."

"That's right, Zula, you come on and move back down South and Cecil'll have you in church three, four times a week. You know how much you'll like that!"

Everybody laughed, then conversation turned to our new home under construction.

Gramma said, "I guess Fern's picking out furniture by now."

Oh yes, she was. Mother was devoting considerable time and effort to her stack of magazines, tearing out pages, making notes, already decorating in her mind. I asked Leslie if he liked where his room would be in the new house and did he know what color he would be painting it.

"I don't care."

"You do."

"No, I really don't."

Gramma went straight to the kitchen where Daddy handed her one of the big aprons both of them preferred, and soon the two of them were cooking. When I got up the next morning, Gramma was already out in the kitchen with Daddy, and though I couldn't hear their words clearly, I caught the edge of a conversation and realized it wasn't the tone they'd adopted years ago as their particular style. Daddy wasn't animated the way he generally was of a morning, telling stories, laughing, whistling. I hesitated before going in there for my coffee, and finally when I decided to go ahead anyway, sure enough, their conversation stopped.

I took a section of the newspaper out to the front room. Leslie had found other sources for his morning coffee. He claimed he had to leave early for his paper route, and then he'd go off with his new high school friends someplace where coffee and pie were served for breakfast. It was the first time the three of us, my brother and Daddy and I, weren't sharing conversation and a bite to eat together while Mother slept.

The second morning after she arrived, Gramma K and Daddy again occupied the kitchen table, but this time Daddy heard Leslie Ray start out the front door, and he called for both of us to come in there. We sat down, and without any preamble, he said, "Leslie Ray, your Gramma has invited you to come stay with her for a while out in California."

Leslie Ray didn't look at Daddy or Gramma K. He looked at me. As soon as Daddy finished saying his piece, my stomach caved in because nobody had said my name. It was immediately clear I wasn't part of this plan.

Gramma said to Leslie, "If you want to."

If he *wants* to? Both of us would give anything to leave. If he *wants* to? To his everlasting credit, it was my brother who spoke the obvious.

"What about Nita Faye?"

"Well now your Gramma can't take both you kids . . ."

Gramma said to me, "You know I'd love to have you too, but . . ."

As soon as she got out that part of her sentence, I erased Gramma K from my very short list of names a person could trust.

I said, "For a *while*?"

It wasn't a question so nobody bothered to address it. This was the worst thing that had ever happened. I couldn't imagine life without my brother. We were the us in "them and us." We weren't done raising each other. Him living all the way across the country was unimaginable. Someone should have yelled at Daddy. Do you really think you'll ever get your son back again? Staying *awhile*? Leslie going to California would be goodbye.

I would be losing my entire family when he left, but I wouldn't ask him to stay, even if I thought there was a chance of persuading him. I never blamed Leslie for the look of joy on his face when he heard Daddy's words, but I was angry and hurt that he'd been chosen to receive the key to freedom and I hadn't.

If it had been me she invited, I couldn't have done it, couldn't have gone to California without Leslie Ray, but things were different with him. He was older, had gone farther down the road away from our parents, had turned his back on their teachings early, and the real deciding factor was that he'd turned all his fury on Mother, a situation Daddy was never going to abide.

When Daddy called Gramma K to Bogalusa on this emergency errand, the two of them became unlikely and mismatched conspirators, but surely it would be painful for Daddy to release his boy into the home of a sinner, knowing his word would carry no weight with my brother after he left the South.

The two conditions that took away my best friend were unfixable from Daddy's point of view. First, Leslie Ray hated our life and was saying so all over town. All Daddy's efforts to rein him in had failed. Second, his temper was as big as Mother's, and that threatened Raymond's Doll Baby.

I don't believe Leslie Ray expected that Gramma K would fill any of the emotional gaps left by never having a real relationship with an on-duty mother. We knew our own mother had also never had a real mother, and she carried unhealed wounds from it, so this very gramma who was offering to spring my brother from his religious prison was no more suited to impart warmth and wisdom to him than Sister Fern was.

Daddy and Gramma had worked out all the details and that meant they were both prepared for the ramifications, including whatever I would feel on hearing their words. No reaction from me, however, would move them away from their plan. After all, I wasn't as combative as Leslie, so they could deal with me later, if at all.

Updates were delivered over the next few days, as if this whole trip was just another adventure. Train tickets were bought. Leslie and Gramma would take the train out of New Orleans soon.

Leslie Ray and I spent those days together, and our parents left us alone, asked nothing extra of us. He started packing some boxes we were to send along later, but Gramma K intervened, telling him he didn't need to bring much of his old stuff because she would be buying him new clothes. Life with Gramma K offered him other advantages. There was talk of a car, since he was driving age. Every detail she added made it worse. Every detail took him farther away from this life.

One day, through a haze of resentment, a revelation arrived. Didn't any of them see that Leslie Ray was the trophy in the incessant competition between Mother and Gramma K? Daddy had just handed Gramma a giant victory over his own wife. California won. Freedom won. But it was Gramma K who would be leaving Louisiana with the prize possession, the handsome firstborn son, the intractable, unreachable Jones boy.

I didn't blame the trophy for agreeing to the new shelf he would occupy. How could he not agree? I wasn't trying to make him feel bad, but every time the subject of his leaving came up, I cried.

He said, "I'll write to you all the time."

"You swear?"

"Swear."

"Not postcards. Letters."

"Letters."

"And tell me everything. What high school is like in Glendale, what they're wearing, what songs are popular, and take some pictures of your room when you get it fixed up."

"I will."

"When will you come back here to visit?"

This was a sticking point. We both said over the years that if we could get away, we would never return to this life, so trying to pin him down about a visit was as close as I came to making him feel guilty.

"You're gonna *have* to come back to visit. I can't come out there."

"Yes you can. Take the train."

"It costs too much."

"The bus then."

"They won't let me."

Mother stayed clear of all discussions about Leslie leaving. She never participated in any planning. In fact she left the room when the subject came up.

When the time came, Daddy said to me, "Come on, you might as well ride over to New Orleans with your brother to the train."

I said, "No, I won't go."

I cried when the car pulled away and didn't stop crying for months.

Chapter 28

The Pink House

Bogalusa, Louisiana, 1956

I no longer saw Gramma K as anybody's savior. True, she was Leslie's champion, but much of that I attributed to her competition with Mother. I expected nothing further from her. I held no illusions that Gramma would facilitate any part of my future.

When the workers broke ground for our new house, it felt like any other parsonage, fine for somebody else's family, the people who would probably live there next. We'd moved so many times, left parsonages, left towns, changed states, it was impossible to believe it wouldn't happen again.

From the day Brother Janway introduced us to the Bogalusa relatives of people in his Westbank church, Leslie and I were taken with the Quaves. Two of the Quave girls, Janice and Shira who were first cousins, went to school with me, and we became close friends, sisters from the start, them with their shiny black hair and dark eyes and sweater sets and me with my red hair and freckles and cotton preacher's girl dresses.

We were inseparable. One of the cousins remained Catholic and there were distinct differences between the Catholic Quaves and the Pentecostal Quaves. The Catholic cousin crossed herself every time she passed her church. The priest was unhappy about her consorting with my family. He said Catholics couldn't come inside our church, not even for a Singing, which wasn't really a church service. She promised she wouldn't sing a hymn, wouldn't participate in any of our prayers and would only listen, but he said no. The similarities between what Daddy preached and what her priest demanded, the insistence on one door that leads to the hereafter with all other options closed, were not lost on the three of us girlfriends.

While keeping one foot safely planted in their own home lives, Shira and Janice found ways to mix me in. Lies and secrets and subterfuge, the long-time mainstays Leslie and I had relied on, were also employed by friends who wanted to spend time with me but whose people felt Daddy's beliefs were wrong.

Frances Roussel (Roo-say), another school friend, became our fourth, but her parents also forbade her to come inside our church or my house. Her parents confessed to the priest about visiting our tent revival when we first arrived. He let that one go, because at the time we were only curiosities passing through, but now we were the dreaded harbingers of the Personal Jesus movement that was sweeping the South.

I wanted to dress more like the cousins, but when I asked for new clothes at home, other than the ones Mother felt like designing, it always ended with unpleasantness. Sister Fern's design sense was as unusual as everything else about her and as odd, though in a completely different way, as Gramma K's knitting and crocheting projects. I gave up asking about clothes. Instead I left for school wearing something Mother made, and Janice and Shira brought things from their closets for me to change into in the bathroom at school. I reversed the process before coming home.

Sneaking out also helped. I didn't follow in Leslie's footsteps exactly, but I found ways to get answers to my questions. I snuck into Catholic church to see what went on in those grand buildings. Our buildings had always been modest, though that, too, was changing. With preachers like Brother Daly starting off in new directions, others were following and Pentecostals were putting up bigger and bigger buildings with everything a theatre might have.

One day after school I found Mother at the sewing machine, fashioning her favorite colored sheets into window hangings and bed covers. She used to buy parsonage curtains with church funds at the local mercantile or J.C. Penney, if there was one in town.

I asked, "Why are you sewing curtains for the parsonage?"

Her reaction was stronger than the question warranted.

"It's *not* a parsonage. It's *our* house."

"But the house is right by the church and Daddy's the pastor."

She said another house could be built later to serve as a parsonage for the preacher who would follow Daddy, if we ever wanted to move.

"If we moved, could we still come back here?"

"Of course."

"So this will be our house forever?"

"That's right."

When Daddy told her it was all right for her to pick out furniture for the house, she'd already done it.

"These are the ones I want. Special order from the Maison Blanche in New Orleans."

Daddy turned his attention to the *Times-Picayune* page she waved in front of him, an ad which had been folded and unfolded many times. It featured a sketch of a fancy couch and matching chairs. She bubbled over with the wonder of buying new after all the years of living with someone else's belongings in church housing. She asked him to hold the ad while she moved to a wall and spread out her arms.

"See, Raymond, if this was our new house, that chaise would be right here."

She hopped around, a bird plucking compliments to add to its imaginary decorated nest, and she landed on a spot kitty-cornered from the chaise.

"And see, the other chair can go right here. Do you see? Raymond, can you see what I mean?"

She moved to another location.

"Or it could go all the way across the room, like this."

This was the happiest I'd seen her since we arrived in Bogalusa.

"You go ahead and order them, Sugar."

"I'll get them covered in pink brocade. Won't that be beautiful, Raymond? It'll take a few more weeks, but it'll be worth it, won't it?"

The two of them walked off together, discussing whatever it was they needed to decide next about the new house.

Junior was in charge of the building crew and he stopped by regularly to receive new questions, new instructions.

". . . and I want a pink bathtub and a pink sink and even, excuse me, a pink commode, if we can get one in pink."

"Oh yes they come in pink."

"Black tile around the tub. Can you do that, Junior, make the trim around the tub out of black tile?"

Finally her furniture arrived. We went over to the new house to receive the pieces. Daddy dropped us off. I put my coffee thermos on the front steps and sat down to wait.

"Hey Nita Faye."

"Hey Junior."

"Let your mama know I'm here, will you?"

I went inside to get her and she ran right past me when she saw the Maison Blanche truck. Junior helped a delivery man lift the pieces into the front room. The chaise was bubblegum pink, with a curved back, and its legs were shaped like funnels, in blonde wood with golden caps on the bottom. My first impression was all that pink! Second impression was that these pieces were supremely impractical. Mother's first impression, however, was love at first sight.

"Oh Junior, isn't this beautiful?"

She stretched out on the longer piece, bounced back up, and patted the seat beside her. Junior smiled at her.

"Try it!" she urged.

"No thanks. Well—all right then."

He dusted off the seat of his pants and sat. The two decorating conspirators smiled at each other.

She said, "Isn't this a beautiful fabric? So unusual. Feel."

He rubbed the chaise carefully.

She continued, "It's raised, and look at this tufting on the back."

He ran his hand over the fabric. "Bumpy."

"Exactly! It's brocade."

"It's *supposed* to be bumpy, then?"

"Yes, it is. It's very elegant. I never had a new couch before. I never had *any* new furniture. Did you, Junior?"

"Things I build from time to time. When Margie wants something new."

"Marge is a lucky woman. She *is*. Did I hear that you made her a dining room table?"

"I did."

"And chairs to match?"

"Oh sure. Gotta have matching chairs."

"And then Marge covered the chair seats herself?"

"She's good like that."

"I'm gonna learn how to do that too. Upholstery. That's one of the things I'm gonna teach myself now we've got our own home. I'll probably learn to crochet too. My mother wants me to."

"Miz Jones, you got to pick a color today for the outside. I brought some more samples."

She glanced at them.

"Not any of these."

"The painter's needin' to get started. Once he gets here we got to pay him for the whole time every day. Can't bring him all the way over here and—"

"I know, but these aren't right. I want the house to be *this* color."

She patted the chaise.

"Pink? Miz Jones, I mean the *outside*."

"Yes, the outside. Pink outside and a sparkly white roof, you know the kind?"

"I've seen them."

"So pink outside and a white roof. Okay?"

"Okaaay. But that's a whole lotta pink."

"Pink's the most important color today, Junior. Everybody's wearing pink and black. Elvis Presley had his picture made in a pink shirt and black jacket that looks exactly like an outfit I designed to sing in. Junior, can I tell you a secret?"

"You like pink?"

"Yes I do but this is something else. I just finished writing a new song. I'm gonna tape it and send it around to people and see if somebody famous will record it."

"Miz Jones, you oughta be recording your songs your own self. Nobody sings like you do. I oughta tell you what my Margie says. No I better not."

"Oh yes, you better."

"She heard you sing on the radio Saturday morning over at WHXY and she says, Margie says to me . . ."

"What?"

"She says, Junior, that's Rev's wife on the radio. I say, yes I believe it is, and Marge says, Miz Jones sings like a man. And then she says, she sings like a *colored* man."

"No! She did NOT!"

Mother put her hand over her heart.

"Junior, please tell her I am honored. Do you want to hear my new song?"

"Course I do."

"I got the idea from my mother."

She picked up her guitar, strummed, and sang,

Don't try to cross that river that you cannot see

Don't try to tunnel through that mountain that may not be

She stopped to explain the arrangement she heard in her head.

"And then backup singers come in behind me and then . . ."

For by tomorrow all your fears

May up and slip away

All the clouds of darkness

May turn to day

For all the trouble you have feared

You'll find there's grace to borrow

So let tomorrow be until tomorrow

Junior, always an active listener, said, "Uh-huh. You tell it."

She asked, "Soooo . . . what do you think?"

"It's a good one. You sure do turn a song into a lesson."

"It's the way my songs come to me. Back when we were getting our last baby and I was so sick, I called up my mother and she was upset that I was expecting again because sometimes I have a hard time—"

"I know you do."

"—but then when I told her I was scared about it she said, 'Don't borrow trouble. Let tomorrow be.'"

"I don't know how you do that. Write a new song as good as any on the radio."

"It's my gift from the Lord, Junior. All my songs *will* be on the radio. I know they will."

Chapter 29

Prodigal Son

From the moment the car pulled out of the driveway headed to the train station in New Orleans, my brother's address was Raymond Avenue in Glendale, California, and I would soon be living somewhere on Avenue F in Bogalusa, Louisiana. Our pink house was so new, there wasn't a street number for it yet.

After Leslie left, I stopped singing with them. I still performed once in a while by myself, but no more duets, no more family harmony. I wasn't sure California would have worked out for me anyway. It hadn't fixed everything for my brother so far. He still fought the same battles he had before leaving the South. The battles now had different names, but he fought on.

We talked long distance and kept our conversations secret. He called a friend in Bogalusa who brought the message to me, and I went over there and called collect to Gramma's number.

From the reports we received via cross-country traveling relatives fresh off Route 66, it seemed Leslie did what he pleased at her house. He told me himself about his misdeeds, neither bragging nor remorseful. He drank beer, drove his car into a bunch of garbage cans, and got arrested. Gramma bailed him out, took his car keys, and hung them on a nail on the back porch for a while. He said when they walked past the nail with the keys, they both laughed, but she had the good sense to keep them there awhile.

When his keys were returned, he went to Bob's drive-in, where everyone hung out weekend nights. He got into a fight with boys from the rival high school across town and was asked by the manager to stay away for a while. Gramma hung the keys on the nail again. Gramma's brother, Uncle C.F., came to California with some of the Southerners who found work at Lockheed in Burbank and sometimes he showed up at her Sunday suppers. He took Leslie aside one day. Leslie told me about it later.

"You're not showing your Gramma respect, son. This is not how a man behaves."

Leslie quit getting into trouble and got himself a job at Bill's Ranch Market, where he illustrated their sales signs in the late afternoons after basketball practice. He was proud of the artwork he created for the market and they were proud of him. The store presented him with a personal apron, the kind with long strings that wrap around from the back and tie in front. It had his name on it next to the store logo. He hung on to that apron for decades and wore it long after the ties were shredded and had to be replaced.

Though he sent me long letters, as promised, I'd only received two photographs. One was him leaning on his car. The angle was more car than brother. The other was him in his Bill's Ranch Market apron, and he had evidently instructed the photographer to concentrate on the logo, because the photo showed only the apron and no Leslie.

The next time I saw him he was a stranger walking through the door of our new house, a different person wearing California clothes. The growth rate of a high school junior cannot be overestimated. I had no idea a person could change so much in a few months.

He paid polite attention while Mother showed him pictures of everything she planned to do in the future in the pink house. He complimented her on her decorating ability, but then he'd barely unpacked when he told me he was ready to leave again to go back to his real home in California.

That first visit back to the South was because Daddy demanded it as a condition of Leslie Ray going to Gramma K's. He required Leslie to return within a certain period of time and spend at least a week with us. I don't know what Daddy hoped to achieve with the enforced visit.

Here are some of the things my brother did while he was back in Bogalusa. He went fishing with Daddy. We all went over to Westwego to visit the Janways. His nights were spent at WIKC with Bill Siegelin, where they played their favorite jazz records. He took my friend Janice on a date.

Daddy handing Leslie Ray his car keys during that visit was the last vestige of our childhood, gone. It was odd to be in the passenger seat with my brother driving and Daddy nowhere in sight. We rode around a lot, and after the first chunk of time we spent alone, he stopped being a stranger.

The two of us crossed Pearl River just a few miles away into Mississippi, to go to Picayune for pie and to Poplarville for barbecue. I wanted to know what it was like living with Gramma K. If it was different from when we stayed there as kids. He said her temper was bad, her headaches and her moods lasted for days, like Mother's, but when Gramma was upset, he could get her laughing, and besides, Gramma's moods didn't matter as much to him as Mother's once did.

At first he defended Gramma K until I reminded him that I'd known her all our lives too and there was no sense pretending with me. He didn't take any of Gramma's traits personally. There was one other big difference. On Raymond Avenue in Glendale, he was obviously in charge.

He spent a lot of time with The Baby. Every day she showed him another important part of her life. She took him by the hand and led him toward whatever interested her.

"Look!"

She pointed him toward a patch of something growing, tiny sprouts pushing up where Daddy was teaching her while he planted a new garden. Sometimes it was a pile of rocks she gathered out of the way of Daddy's plantings, stacking them over to one side. Sometimes it was crawly things she collected in a coffee can until everyone admired them, then she was on to the next stop.

The driveway sloped just enough to let her gain speed on her tricycle from top to bottom. Parked at the bottom next to the house was the family car. By the time she reached the bottom of the incline she was only able to stop by sticking her legs out straight in front of her. When she landed, she knew how to bend her knees to soften the impact most of the time. Sometimes, though, the thrill of it all clouded her judgment and she tried some straight-leg stops.

She showed Leslie her tricycle parked in the hall outside her bedroom door.

He asked, "How come it's inside? Is it broken?"

"I can't ride today."

"Why not? Did you hurt yourself?"

"I hurt the car."

"You rode into the car?"

"Uh-huh."

"And then . . . ?"

"Then Daddy said don't do that."

Once her riding privileges were restored, since she was forbidden to coast down the drive, the long hallway became her speedway. From her bedroom, she roared up the hall into the kitchen, parked her trike, climbed onto a chair, ate whatever food was presented, asked to be excused, mounted up again, and was off doing laps, hall to front room. She hadn't mastered turning around in a small space, so she dismounted in the front room to turn around. Some guardian angel must have protected her from bumping into Mother's Maison Blanche furniture because Lord knows what would have happened had she ever used one of them to stop herself.

Her riding made considerable noise on the wood floors until finally one of us insisted she go outside and play. That was not a satisfactory solution. The only other smooth surface available was Avenue F at the top of the driveway. As soon as we looked away, she dragged her trike up there and pedaled off. We'd all chased her numerous times. Leslie didn't believe she could outpedal him, though we assured him she was a little speed demon. She took off and it took him longer than he thought to get her back home.

She barely remembered our old rented house, so Leslie showing up at the new pink house was exciting. It was all hers to show off. A new audience to see her treasures. She was his shadow. He was delighted. He complimented her.

"You go very fast, don't you?"

"I like to go fast."

Those two, the oldest and the youngest, loved everything accelerated while I, in the middle, preferred life a bit more placid than it was proving to be so far.

Daddy took Leslie into the front room to demonstrate his combination hi-fi and radio, housed in one big glossy wood cabinet. Favorite records were in metal stands nearby. When Daddy and Mother sat down together in the afternoon, him with his tea and her with her coffee, he played the Ames Brothers' "Naughty Lady of Shady Lane" and "It Only Hurts for a Little While." One of them would choose a favorite, put it on, and they'd discuss what each of them thought of the songs, or they'd sing with the record.

For Leslie, Daddy pulled out a record I didn't know he owned. It was instrumental. No vocals. It was straight-up progressive jazz. He must have bought the record in an effort to renew a conversation about the music Leslie loved. He put it on the turntable.

"I want to understand why they do the way they do."

Leslie laughed.

"Daddy, I'm not sure I can explain this any better now. I'm not one to say, since I don't play."

Daddy insisted.

"Well, take this part right here. Why do you reckon they take off like that right at that spot?"

"Because they like the way it sounds? I'm not sure."

"Does somebody in the band decide when to come back to the melody?"

"I don't know how that works either, Daddy, but I'll find out and let you know."

"I am trying to understand it, but I can't. Now you take country singers and band singers and blues singers, and groups like The Harmonizing Four and the Ames Brothers, I can listen to all of them and understand everything they're doing, but something like this, well . . . do you s'pose all of them read music so they can look at it and decide when to come back together?"

"That's a good question, but wouldn't you think some of them might play by ear?"

"I don't see how. I play by ear and I could no more do that."

Leslie seemed touched that the conversation was even taking place. I was surprised by what he said next.

"Daddy you don't *need* to play like that. Maybe these musicians want to sound like something they haven't heard yet and jazz gives them the way."

The two of them shared versions of that conversation for years. During that first visit home, Daddy moved Leslie Ray into the role of visiting relative, a peer, and broached no discussions of the past, but Leslie was still only barely cordial to Mother the whole time and I think if he'd stayed longer than he did, their old stew would have boiled over again.

When he left, he didn't leave any personal belongings in the new bedroom designated as his. He promised to keep writing and he did. Sometimes he sent a list of things he wanted me to read or listen to or learn how to do. There was a way you dressed and talked in California and being from the South was something you got teased about when you started high school there. He was teased plenty about his accent at first, he said, but he punched the ones doing the teasing and now they were good friends.

He said I needed to listen to The Four Freshmen a lot more, and if I couldn't afford to get myself my own copy of *It's a Blue World*, he'd send me one. He also wanted me to pay attention to the Hi-Lo's because they had a song called "Have You Met Miss Jones" that I would like. And did I remember Ella Fitzgerald from when he played "A-Tiskit, A-Tasket" for me? He said her new album was even better.

He told me Wallichs Music City in Hollywood had separate listening booths where you could put on any record and hear it before deciding if you wanted to buy it. He said he'd drive me over to Hollywood and show it to me when I came to visit.

On the matter of driving, how was I doing with my Driver Education class? Did I know how to drive a stick shift? Because his car in California was a stick, and he'd need to show me what to do about the traffic. I was miffed that he asked, because in Louisiana you had to pass your driving test with a stick shift so of course I knew how, and I already had my learner's permit and he had only been gone a few months and ought to remember that.

Chapter 30

Johnny Cash Will Make All the Difference

Daddy came back from the post office.

"Mail's here."

She opened a big envelope.

"From Governor Davis."

She held up an advance copy of the sheet music for her song. A letter was attached. She skimmed ahead.

"... and Johnny Cash recorded 'I Was There When It Happened' at Sun Records."

She stopped, struck by what she'd just read.

"Johnny Cash! My song!"

Daddy's reaction had everything to do with what Johnny believed. He agreed having a man like Johnny sing a song you wrote could be a good witness for the faith.

"I hear John's a good man. Reads the Word. Good to his Mama. Loves the Lord."

Johnny and Elvis were filed into the same compartments in Daddy's assessment. Faith and respect for their elders.

The news about Johnny filled her with excitement because of the role he might play in the realization of her dreams, and unless Daddy thought Johnny was a good man, he'd never have encouraged the relationship. This news was immediately celebrated.

Johnny Cash was already famous and with him recording the song, Mother and Governor Davis would share royalties and would also be able to sell more sheet music. The Governor appeared on television shows and made movies and toured everywhere, while Mother, having adapted to our new life in Bogalusa, no longer toured. Mother's biggest audiences were now in New Orleans, but having written a hit song could expand her horizons.

"I Was There When It Happened" was Johnny's favorite, the Governor said. He learned it from listening to the radio. It was the song Johnny sang with the Tennessee Two when he auditioned for Sam Phillips at Sun Records in Memphis, since it was the only song they'd practiced enough before they recorded. She read on.

"Governor Davis will be coming to Bogalusa to the Auditorium and wants us to appear. Raymond, won't that be exciting? The man who wrote 'You Are My Sunshine' is asking us to play on the same bill with him!"

"I told you before, Doll Baby, I don't feel right anymore about playing outside except for church work. You go ahead."

"But you *have* to come, Raymond."

"No, honey, I *don't*. I'll be at a meeting that night."

"You don't even know which night. I didn't say it yet."

"Whenever it is, I'll be busy. I'm pastoring and that's what I'll be doing. I'm sure Jimmie Davis knows plenty of guitar players that'll keep the beat going for you."

"Honey, do you know how important this is for me? My own records will be here any day now and I can sell some when I sing, the way other people do. That's why we saved up to make the records, so I can sell them when I sing."

"You continue on ahead and do that."

A few days later several boxes arrived. Junior went to pick them up while Daddy was out on a sick call. Mother said leave them on the front steps 'til Daddy gets home. When she heard the car, she ran to him.

"Look! They're here! My records! I promise I'll pay back every penny they cost. Raymond, will you take a picture of me? I'm gonna pose with the boxes of records before I even open them."

An invitation came from Brother Daly for Sister Fern to join in a Homecoming Jubilee in New Orleans, a huge two-day event featuring famous quartets and musicians. The backup band, he told her, would be worth the trip. And he had a new choir director who'd already taught them Fern's songs.

She worked late several nights getting her clothes ready. She told Gramma K on the phone that one dress she was considering was that black one with the fuller skirt but, of course, there was also a favorite red jersey with the sweetheart neck. The movie star neckline adapted into a more modest version by Fern revealed only a bit of skin, but because of the way she was constructed, hints of pulchritude were just a breath away.

Backstage in New Orleans, friends dropped in. Mother had a dressing table, but since she didn't wear makeup, she spent most of her time in front of the mirror trying to win the battle of her curly hair versus New Orleans humidity. She tugged and pinned some up on top and finally turned away from the mirror with an unhappy face. That was Daddy's cue to remind her they were doll baby curls and she was his Doll Baby with big ol' doll baby eyes, and she calmed, as always, as if she hadn't heard it all before.

Brother and Sister Janway stopped in to say hello.

Brother Janway said, "Guess who's coming tonight? Our old buddy, Kousin Karl."

Daddy said, "Are you sure? Last I heard, Karl doesn't want anything to do with church music anymore."

When Kousin Karl came through the door, Daddy shook hands and nodded and waved to the musicians just outside in the hall where they were tuning up and telling each other their road tales. The announcer's mic went on. That was our cue to vacate.

"Welcome to Canal Street Tabernacle!"

The band swung into a fast version of "I've Got That Old Time Religion in My Heart," not the one that says "gimme that old time religion," but the one that you could play at any tempo, sing it alone or with parts, and just a few bars into it, everybody was up off their seats.

Mother would appear early this first evening, and again later in the show, then we'd stay over in a hotel room arranged for us at The Roosevelt, the first hotel we'd been to since our visit to The Shamrock in Houston. This time we'd get to spend the night and Mother would sing again the next afternoon.

Daddy and the Janways and I sat together. Rita Pleasance and her family came over from across the river. A sizeable section was occupied by members of our Bogalusa congregation who had only seen Mother sing in church. We watched her stride across the stage in her clingy red dress with her back porch in motion. When she was up there she turned into touring Sister Fern and I thought that would be a big surprise for church people who hadn't met that person before.

In Brother Daly's palace for Jesus, the lights loved her and she loved them back. A spotlight followed her and landed smack on big rhinestone clips at each corner of her trademark neckline. Those clips twinkled so much, they were all I could see on the bosom of the wife of the preacher who taught against personal adornment. I'd be surprised if she had mentioned to him that she'd be wearing jewelry for the first time since they converted to the faith.

The band played, the choir sidestepped in time to the music. Sidestep over and clap, sidestep back and clap, the way Black choirs did. Some of our white Pentecostal church choirs had adopted that maneuver fairly recently. A few years back, our choirs were made up of mostly older churchwomen with frail vibratos, aided by an occasional male bass or tenor, and on Sunday morning, it would be ten old women and two men, standing quite still, yet they managed to put out music that stirred the spirit, a testament to the notion that the spirit can sometimes be stirred, as Daddy claimed, through pure intention.

In Black churches it felt like everyone was always in motion. The preacher crossed the platform many times exhorting, and choir singers moved around and clapped, and when they sang a slow song, they swayed. I wondered, how do they do that? How do they all know which direction to lean? They did know, all of them. Now here we were in New Orleans, with a big choir, all white, moving the same way Black choirs had been moving forever.

Sister Fern launched right into a favorite, "Just a Little Talk with Jesus." She always opened with a familiar one, even if her arrangements were much different from the original. She moved from that one into a new song, offering a spoken verse within, a devotional recitative, a testimony, a poem within a song, as was the style in Southern gospel circles in the late 1950s. In New Orleans she gave the audience the song she'd just finished writing in Bogalusa. She sang a chorus of "Let Tomorrow Be," then she did the spoken word portion.

For by tomorrow all the fears may up and slip away
And, you know, all the clouds of darkness
May somehow turn to day
And for all the troubles you have feared
You'll find somehow there's grace to borrow
So why not let tomorrow be until tomorrow

The choir hummed and sang background oohs and aahs, and when she got to that spoken word part, some people in the crowd were dabbing their eyes. When the audience applauded so long and so loud and wouldn't quit, the MC called her back out and held her hand and reminded them she would be singing again later. They kept applauding. He kept saying she's coming back soon.

Karl stood back a ways, looking up at the stage, beaming at her. After the Singing was done, in the dressing room, I gathered personal things to take to the hotel with us. Karl stuck his head around the door and said to Mother, "Now that's the way I like to hear you. For a minute there I thought Sister Rosetta had stopped by here."

Mother had kept track of Karl even before his new California television program was announced. Scouting for record labels was often done by disc jockeys and studio musicians and performers who shared income with songwriters. It wasn't a stretch for Fern to believe Karl might put her name forward, especially since the word was out about Johnny Cash liking her music so much, and Karl had already mentioned hearing about the Sun recording session.

She said, "I'm so tickled to see you! I thought for sure you'd forget about us around here once you got out to Hollywood."

"Passing through, Fern. A musical pilgrim, that's what I am."

Daddy asked, "What brings you to New Orleans? You working with people around here?"

"Got a singer to hear over at the Blue Room, then on to Memphis, then Nashville, the Opry."

Mother asked, "Do you have a card for an old friend?"

Karl dug one out of his pocket.

"Here's the Nashville number. You want the California number too? They always know how to find me."

Mother opened her purse and wrapped Karl's business card in a tissue, treating it like a treasure as she tucked it inside the black satin clutch Gramma K made her for just such occasions.

Chapter 31

Saturday Night and Sunday Morning

1957

They were at the kitchen table, the shiny red Formica one with chrome trim around the sides and matching chairs that she saw in a magazine and had to own. He had notes in front of him, his open Bible, and a cup of tea. She joined him earlier than usual that morning and poured a cup from the coffee he had ready for her. A kiss on top of his head, then she took a seat and reached across for his hand, urging him to lay down his pen. It was a big leap from good morning to what she had on her mind.

"I've been thinking about California. Everybody's out there now. Even Governor Davis goes to California to sing on television programs."

"You want to go visit your mama? We'll work it out, Doll Baby. I know you're missing her. You want to sing at some concerts while you're there? Stay awhile? Go ahead. I'll get somebody else to play piano for church."

"No, I don't mean *visit* California, honey. I was thinking we should *move* there."

I was about to leave for school, but that stopped me. I waited to catch every word.

"Move? Move to California? To sing? I don't hardly see how you could sing much more than you do now and still help me with the church."

"But, honey, think how many sinners are out in California that need salvation. They're putting church songs on national television. Tennessee Ernie ends every one of his programs with a hymn."

"Television? You know how I feel about television."

"But you see how television can work. Look at Brother Daly. Shut-ins get the Word even if they can't go to church. In California, there's more gospel concerts and they already asked me to be on Cliffie Stone's program and there's Cal Worthington's and Tommy Sands. Everybody likes our music. It's time to get my songs heard."

"You know good and well my work is here. Your music is plenty popular right here in the South."

"There's more record companies out there. Maybe I could get a record deal and then I wouldn't have to carry my own records around in boxes everywhere. Oh, Raymond, I am so tired of being poor."

"I don't think it matters one iota how much a person has."

"It does, honey. Sometimes it *does* matter. If all you've ever *been* is poor, it matters a lot."

"Now you don't mean that. I know you don't."

"Yes I *do* mean it. I've been poor my whole life. And here God gives me a talent that can maybe make us some money. You say yourself all talent comes straight from the Creator."

"And you need to dedicate it right back to Him. If you're thinkin' I will ever agree to you recording worldly songs, well I won't. It's just wrong, Sugar."

"I never said, never *once* said I want to sing anything but gospel. I'm not looking to sing other music in public, but I *do* want to sing every place I can."

"I don't know who's trying to persuade you. Is it Karl?"

"*Persuade* me? I'm tired of everybody thinking I can't make up my own mind. My mother keeps pickin' pickin' pickin'. How if I hadn't married you, I'd have my own television show, I'd be making records. Karl says if I'd sing some other kinds of music he'd have me a recording contract already, and you remind me every minute how I'm supposed to believe. I don't need any of you telling me what to do anymore. I've got my own opinions about all of it. *All* of it."

"Honey, we both still believe the same way, don't we?"

The answer was so quiet, I could barely hear it from where I stood.

"I'm still a believer, of course I am, but it's different now."

"Our faith is tested sometimes. We've talked about it and prayed through it many times. This is when we have to trust in the Lord even more. Don't you believe that? If you believe that, why are you talkin' about going off on your own? Sounds like you'd just up and leave without me."

"Oh no, honey. I don't like to be away from you a day of my life. I can't hardly sing when you're not with me. We could go together. Could we talk about that?"

The chair scraped so loud against the new linoleum, I knew he'd jumped up.

"Talk about WHAT? About throwing away everything we've worked for our whole lives? What do you want me to do, Fern, sit around waiting for you to decide what you're gonna do next? Don't talk to me about moving someplace where I might not be needed. God called me to preach right here and that's what I intend to do."

"Raymond. Honey. Please sit down. Please listen to me. Sometimes I think you feel like preaching is *everything*. The *only* way to testify. I feel like music is just as important in the Lord's work. When I make records, radio stations will play my songs and this time I'll be the one singing them. I know it."

"We can't be sure it'll turn out that way. Even Karl told you that. Your songs are for *church* people, honey. You're actin' like that's not enough for you anymore. You knew when we came here you'd be a pastor's wife, and when I asked you about moving here in the first place, you said yes."

"I am trying. I sing in church. I play piano. I go to the Women's Missionary Council meetings on Wednesdays. Sometimes."

"Sometimes? Twice."

"Sometimes I just don't feel up to it. Maybe being a pastor's wife isn't my calling, but I don't know what I'll do if we have to be apart."

"What do you mean 'apart'? You are sittin' in your brand new house with your brand new furniture you wanted and you're talking about being apart?"

And right about there, it seemed like somebody else was saying things using Daddy's voice. He was talking to her a way I'd never heard him talk. He was no longer placating or trying to soothe his high-strung bride. It even sounded like he had thoughts of his own saved up for this occasion.

"We've got a congregation counting on us. This is where our work is. *This* is where we live. You've got no reason, NO REASON WHATSOEVER to talk about going off to make a record or sing on television or some fool thing. You've got a church that needs you and kids to raise. I'm sick and plumb tired, Fern, of raising *you*! You're a married woman and a preacher's wife. Now START ACTING LIKE IT!"

That was the first time I ever heard Daddy raise his voice to her.

"Don't you talk to me like that! You have *never* talked to me like that before."

"Well maybe I should have."

"You sound just like my mother!"

"You can pout all you want to and stomp around here all the livelong day, and you won't make me change my mind. Your place is right here."

"You ARE just like my mother, taking that tone with me. Just like Mother. Nobody lets me do what the Lord intended me to do. Use my voice. That's all I ever wanted, just to sing."

"I never held you back. I got you out of your Mama's house, didn't I? I help you with your music. BUT I WILL NOT GO ACROSS THE COUNTRY just so you can have a pink Cadillac."

"Know what's wrong with you, Raymond? You've got no ambition. Your people, they don't—"

"Don't you be talkin' against my people!"

"Look at your Mama, poor little beat-down thing—"

"Don't you EVER talk against my mama, you hear me? Not one word! That woman never said an unkind thing. It wouldn't hurt you to be more like her. She cooked breakfast for ten young'uns every morning before good daylight, then picked cotton out in the fields."

Mother should have known not to slander anyone named Jones. This was one of the earliest lessons Daddy taught, about having respect for your people, not talking bad about them to anybody. You had to be careful when speaking about kinfolk. Leslie Ray and I learned that lesson quickly. If you started with a criticism, before you could finish a sentence, Daddy would say telling tales is not right, and he'd quickly turn that into a devotional, accompanied by scripture, and after talking to you awhile, he'd suggest you go to the Bible for some related reading.

"I'm not slandering her name. Not a bit of it. I'm saying she thinks everything you do is perfect, so she never pushed you to finish school. To get ahead."

"You ashamed of your husband, Fern?"

"Of course not. I'm just thinking about all you *could* be. People listen to what you say. Everybody likes you. I know you can find a church to pastor in California."

"You mean a big church with television cameras, where you can sing for thousands of people?"

"I promised you when you got your calling, I won't sing anything but church music, and even if you quit pastoring, I wouldn't be out there singing any other kind of songs. I mean to sing *gospel* in California, honey."

"I'll help you all I can with your music, but I will not move, Fern. The subject is closed. I'm not going to California."

"Maybe I'll go out there by myself then."

"No you will NOT, Fern. We're not moving. You hear? The only place I'm going right now is out of this house."

"What am I supposed to do?"

"I don't much care. I'm going fishin.'"

Chapter 32

Down by the Riverside

Daddy fished as often as his days allowed. He fished alone, he fished with men from church while they conducted business by a creek or a river or a lake or a bayou, but his favorite fishing partner was Junior.

Leslie Ray and I were the original worm diggers. From the time we were tiny, we reaped a rich harvest of wigglers where they lived in the dark soil right up against the house, some so big they seemed like baby snakes. We put the squirming things into a coffee can with dirt in it, then we put the can in the bottom of the ice box next to the bundle of clothes kept dampened for ironing. If one of our sturdier specimens managed to navigate to the top of the open can and find its way into the laundry, then we got to hear Mother holler for someone to come fetch it, and that didn't disappoint us. She was afraid of so many things, worms were way down on her list, but it was still satisfying to provoke the squeal, followed by the call for Raymond to come fix it. If he wasn't around, she went down the list. "Leslie Ray! Nita Faye! You better come get this thing!" By the time we moved into the pink house, even The Baby was a worthy worm wrangler.

Now it was Wordell and me digging up worms. Daddy and Junior were going fishing the next day and they said we could go too. We'd leave right after school.

We climbed into Junior's truck, Wordell and me in the back. At the river our daddies stood side by side, fishing poles in the water, not caring all that much whether one of them got a bite. Wordell and I were nearby, having a contest to see who'd get a tug on a line first.

Junior said, "That's a good song Miz Jones is working on."

"Which one is that?"

"The new one."

"Which one did she play for you?"

Junior sang a line from "Let Tomorrow Be."

"She just now sang that one over at Brother Daly's."

"Everybody liked it?"

"You *know* they did. Sometimes, Junior, I think how much easier life would be if I'da picked another line of work."

"A call to preach is a sacred thing."

"No money in it."

"Money's not everything."

"I b'lieve my wife feels different, Junior. I don't need much, never thought I'd have much, but seems like she needs more. *Wants* more."

"Miz Jones likes to buy things once in a while. That's how women do. But that's not the most important thing to her. That woman's crazy about you and you know it. And her songs, you see how she gets, the way she is when she's got a new song she likes. And when y'all get done making that new record . . ."

Mother and Daddy spent many hours in Brother Daly's studio, recording some of Mother's own songs, but also others they sang as specials in church. She wanted an album patterned after their radio shows, with some audience favorites and some new material. They'd already decided the album title would be the same as the radio shows, *The Joneses Sing*.

The sessions came about quickly because Brother Gene Thompson was working nearby. He was the most renowned guitarist in our circle. He pastored in Arkansas and we held revivals for him. In between he played guitar at bigger and bigger churches and now he had a following of his own. Mother and Daddy were eager to sing with him again.

Brother Daly said the studio was theirs for as many days as they needed and introduced them to his chief engineer "who knows all about great sound." The Revelators sang backup. Brother Daly sweetened the invitation to get the quartet to the studio when he booked them on some television shows and auditorium appearances nearby so they could sell their own records.

To my ear, the most unusual treatment of a song on the album was Mother's recording of "Whispering Hope" with a church organ. She'd never recorded with an organ and her version of the old hymn with The Revelators and Brother Thompson playing steel guitar was a personal favorite.

"When Miz Jones has the new records ready, she's gonna be happier staying around here, singing over in New Orleans where she can sell them."

"Junior, lemme ask you. Now you say exactly what you think."

"You know I will."

"Do you believe writing songs is a sacred calling? Important as preaching the Word?"

"I'm gonna tell you a story."

"Go on then."

"I was working over in New Orleans at the tabernacle and it'd be hot of a afternoon and the band would be in there playing."

"Lord yes, hot *and* humid this time of year."

"And the doors'd be open and the choir'd practice and people'd start coming in to listen. Walk in off Canal Street. With they grocery bags and all. I'd take a break, go down to the corner, get me a Co-Cola, come back, and the place'd be filling up—listening to the band and that choir."

"Well, Junior, you are talking about a cool place to rest on a hot day."

"That's not all. Did I say I was done?"

"No you didn't. Continue on."

"The next Sunday I had to go over to fix something, I forget what, and the thing is I seen some-a them same people cleaned up and setting in the pews. At Sunday service. They came back."

"I take your point about music being important, Junior, but some of those people might have come out to hear Brother Daly preach."

Both shook their heads no, that wasn't it.

"Did I tell you, Rev, about the new songbooks he got?"

"Fancy?"

"Oh yes, fancy and then some. Dark blue like the new choir robes—"

"How many kinds of robes do they have now?"

"Wait, I'm fixin' to make my point here. Right there on the bottom of the new songbooks, in gold letters, mind you, can you guess what it says?"

"Lemme see—'Jesus Saves'?"

"No. His *name*! Brother Daly went and put his name in gold on the hymnals. You know how we talk about that place being so—unusual—but, Rev, they're saving souls over there. That's a direction I could see you taking on down the road. You and Miz Jones with your music and your preaching."

"Fern's already brought that up more than once, how we could pastor a big congregation. She is trying Junior, she really is trying to think of ways we can both minister the way we feel called. But me in a big ol' building like that? I got no interest in that kind of ministering. No interest in television. I'm a country preacher. Blessed to be one. That's what I am."

"Well Brother Daly's place is full. They're turning some away. Gonna have to add more services. He's got all those singers and musicians and some people do say, maybe music can save your soul."

"You been talking to Fern. Whoever said it, she's the one repeating it all the time."

"I've seen it happen, Rev. You've seen it too."

"Junior, I got other troubles. About California."

"About your boy? I know that, Rev, I been knowing that, but I don't tell nobody your business."

"Both of them so hotheaded, I had to let him go. I was afraid for him and his Mother to be in the same house."

"That'd worry any man's soul."

"Fern's all tore up about California."

They were having two different conversations, with Junior guessing the latest trouble might be something new Leslie had done, or Fern missing their son, but Daddy was past that topic entirely.

"She wants to live out there."

"*Live* out in California?"

"That's what she wants and I don't think this will pass."

"Well, I'll be! I reckon we shoulda seen this comin' a mile off, but listen, she's using all her talent doin' what you asked her to do and you got no reason to worry about her fixin' to backslide."

"I never said I was afraid of her backsliding."

"You never said it, but you act like it and I don't know why. She coulda got her a contract like the rest of them, probably have some hit songs on the radio, if she'd sing different kinds of songs. But she didn't even try to go see about that. I don't see no sign, no sign a-tall of her puttin' one foot outside the faith."

"There's other things. I don't know if I should say."

"You can speak your piece with me."

"Even after I asked her not to, Fern went out and started looking for a recording contract."

"I'm sure she's only talkin' to gospel people. Because she's got new gospel songs ready to sell. Where is she looking? Memphis?"

"California. Maybe I should've let her go over to Memphis when she wanted to so bad."

"Where Elvis and Jerry Lee and Johnny Cash and them make records? Naw, you was smart to keep her outta there."

Junior attempted to lighten the atmosphere.

"The way she looks and the way she sings! Them people at Sun Records, if they got the sense God give a donkey they'd lock up that recording studio with her in it, throw away the key."

"No, Sun Records already said they won't take on gospel singers, but Fern found out Sam Phillips who owns the place knows everybody else in the music business."

"If she was to sing for him one day, I'd like to see his face when he hears her."

"I shoulda carried her over there myself. She sent him some songs and on the tape recording it's her singing them, so he played them around for people and now she's got somebody telling her she might get a contract in Hollywood."

"Who? Who said that?"

"Mac Wiseman. You know his music?"

"Guitar player?"

"He's a singer too, makes records, and now he's working for Dot Records and they're fixin' to move their company to Hollywood and they're looking for songs and she sent him some. Junior, if she has to be in Hollywood, I don't hardly see that I've got a choice."

"About what?"

"I might have to go with her."

Wordell and I, who generally had no trouble ignoring other conversations and sticking to our own, were both on alert. We stopped talking.

"Leave Bogalusa? Leave? But, Rev, your church ain't even finished yet, and you just now got things going good in town. The Cajuns love you, the colored, they respect you, even the Catholics don't hate you too bad anymore."

"I don't have the fight in me. I can't keep arguing with my wife. It just about kills me to fight with her. If you could see how happy she is about people taking an interest in her music. But I can't keep building up churches and leaving them. If I was to leave this one, well I wouldn't even expect the Lord to send me another one. I can't talk to anybody else about this."

"You don't need to tell nobody else."

"I haven't made up my mind."

"You think it over and pray on it some more and then you go ahead and do what you need to do, Rev. You and me, we know who's in charge. You stay close to Him and He'll take care of you *and* your troubles."

"I'm worried about letting the Lord down too, Junior. Giving up my calling. What will He think of me? You pray for me now, you hear? Ask God to keep this church going strong even if we have to leave. And if we move, you gotta promise to check on that new yard we put in. I couldn'ta done it without you."

Out of everything the two men said that day, it was the part about the yard that was saddest. Daddy was a natural-born grower of anything, and while the pink house was going up, at the same time Mother was ordering furniture from New Orleans and writing songs and sewing bed ruffles, Daddy drew on a piece of paper exactly where the vegetable garden would go, how much grass to plant, how far back the yard could go before the marsh took over, and it was the catalogues filled with colorful bulbs that he saved for last. Whatever bulbs he couldn't beg or borrow from friends' gardens, he would order as funds permitted. He complimented a churchgoer on the array of irises in their yard, accepted any bulbs offered, and when there were blank spots, he planned to order more, plant them, and watch them grow. Daddy planted everywhere we lived, even if we weren't always there long enough to see the blooms.

"Junior, I'm worried about lettin' the Lord down if I go away from here. Am I a good husband? I worry about that. And can I stay true to my convictions? Remember me in your prayers, will you?"

"I'll say a word. I always do."

Junior laid down his fishing pole, propped it up carefully with a rock to hold down the dry end, and pulled his harmonica out of a pocket. Music was part of every fishing trip. Though this trip took an unexpected turn, the habits of the musical fishing buddies held sway. He blew a note, then a few more.

"What's that you're playin'? 'My Heavenly Father'? Start it up again."

Junior repeated the first few notes. Daddy sang.

I trust in God wherever I may be
Upon the land or on the rolling sea

Junior sang along.

For come what may, from day to day,
My heavenly father watches over me.

Daddy called over to me and Wordell.

"Young'uns, get your poles. We better get home. Fix us some supper."

He shook loose the rest of the worms from our coffee can onto the riverbank.

"No luck. Didn't catch a thing."

Junior pulled up his pole.

"Not a one. We'll get 'em next time, Rev."

Chapter 33

Leaving Louisiana

1957

I went across the road to Shira's to use her phone to call Leslie Ray. Her mother always let me use their phone to call my brother, and when I offered to pay for the long distance, she said no. From their hall phone I reported to Leslie every detail from Junior and Daddy's conversation.

He said, "I sure hope they don't move out here."

"Me too. I don't want to move."

"I don't mean *you*. You'd like living in Glendale."

"I don't think living with Gramma would be any better than here."

"Sure it would. She doesn't preach all the time."

"Not to you."

I wasn't done with Louisiana. I had years of high school to look forward to with my best friends. My brother and I both thought Junior would remain the one person Daddy would confide in about this decision. We figured he probably wouldn't mention it to Brother Janway because he was the one who arranged for us to come to Bogalusa in the first place. We decided to pin our hopes on Junior being able to persuade Mother and Daddy to stay where we were.

We talked often over the next few days, wondering about other conversations that might be taking place about something as big as a possible move to California. Or maybe there was already an end to it. I never heard another argument in the house so I preferred to believe the idea of leaving would go away. After a brief report at the start of each conversation with my brother, he and I returned to our usual talk about us, what we were interested in and what we were doing and reading and listening to.

A few weeks later on Sunday morning in church, Daddy and Mother sang a duet, one of his favorites, "I Don't Care What the World May Do, I'm A-gonna Praise His Name." After she sat down he asked her to go to the piano. He said to her, "Blessed Assurance," and she played the chorus softly, while he talked to the congregation.

"Y'all stand with me. Let's sing this one."

Mother's chords led us as we sang the chorus with Daddy.

This is my story
This is my song
Praising my Savior
All the day long

He motioned for everyone to be seated again.

"I was a very young man when I heard my call to preach. With a wife in her teens. She gave up a lot to follow me."

He took his billfold out of the inside pocket of his coat and removed a card.

"This right here—this is proof of my ordination."

He read from the card.

"This certifies that Reverend Raymond D. Jones is an ordained minister, fully authorized to perform . . ."

He stopped reading, but held on to the card, held it up higher so everyone could see, then walked the platform back and forth from side to side holding up the card.

"This says I can marry you, I can say words over your departed, pray for your healing, and because I'm ordained, you know I care enough about my calling to keep studied up and prayed up. Every year I get a form in the mail to renew my ordination. Next time, when they mail me that form, they'll be sending it to California. That's right. California. I don't know where I'll be preaching next, but I'll carry this card with me as long as I live. My wife has heard a calling of her own, and she needs to answer it. I believe she should. And I believe I ought to support her work, just the way she came with me wherever my calling took us. She followed me, even when we didn't always agree. But we held on and worked it out together. And now I am on my way to California."

He put the card back into his billfold, put the billfold back into his pocket, and though it only took seconds, the quiet made it seem like forever.

No, they hadn't told me of the decision in advance. I was hearing about it at the same time as the church people. Though it wasn't unusual for them to make decisions based solely on their calling and not on what the impact would be for their children, this announcement that would change everything about my life set me seething. Instead of my usual tears and sadness, I felt what Leslie must have felt all those years, the rage of helplessness.

From somewhere in the congregation, a sob broke through, a big, loud, gulping cry. No need to look around to identify which member it came from because it echoed what all of us were feeling. On hearing any sign of distress, Daddy from up front would normally stop and call out a member by name, in a gentle way, "Sister Thigpen, are you troubled? Let's stop right here and say a prayer for our Sister in the Lord," and that's what we'd do, but this time the sound hung there unremarked.

"Y'all have *got* to take care of each other, y'hear?"

No matter how many times you leave, the next leaving is always the hardest.

Everyone expected Johnny Cash's version of Mother's song to change things in our Southern music circles, but it hadn't been released yet. Sun Records didn't allow that to happen. Sam Phillips said he wouldn't release Johnny singing gospel until he had recorded some other kinds of music. Sam said it was harder to get radio stations to play gospel, and he wanted Johnny to record something else, maybe something gritty, something where the big guy with the deep voice had been done wrong and got the lonesome blues. Something like that. Johnny put up a fight to keep singing gospel. He left Sun to sign with Columbia Records and only then did Sam release "I Was There When It Happened."

Before Johnny's version of her song was heard on the radio, Dot Records had already offered Mother a recording contract. When the contract arrived in the mail, it wasn't because Johnny or the Governor or anybody else recorded her songs. She got her deal based on her own initiative, her own voice, singing her own songs. It wasn't Kousin Karl who negotiated for her. It was Bluegrass legend Mac Wiseman who took her songs to Randy Wood, president of Dot Records. Mac was an A&R (Artists and Repertoire) man for Dot. His was the department responsible for scouting. A&R people stayed in touch with music publishing companies to find new songs for their established singers to record, and it was through composer channels and the demos she recorded that Dot heard Mother sing.

After digesting Daddy's shocking decision to go to California, I was even more surprised about how much I didn't want to go. I missed my brother awfully but I was a Southern girl all the way through. Janice and Shira and I saw each other every day. When Leslie Ray left, the Quave cousins were the place I ran to. They were more kin to me than the kin in my house. I couldn't imagine fitting into life in California the way my brother did.

Daddy and Mother shared with me only the most rudimentary information about our move, mostly about leaving behind my possessions again. We would pull one small trailer on Route 66, then we would stay at Gramma K's until we found a place of our own. I was eager to see my brother, and more eager than ever to learn his thoughts about achieving freedom (without tossing knives around the backyard), but nothing assuaged the goodbye grief.

We were in the pink house only a few months when we started loading up the trailer. The men connected the trailer to our sedan, and we packed it with clothes and music equipment and boxes of what would be needed first in California. Junior would ship more things later so Daddy said to keep the packing light.

The Baby roamed around tugging her tricycle with her. I knew what was coming and I didn't want to hear it, so when Daddy squatted down by her to have a talk, I turned away. The Baby was about to learn that her red tricycle wouldn't fit into the trailer.

No matter how many times you leave, the next leaving is the hardest. My red rocking chair in Georgia and her red tricycle in Louisiana were both now added to the growing list of symbols that meant goodbye.

Mother went from room to room crying. We could hear her in there. It wasn't a stretch to imagine her telling her pink furniture goodbye. She came out and took Daddy aside. Though I couldn't hear what was said, it was obviously something Daddy could make right because he hugged her and she stopped crying.

Daddy and Junior started pulling stuff out of the trailer. Boxes and boxes, carefully packed to distribute the weight, were removed. Then the two friends went inside and came out carrying the pink brocade chaise and chairs.

We never returned to that house. A Bogalusa real estate agent was engaged. Mother showed everyone the newspaper ad she was so proud of. There was a picture of the "Darling Pink House." (She wrote the copy herself.) She insisted the realtor place the ad in a prominent position in the newspaper, though surely his commission from the sale of our modest home wouldn't occasion an ad that size.

Mother's ad described features in grand style. There was, she mentioned, a sparkling white roof and bright green grass and a vegetable garden and a flower garden. The flower garden at the time was mostly new soil Daddy brought in to plant his irises. She was advertising the promise of future blooms.

Our trip was extended an extra day because the car didn't like the trailer and a mechanic had to reconcile the two of them. We crept along over days and nights and flat tires and quiet conversations in the front seat and me keeping The Baby occupied in back until we were finally on the last hundred miles.

When Daddy and Leslie Ray greeted each other, the sun came out, as if between them there had never been a cloud in view. It wouldn't last, but at the moment it seemed promising. The two tall, good-looking Jones men beamed at each other and headed to Gramma K's kitchen to catch up.

We arrived in Glendale to a welcome repast. Gramma had cooked one of everything each of us craved. It was the stitching-up we all needed after our ragged departure from the South. After we ate and cleared the table, Leslie said to Gramma, "We'll be back to do the dishes." To me he said, "C'mon. I wanna show you something."

He had created an apartment in the garage. He had a couch out there and a table and some lamps and everything else a high school senior held dear. Of course there was a record player with many albums beside it, because he was never more than a step away from jazz.

He didn't want to stay in the same house with them. He planned to keep living his own way, and he said if he was in there with them, it wouldn't be long before the subject of religion came up. They'd disapprove of everything he did and Daddy would remind him that without salvation he would go to hell and Leslie would lose his temper.

Leslie said he didn't like disappointing Daddy, but he hadn't set foot inside a church since he left the South and he never would again and there was no use talking about it. If Daddy asked him, that's what he would have to say and he didn't want to say it again. Leslie had thought about this a lot.

He said, "I like Daddy."

"Me too."

"I wish he liked me more, but he probably won't unless he's sure I'm going to heaven."

Leslie and I continued to handle the conflict between their beliefs and ours in different ways, but both of us agreed on one thing: Daddy was kind and accomplished and silly and good company when he wasn't lecturing us, but he preached at us too much and always came back to the scripture in Proverbs that said, "Train up a child in the way he should go and when he is old he will not depart from it."

Daddy clung to that notion while we'd long since left behind any pretense of believing the way he did. I told Leslie I believed there was a God, but I didn't think there was only one way to be a good person. By the time we moved to California, I'd met lots of good people and some of them never went to church. But Leslie Ray was done with all of them, Father, Son, and Holy Ghost. As for heaven and hell, that was a discussion we would carry on forever.

Chapter 34

California Kids

Glendale, California, 1957

Leslie Ray was a senior at Herbert Hoover High when I enrolled as a sopho-more and it turned out he was one of the cool kids. He and his buddies were a rowdy group that migrated to Bob's drive-in on Colorado Boulevard every Friday night and girls followed.

Glendale was a prosperous bedroom community where sons and daugh-ters of wealth drove their own cars to school and the student parking lot was filled with automobiles owned by teenagers.

The campus was a city with two thousand students. Everyone looked alike and dressed alike and talked alike. I seemed to be the only one that year with a Southern accent. Leslie said he would help me lose it. It was mostly a trick with the vowels, he said, and then where you put the empha-sis was important. It wasn't "PO-lice," it was "po-LICE." Not "FI-nance," but "fi-NANCE." No more "win-duh" or "mir-ruh." No more "yessir" and "yessum," except in front of Mother and Daddy. "Y'all" and "all y'all" were gone. The Southern California greeting "Hi you guys," which sounded to me like "Hieeee you guyeees," replaced "How's your Daddy'n them?" and "Your Mama doin' all right?" Leslie Ray had lost his middle name and his drawl and if he could, so could I.

The Baby started kindergarten where she was appointed some kind of monitor one day a week, an important job, one she said that she needed to practice at home, making people stop in the house and stand next to the wall until she said okay, go. We still called her The Baby and told her that might well continue to be her name in the family for good. Our people often called the youngest in any family The Baby, or Sister or Brother, and you could sometimes know people a long time before finding out their real names.

Though Mother spent most of her time with her own pursuits, she found time to make little dresses that were reminiscent, in an awful way, of the same designs she made for me. Adequate for a five-year-old years ago in the South, but it remained to be seen how this California little one all these years later would take to puff sleeves and back sashes.

The Baby was, in Daddy's words, "a spark plug." Leslie and I thought maybe we had turned cheeky and rebellious early on because there were two of us born close together and we could double-team them in the hope of wearing them down, whereas this youngest one was a handful all by herself.

In the South, our school lunches, subsidized by the government, cost fifteen cents, and what was put on our trays was what we ate. Mondays featured red beans and rice and cornbread and that was fine with me. It was what we'd be eating if we were home at dinnertime. Hoover's cafeteria offered choices of entrees, vegetables, salads, and desserts. Instead of reaching for the meat loaf, a luxury in a little cardboard boat, I celebrated my right to choose, spending all my lunch money on giant oatmeal cookies.

At Hoover, seniors didn't walk the halls with sophomores nor have anything at all to do with them except for school assemblies. There was even a separate area of campus called Senior Glen, where only they could lounge, so it was a surprise when one line over in the cafeteria, there stood Leslie, frowning at me.

"Is that all you're eating?"

"Yep."

"Do you have enough money for something else?"

He reached into his pocket.

"I have plenty."

"You ought to eat better than that."

A few days later he told me he observed me stopping in the hall to talk with certain people and wanted to know why.

"Because they said hey."

"Then do they ask you questions about where you came from?"

"Sure."

"Do they ask you to say words for them?"

"Yes."

"Do you do it?"

"They're just being nice."

"No, they're not. They want to hear you talk because you sound different."

"What's wrong with that?"

"You need to be careful who you talk to at school. Figure things out before you call somebody a friend."

"Figure out what?"

"Who's making fun of you. When I first got here, I kept my head up when I went down the hall, didn't look right or left, just kept walking, let them come to me."

That was always a major difference between us. He held himself apart until carefully, carefully, he found the spot where he would excel. I mixed and mingled with everybody and took some knocks but kept approaching people the same way forever.

He started calling himself "Les," so the first time someone at Hoover asked my name, I answered "Anita" and left Nita Faye standing outside the building at the front entrance, alongside the two giant lion sculptures.

It took exactly one day to learn another California school custom. When a teacher called my name in class, I stood and answered, "Yessir." Everybody stared until he said I could sit down. In the South when addressed by a teacher, the requirement was to stand and reply "yessir" or "yessum." I asked Leslie about it. He said to stop doing that. I said I better ask Daddy. He said why, Daddy won't be at school, so on my second day at Hoover, I began to assimilate California teenage behavior, which was farther removed from family traditions and Southern customs than anything I imagined from Leslie's letters.

I started Hoover High barefaced and soon added makeup (and lying about it) to my routine, putting it on in the morning in the school bathroom and scrubbing it off in the afternoon.

Leslie was polishing my driving technique, teaching me how to merge, how to enter lanes of traffic unlike anything we had in Bogalusa. I was terrified. I couldn't see how a person could shift gears, edge into a ribbon of speeding cars, shift again, speed up, and blend in without crashing. That part of my education continued several weekends until he grew impatient and said, "Go, go, go! Stop being such a baby." So I did.

We moved into a house on Sonora Avenue, a mile away from Gramma K. Ours was adobe with a tile roof and it occupied the front of a long double lot that continued all the way to the next street in back. There was a log cabin in our backyard, a tiny building where I could be alone with my radio and records, my books and my notebooks. My parents were just as happy about my lengthy absences from the main house, as long as homework got done. They hollered from the back porch when they needed me.

The interior of the main house was all graceful Spanish arches and curved nooks. Mother turned it into a shinier version of her pink house. She added glass-topped tables, lots of them, and at the windows she hung giant swags, hot pink around the edges with copious amounts of white sheer panels in the center. She called them Venetian drapes. At every window there seemed to be yards of fabric folding in on itself the way a theatre curtain does as it rises.

In the driveway was Sister Fern's pink Cadillac, long and heavy, with fishtail fenders in back. She got a record contract. She got a pink Cadillac. That was the deal.

Of course I ran over to see Leslie and Gramma K to unleash all my woes and of course Gramma reciprocated by sharing rumors and opinions. She was never reluctant to engage in speculation on any topic concerning our parents, with or without actual knowledge of events. Leslie and I knew how easy it was to get her going and we did it on purpose.

Once in a while, when Leslie was unavailable to accompany her places,

Gramma K took me. Of course we didn't observe any family rules when we were together. We were a pair of miscreants sneaking out to the races at Santa Anita and Hollywood Park.

As good as it was to reunite on a regular basis with Leslie, my heart was broken about the sudden wrenching away from people I cared about in Louisiana. Even with him leading me through some of the California wilderness, I was a stranger in a strange land, grieving what was left behind.

The two Quave cousins stayed in touch. One was good on the phone, the other wrote long letters. Long-distance phone calls were expensive and I wasn't allowed to call back very often, so I relied on the writing cousin to fill me in. The three of us promised to get together soon, somewhere, somehow.

Daddy and Gramma spent a lot of time together. She didn't drive much so when Uncle Jim traveled Daddy took her grocery shopping, carrying her bags and unpacking them out on her back porch, which was lined with shelves. She'd turned the whole porch into a pantry. She shopped sales at several stores every week, buying multiples of everything.

"Zula, you got—let's see—must be one, two, three—a dozen bottles of ketchup out here already!"

He unpacked another bag.

"Zula, you already got four cans of cream corn. I don't know where I'm gonna put these."

She said, "Used to be I couldn't afford one can of anything. Now I can."

She had traveled West seeking a better life during tough times in the South, and her pantry was one representation of her achievement. Her determination to never be poor again was handed down to Mother, who also preferred to own multiples of everything. Mother also insisted on certain brand names, specifically the things she couldn't afford as a child.

When there was money for store-bought canned goods, our cream corn was always going to be Del Monte and the corned beef Daddy used for his stew was always Libby's, the same label that was on the cans of deviled ham on our own California back porch. At our house there were also cans of Spam and Vienna sausages and a big block of Velveeta and jars and jars of Kraft pimento cheese in the decorative glasses we saved to use for juice and for holding flowers on the kitchen table.

Since Daddy never said a discouraging word about Mother, we wondered how he could spend a day with Gramma without her chiming in on the subject of Fern, the way she did with us and all our other relatives now living nearby. Daddy and Gramma K cooked together. They shared recipes and techniques and food stories from their own growing-up years. Fear of poverty aside, both Gramma and Daddy still preferred to cook the foods of poor Southern people, turning their dishes into celebrations.

Neither of them had a sweet tooth, so they didn't make many desserts.

Gramma's two standbys were fried pies and gingerbread and Daddy's only regular dessert offering was rice pudding, so for family get-togethers they implored Mother to create her pies and cobblers and her risin' rolls. Once in a while in the wee hours in the house on Sonora, the fragrance of yeast woke us, as it once did in Murfreesboro, to the delightful prospect of loaves of bread set out for baking.

The everyday Southern workhorse breads, the skillets of biscuits and cornbread, were still made every morning by Daddy or Gramma and covered with a dishtowel. They were there all day to be used as needed. Each of those two fine cooks had favorites from the other's repertoire.

Daddy cut off a chunk of Gramma's pork roast and said, "Zula, I hope you made us some of your smoky sauce."

"It's right over yonder in that pan. Raymond, how about some fried cornbread?"

He dropped spoonsful of hot-water cornbread dough into a sizzling skillet of lard, turning them into golden, crunchy perfection so fast they were ready before our food could get cold.

Unlike Gramma, Daddy didn't seek approval for every dish. He deflected compliments, putting his skills down to years of practice as a short order cook, riding trains from state to state, stopping to work at diners and cafes and even one fancy hotel in Santa Fe he'd tell you about if you asked. Those of us who ate his meals every day would say cooking was one of his gifts, a calling, a cornbread ministry.

At Gramma's house, Daddy supervised everything that needed planting or repotting or pruning or tending to. She complained about her gardener and Daddy made a point of being there the next gardening day. From inside the living room, we watched him out in the yard shaking hands, grinning, patting the gardener on the back, and in future weeks, the gardener let the grass reach exactly the height Daddy decided was healthiest in Southern California's climate.

Daddy declared his affection for birds-of-paradise, which became the focal point of his garden. He created a path from the steps, around the cabin, all the way to the fence in back, and lined it on either side with bursts of plumage, showing them off to a visitor. Cousin Floyd, Paw Paw's Louisiana farming partner, was treated to the spectacle during a visit.

"Don't that beat all! Plants that look like birds!"

Daddy tasted his first avocados and declared he would grow himself a tree full of them. Artichokes also interested him and an abundance of citrus fruit graced the bowl on the red Formica table in our kitchen nook.

He asked the produce man at the store to stop cutting the tops off turnips and save them for him. He had trouble finding all the kinds of greens he wanted to cook, but eventually he convinced enough produce people in Glendale to provide an abundance of collards and turnip greens.

On Sonora Avenue, Mother played piano and sang and decorated and designed clothes. She took long baths and let the Ivory soap float on top, which was previously against the rules in the South, where we were forever cautioned about resources. She still hadn't learned to drive and often asked Daddy to take her over to Gramma's where the two women continued their attract-and-repel relationship, which we heard plenty about later in both houses.

"Your grandmother's so ugly to me. I don't know why she has to be that way."

I also heard many phone calls from the cubbyhole in the hall, with one or another of our parents asking "When can you come over for supper?" and "You haven't been by in a while," and of course they were talking to Leslie, who managed to continue living the life he had before we arrived. He had moved back into his room in Gramma's house and he joined us for supper sometimes when we went to Gramma's, but he didn't often accompany her when she came over to eat with us.

Daddy was invited to preach at all the churches in his sect in Southern California and there were more and more of them. Pentecostals were setting records for maximum attendance, and they continued to pioneer in televising everything, every Sunday worship, every prayer meeting, every Bible study, every altar call, every healing service, along with frequent pleas for money.

Daddy was still uncomfortable about religion mixed with television, though the denomination reported increasing numbers of conversions and baptisms and gave some of the credit to those broadcasts. Daddy's kind of ministering took up a preacher's whole career in order to reach a few thousand souls in a lifetime, and these big churches with television shows may have equaled his career total in just a few broadcasts.

A huge musical migration from the Deep South filled Southern California with gospel and country pickers and singers. Mother checked in with everyone she knew and someone referred her to a record company that might want to distribute their first album, *The Joneses Sing*.

The company was called Christian Faith, and they not only operated as a full-fledged distributor, releasing popular artists' "inspirational" recordings, but they also allowed their artists to buy albums at a discount to sell themselves. Mother and Daddy hopped in the pink Cadillac with their master tapes and struck an agreement with the company.

Next they needed a picture for the album cover. They went to see a Glendale photographer and came away with happy pictures of the two of them, standing back to back with their real smiles showing. They both agreed on the pose that would be the cover and they both liked the idea of the cover being black and white.

No one suggested their self-made album would ever be competition with whatever she did for Dot, since it was common practice for artists to arrive at major labels with recording sessions in their past, and besides, she wanted an album with Daddy and he was no part of her Dot deal. Soon boxes of the album *The Joneses Sing* were stacked in the cabin out back where I now occupied less space.

KFSG, the radio station founded at Angelus Temple by Aimee Semple McPherson, offered The Joneses a show and Daddy was pleased to say yes. He was, of course, accustomed to saying a word or two about Jesus into radio microphones. Mother had memorized Sister Aimee's career, had once designed herself a dress to sing in featuring flowing sleeves she saw in a publicity picture from Sister Aimee's glory days. Though Mother didn't agree with all of her shenanigans, she admired how far Aimee had come as one of the few women in the country who owned a radio station.

They took their instruments to the station in Echo Park every week. The station engineer was a fan, and he spent a good deal of time setting up a studio for them, positioning mics just so to pick up the instruments. He took pride in the many letters they received and how many song requests were phoned in during their program. They could sing and play any hymn and any obscure spiritual and any of the currently in vogue Christian music now heard on a few radio stations. Before the end of their show, they wove in at least one of Mother's original compositions.

The few times my parents couldn't do the show live, they asked me to do it. I didn't want to, but I did. It was announced as *The Joneses Sing* but it was just the one Jones—me—and the only song I sang live was their theme, "Look Away to Jesus." The station found me a piano player over at the temple. I played songs from *The Joneses Sing* album, but their recordings were only about two minutes long. Stretching to fill time, Wally, the engineer, activated the talkback button and told me who was on the phone so I could chat with listeners about their favorites.

I attended church with a friend I met at Hoover. Daddy said he'd need to know more about the teachings or I couldn't continue. I was to have a talk with the pastor about their beliefs and then he'd decide if I could keep going. Instead I visited a class taught by the youth minister, Rev. Curtis Correll, and found a welcoming group of teens involved in discussions about kindness and helping one's fellow man. Not a speck of hell and punishment. I would do whatever was necessary to get to stay there.

A trend at the time was wearing a small clear globe on a chain with a single mustard seed inside. I saw them at school, at church, downtown, everywhere. They were based on scripture about what a little faith can do: "If you have faith the size of a mustard seed, you will say to this mountain, 'Move from here to there,' and it will move and nothing will be impossible to you."

This one idea, one gesture, one gentle reminder was a revelation to a teenager raised on dire predictions. Daddy decided my new church was almost

Full Gospel enough and said I could continue. In fact my new church was miles away from the way I was raised.

Daddy immediately put vegetables in the ground out behind the cabin. He knew instinctively how to adjust his crops for California. We watched him digging and pushing soil around and watering.

Leslie asked, "How do you know what'll grow back here?"

"Born a farmer, son, always a farmer. Just like my Daddy."

He teased Leslie and me while we watched him do all the work.

"Maybe one of you could be a farmer too, if you'd get down here in the dirt."

In Murfreesboro we'd cherished our time in the garden with Daddy but everything was different now. We were different. We were happy to eat whatever he harvested and quick to compliment him on his delectable crop, but we no longer hoped for large chunks of his time and attention as our interests moved farther and farther away from his backyard on Sonora Avenue.

Daddy plucked a mint leaf from the plant in the tub by the back door, put his gardening shoes on the porch, and headed into the kitchen. We followed and found Mother at the table, about to bounce off her chair. Dot Records had called to tell her they wanted her to record in Nashville. She was booked at the Bradley brothers' famous Quonset Hut Studio with Nashville's A-Team musicians. The players Dot wanted were all scheduled to work with Elvis that same week over at RCA, and Mother needed to get there as soon as possible to take advantage of their availability. In a couple of days she was on the train.

Nashville, 1958

She called every day from Nashville and told Daddy about each day's session and he told us. With Mother away, Leslie was all of a sudden available to have supper on Sonora Avenue. One night Gramma brought a new Mexican dish she was experimenting with and another night Daddy answered back with one of his specialties. We feasted while Mother sang.

The first few days in Nashville, Mother was confident and excited, but as the visit lasted longer, she began trying to talk Daddy into going there to be with her. Sometimes she called and they said goodnight and hung up and a little while later she called again.

If we were in the room when they reached the end of their phone conversation, we could tell she was crying because of how he soothed her, using the same words and phrases and tone he always employed when she was distraught. After a while, after he surely must have exhausted his supply of "Doll Baby" and "Sugar" and "Mama-gal," I'd ask how Mother was doing and his answer contained minimal facts about her recording sessions but a good deal of talk about how lonesome she was.

She was dazzled by the amount of talent packed into the studio, all the musicians responsible for the Nashville sound. Their sessions for her album were recorded live-to-tape with Sister Fern standing right in the middle of the musicians and backup singers. She asked an engineer for playback every night, holding a phone toward a speaker so Daddy could hear. He smiled about whatever he was listening to.

The piano player on Mother's sessions was Floyd Cramer, who already had records of his own, and who created an unmistakable sound everyone was asking for. Mother said Daddy just had to hear Floyd. His "slip-note" style, she said, reminded her of a yodel. This, of course, went straight to Daddy's heart. He tried over and over to teach Leslie and me to imitate Hank Williams's catch-in-the-throat on "Lovesick Blues" but we never matched Daddy's version.

The Sunshine Boys were in from Hollywood to sing backup for Sister Fern. Singing bass with them on the sessions was J. D. Sumner, who claimed the lowest bass notes in the Southern gospel business. Buddy Harman played drums and Joe Zinkan played bass. Hank "Sugarfoot" Garland, who went back and forth between Nashville and progressive jazz, was on guitar. Daddy mentioned his name and Leslie lit up. The musicians came over from Elvis's sessions where RCA was rushing to complete new material while Elvis was on a two-week furlough from the Army. The players and singers were expected to get in, do their work, then dash to the other studio.

Since Mother didn't read music, she had sung all her songs onto tape and sent them to the label. Dot had them copied on charts for the players, but those guys didn't really need charts. She talked through each arrangement but there wasn't much rehearsing needed with this group. They picked up everything immediately. It was her first time. It wasn't theirs.

Chapter 35

Nashville Nights

Mother was glad to come home after her recording sessions as she waited for the album to be released. She'd soon be back on a train headed to Nashville for the DJ Convention.

She was scheduled to have her pictures taken for the album cover in Hollywood. She chose to be photographed in one of her church dresses. Here she was in the show business capital of the world, behaving all of a sudden like the small-town preacher's wife Daddy had tried so hard to cultivate. As she prepared to go to the studio, the makeup tools she took in her purse consisted of Vaseline and her small eyebrow brush.

Leslie and I relished Gramma's gossipy side and participated with her in criticizing Mother in specific areas of disagreement where we were also experienced, but we were both uncomfortable speculating about how a photography session might proceed.

Mother's struggles with her curls were lately eclipsed by her concern about darker circles under her eyes caused by a recurrence of the blood condition. The circles were darker every year, but it hadn't seemed crucial until we watched her grow agitated in front of the mirror before leaving to meet the photographer in Hollywood. Given her beginnings as a hometown beauty who bought at least one new lipstick or nail polish every week when she and Daddy first married, she knew from experience how much even a little makeup could improve and conceal.

Women in the denomination had begun wearing makeup a while back, but Mother didn't. She left that day for the photographer's studio a barefaced child expecting magic, believing her photo session would produce an album cover that would dazzle, would represent her personality, would make her look good. She was a pretty woman with all those curls and giant grey eyes, and according to Daddy's reassurances, that's what would come shining through.

Proofs from the photo session arrived for approval. We all saw them and told Mother they were fine, but they weren't. The forward-facing pictures, even with studio lighting, didn't look the way Sister Fern must have imagined. We thought Dot would probably insist on retouching them. Gramma K and even Daddy, who never offered anything but compliments, assured her the pictures could be fixed. By comparison, the simple black-and-white image on *The Joneses Sing* album cover looked like art.

Mother was asked to select a photo from the session. She chose a side view. Gramma K, now professing to be a big fan of Daddy, told us Mother's decision to continue the photo session without cosmetic assistance was her wanting to please Daddy.

"Your mama knows how much she owes him. He came all the way out here for her."

What did that have to do with it? we asked. How could looking one's best in a picture possibly offend Daddy, who already believed her to be the most beautiful girl in the world? Why would Mother walk right up to the edge of achieving what she wanted, then sabotage it with bad photos? We didn't have any answers, and we were accustomed to the two of them making their own deals, which seemed to serve them well even while the rest of us lost track of who was owed what.

She decided against retouching and the battle over the album cover was the first of many she fought with her label. Randy Wood, Dot president, wanted the first single release to be Sister Fern singing a cover of a spiritual, either "Didn't It Rain" or "Strange Things Happenin'," but Mother reminded him he'd promised that the first single would be one of her original songs. None of us heard that discussion between Mother and Randy, but we all heard her reaction when he told her it was his way or nothing.

Randy said he couldn't get airplay for her without them agreeing on a single. He claimed to love her music, thought her style was original, distinctive, a white woman singing about Jesus with a rock and roll sound, and he thought the world was ready for that. That's why he signed her, he said.

We hadn't counted on Sister Fern's determination. (Daddy would say pigheadedness if he was talking about one of us kids.) She had gotten this far without a major label, and though this record had always been her dream, evidently the other and equally important part of the dream was hearing one of her own songs on the radio first.

Dot promised her the record would be available to the world before she got to Nashville and they'd also pay for everything while she was there. It was time to leave for the convention and the label still hadn't released her album. She decided to go anyway and promote the record as much as she was able through her own connections in the South.

The release of Sister Fern's Dot album, *Singing a Happy Song*, was so quiet, it was as if it didn't exist. Copies did arrive in Nashville, but with no hoopla from the company, and so began a decades-long struggle between Mother and the much more powerful Dot Records president. She began shaking the trees for any deejays she knew who might play her songs. As feedback came in from radio people who heard the album, one of the first comments was how good it was, followed by surprise that Dot even made the record, since it was so unusual for the time.

Dot's most successful star was Pat Boone singing fully orchestrated, very white, and very safe versions of R&B hits. Fern, on the other hand, wailed when she felt like it and often injected recitative into her story-songs, sounding most like one of the Black preachers she listened to. There was no category for what she did, for her lyrics, for her style.

She was brokenhearted that the label pulled back on publicizing her record, but she didn't give up. She contacted Kousin Karl, who was by then mostly working in television. He still had a soft spot for Sister Fern. He made calls on her behalf to get her bookings at important venues while she was in Nashville. He got her booked on Wally Fowler's *All Night Sing*, which originated from Ryman Auditorium. She was thrilled to stand on the Opry stage.

Gramma K sent Mother off to Nashville with the mink stole she always wanted. Gramma shopped auctions to feed her craving for showy things. It would be exhausting to list all the jewelry she bought at auction, pieces with pedigree and some of dubious provenance. She and Uncle Jim went to a fur auction to bid on the stole. No one in our family would have known whether it was real mink or what quality it was, but that wasn't ever the point. Mother was ecstatic about the gift and promised no matter the weather in Nashville she'd wear it every day.

She was thrilled when people from the South remembered her from all the radio shows she'd been on and the big Singings. They came to get her autograph. She posed for pictures with fans wearing her mink stole.

Karl asked if she wanted to tour other towns while she was down South, places where he could pull some strings. He said Dot should pay for the tour, and if she didn't feel like dealing with them, he'd talk to someone at her label and exert influence. She agreed to sing in several towns.

In Mother's absence the shuttling of food between Gramma's house and ours began again. Daddy stayed home every night to take Mother's calls and repeated parts of their conversations for us. She asked if he would come to Nashville. He told her he knew she was homesick but it would pass. She said no it won't and she missed him too much and maybe she should come home. He said not yet, you waited a long time to get there.

Another night in Nashville for Mother. Another supper in Glendale for the rest of us. Gramma brought a big bowl of chili and Leslie Ray put the greased skillet in the oven to get it good and hot for cornbread. I was at the table in the breakfast nook, and just around the corner The Baby, at the piano, played and sang so loud, it was hard to hear ourselves talk.

She'd started piano lessons and wasn't very far along yet with reading music, but already she had a strong sense of how she wanted a song to sound and she worked it out playing by ear. This involved her ritual of singing a part of a song at top volume while pounding the one chord she did know, until she needed a new chord, which could take some time.

When you were in the other room listening, there were long pauses between her singing and playing when you thought you could resume a conversation but then the song started up again. It was an odd rhythm but it made sense if you'd ever been in the room with her while she taught herself. She sang a melody she wanted to play, then began to position little girl fingers to complete a chord. Left hand, finger down, next finger down, next finger down. Right hand, repeat. Crash that chord. Wrong. Silence during the repositioning of fingers to complete whatever she was hearing in her head.

Hang down your head Tom Dooley

Crashing chords, mostly correct.

Hang down your head and cry

Wait. Wait. Wait. Chord crash. Wrong. Try the original chord, find it doesn't work, reposition fingers, find a better sound, pound it twice just to be sure.

Daddy called to her.

"Can you play a little bit softer?"

"I can't."

She wasn't being disrespectful and nobody took offense. She was just stating a fact. This was the volume she used when learning. We paced our chat to fit into spaces between chord changes.

Hang down your head Tom Dooley

Gramma asked Daddy, "What do you hear from Fern? Did she already call?"

Poor boy, you're bound . . .

"This morning. She's supposed to sing in Memphis next, but she wants to come home."

The end of The Baby's song was near. We paused.

. . . poor boy you're bound . . .

Chord.

. . . to die!

Satisfied for the moment, she turned her thoughts to suppertime, joining us in the kitchen, where instead of asking someone to move over, she liked to climb under the table that was fitted inside the built-in U-shaped banquette. She surfaced between Leslie Ray and me and reached for a slice of tomato from the plate of tomato, cucumber, and onion that accompanied most of our meals.

Daddy said, "Wait for the blessing, please."

Before the cornbread was done, the phone rang again. Daddy dashed to the hall and we all strained to hear his side of the conversation.

"Well, Sugar, we miss you too. Your Mama's here. We're fixin' to eat. I guess I better . . ."

He came back to the kitchen.

"Zula, she wants to talk to you."

We all followed Gramma to find out what was going on.

"Hey, Sister, how you doin'? Uh-huh. Well now you've lived in that humidity before. You know how to handle it. Uh-huh. I *know*."

She covered the mouthpiece.

"Her hair's frizzy."

Gramma handed the phone back to Daddy. When he joined us in the kitchen, he said the other news from Mother was that after a couple more stops, Karl could get her booked on the *Louisiana Hayride* from KWKH in Shreveport. Elvis had already been on, and they were inviting more singers who weren't country. That show was so famous in our world, we never missed a Saturday night.

A few days later, Daddy said he had to go to the train station downtown to pick up Mother. When I got home from school, she came out of their bedroom, said she was tired, then went back in. Daddy moved back and forth between the things he usually did and staying awhile with her.

Mother had run away from the Promised Land in Nashville to come home, spending (I assumed) tear-soaked days on trains in what some might perceive as a defeat. It must have puzzled people who worked to get her bookings to have her up and leave like that. It puzzled us too. They'd extended themselves for her based on their unanimous conviction that she possessed unique abilities that deserved to be discovered.

I wanted to know what happened, why she was home when she was supposed to be singing in the South. When I called Leslie, he said he didn't know but I oughta stay out of that. I asked Gramma if she knew. She said this was the first she'd heard about Fern being back home. I said maybe Mother was just tired. Gramma said, "Hooey! I'll tell you why she came home. Because your Daddy wasn't there, because he wouldn't go with her to Nashville."

Leslie and I disagreed with her on that issue. It had been years since Gramma lived with Mother, while our history with her was still unfolding. We had seen her push, persevere, and get up the gumption to ask Daddy to do a good many things for her, including leave the South.

I insisted, "It looks like she does what she wants no matter what Daddy thinks."

Gramma saw things another way.

"You go on ahead and believe that if you want to, but I tell you what. She can't do anything without him."

We'd watched Mother wade into rough waters before and it seemed to us she could make her way anywhere in the world. The two of them, in fact all of us, had risked a lot on account of her music, yet here she was retreating when she was possibly one step away from what she'd always believed, what she'd always told us would happen.

Gramma K ended the discussion.

"She can't do a thing without him. Your Daddy, if he was married to somebody else, he'd have a normal life, but your Mother, no, she couldn't. She can't get along without him and they both know it. He's got his hands full with that one."

Chapter 36

Fifties Farewell

Glendale, California, 1960

When Leslie moved away from home at sixteen and I left at seventeen, both of us went without regret. Wherever we lived with them, there wasn't enough room for us. After we moved away, we watched the space behind us close as if it had always been just the two of them. She was still the child he spent the most time parenting.

I lasted through my senior year of high school, counting the days. Once in a while Gramma K invited me to sleep on her couch when they were tired of fighting with me, but she never offered me permanent sanctuary.

When I entered high school in California, I began to erase my past, denying my unusual life, refusing to discuss our family's work, and by senior year, it was if I'd never been part of The Singing Joneses. I didn't invite friends to my house. I sneaked around creating my new life, which included makeup and different clothes and complicated stories I told my friends about why I didn't go to football games or dances. I wasn't clever enough to create coverups about staying out at night since nighttime hours were strictly enforced.

I still wasn't allowed pants or shorts. A discussion about gym clothes would have us all on edge. Instead I told my parents not dressing in proper gym attire would get me an automatic F, no exceptions, and there was no sense in them going to talk to anyone at school. They said no. I bought tee shirts and shorts myself, with Uncle Jim driving me to Webb's on Brand Boulevard. I washed them at a friend's house and left them there to dry. So much work just to keep from confiding in anyone at school about the real reasons behind my parents' pants prohibition, that a woman wearing pants needed to get right with God.

I graduated and moved to an apartment in Silver Lake, a few miles and a world away from Glendale. Silver Lake was eclectic, artistic, populated with charming houses on hills, and an altogether exciting place to grow new wings. I typed by day, lied about my age and sang in clubs at night. I visited all kinds of churches and heard sermons where even when the subject of redemption came up, it wasn't accompanied by threats of punishment and eternal hellfire. There was a lot of catching up to do, a lot of information to absorb.

Leslie declared himself still not interested in being inside a church of any kind, not even when I was singing, but he showed up everywhere else I performed, at every bar and every night club.

Uncle Jim remained a grace note throughout our Southern California teens and we remained grateful for his kind availability. If we were stuck somewhere we shouldn't be, or just stuck in general, he was the person to call who might not agree with whatever we just did, or wherever we were, but he'd come get us and he wouldn't tell.

He took my side, which no one in the family except Leslie had ever done. When Gramma K designed for me an ugly, stiff, neon gold net dress she wanted me to wear to sing someplace, Uncle Jim risked life and limb approaching the lioness in her den to plead my case. The dress was so scratchy it left marks everywhere it touched my skin. It was not something any teen would wear.

"What's all this in front?" Uncle Jim asked Gramma while I stood on a stool getting the hem pinned.

The bodice was made of the same stiff net, with so many gathers it stuck straight out.

"To give her bosoms."

"She'll get them when she gets them."

Gramma huffed out of the room. I went behind the curtain hung in a corner as a changing room for her clients, put on my real clothes, and dropped the explosion of net on a chair. Uncle Jim and I went to Bob's to get a burger while she got over it.

Pedro continued to hate all of us. He growled and snapped when we got close to Uncle Jim's chair. Daddy ignored his rebuff, asking "How are you today, PEE-dro?" Spanish filtered through his drawl created another language altogether. In addition to his "PEE-dro," Daddy's "see seen-yer-eeter" was a family favorite.

As I packed to move away from them, Mother yelled at me and Daddy talked in a sad voice about the disrespectful ways I was treating them and about me leaving without their say-so. Though I wasn't yet eighteen, I was by then bold enough to believe I would figure things out.

They still acted surprised at our rejection of their beliefs, though Leslie and I explained to them many times that in our opinion what they'd been asking of us all these years was miles past disrespectful. To us, it was total soul surrender they required, and we refused.

When I left, there was an extended silence between them and me. One day Daddy pulled up in front of my apartment and dropped off a box containing paper goods, an assortment of cans from their pantry, a chunk of ham, an enormous pot of beans, and cornbread in his favorite skillet, the one that traveled with us all over the South. The skillet was significant because I'd need to contact him in order to return it. He didn't say a word about Mother, and no, he didn't want to come inside to see the place.

Leslie and I coordinated our visits to Glendale so we were always together when we went to see them. While we'd distanced ourselves from their beliefs, we still spent an inordinate amount of time together dwelling on our childhood and our reactions to it. Over in our self-imposed purgatory, we weren't able to leave the subject alone. Even the past wasn't far enough in the past to be comfortable yet.

Though we took giant steps into new worlds and put as much distance between us and them as we could, we left with the knowledge that as long as we lived our way and not theirs, we would continue to represent failure to them. We fell into a routine during our visits to their house. No talk about religion. If the subject came up, we invented excuses to leave quickly. Safe subjects were food and music and relatives in the South and whatever The Baby was up to.

After our first medical and dental exams, Leslie and I compared notes. Each visit to healthcare professionals included scolding and what certainly felt like judgments, starting with, how could you let this go so long? We were terse, answering only with the facts. We both immediately clamped down on sharing further information about that topic, even with friends. It was years before either of us volunteered details about our lives on the road.

Every time we answered a question we felt like a case study. "Unusual" is what we'd always been and what we didn't want to be.

We worried about The Baby being left in their care, and whichever one of us verbalized the concern, it was up to the other one to assuage. What about her being raised without a sibling? Maybe she didn't need one. Maybe her situation was completely different since Daddy was no longer a pastor and no longer asking small children to set an example for a congregation.

As for medical treatment, Gramma still considered our parents' faith healing practices criminal, and now that we were all in California, we knew she wouldn't hesitate to violate their orders where The Baby's health was concerned.

Our visits were sometimes months apart, and when we all got together, we were astonished at the enormous changes between visits. It was startling to hear a big voice come from that little girl. Her choice of material was based on whatever she fancied on the radio. She showed no interest in church music until she fell in love with "How Great Thou Art."

One day, according to the way Daddy and Mother told it, the two of them were in the studio corner of the house, singing together. It was a familiar musical conversation they shared close to suppertime almost every day, and you could wander into it, pick up a part, and join anytime. When it was the two of them, they tended toward a soft and slower version of the song.

Oh Lord my God when I in awesome wonder
Consider all the worlds Thy hands hath made
I see the stars, I hear the rolling thunder
Thy power throughout the universe displayed

Some soloists in performance of the song turned dramatic at the chorus. George Beverly Shea sang it big in the Billy Graham crusades. It lent itself to theatrics if you wanted them. Our little sister had never been anywhere near a revival. The only version she'd ever heard was two acoustic guitars and her parents' at-home harmony.

Mother asked during one of our visits, have you heard The Baby's new song? No and of course, yes, we'd love to. Daddy and Mother acted like conspirators when they called her into the room.

"Would you sing your new song for your brother and sister?"

She certainly would. She pulled out the piano bench and slam-played a couple of chords which, if you knew the melody, announced she'd be skipping the verse entirely.

Then came her version, full drama included. Fortissimo and then some. We'd heard her sing since she could talk, but now here was that little body with that huge voice and a texture to it, a style, a mature delivery.

Then sings my soul, my Savior God to Thee
How great Thou art! How great Thou art!

This was the surprise Daddy and Mother held on to for our visit. The Baby's musical talent surpassed my brother's and mine, but in an odd twist of birth order, the one with the big gift wouldn't be performing through her childhood the way we had, performances we'd hated and the very thing she'd have loved. She could sing any harmony part, could learn to play several instruments, make up her own arrangements, and fill a space with what all of us knew was the best voice in the family.

☐

Without any preamble, with no announcements, no hints, no indication to any of us, Leslie went and joined the Navy. He'd spoken always and only about going to college to become an architect, so when he signed up, it was a shock. One day he showed up at my apartment with a carload of belongings he wanted me to keep while he was away. He installed his sound system in the living room for my roommate, Linda, and me to use, and brought in racks and racks of records. He'd be leaving right away for boot camp in San Diego, then he'd ship out wherever they sent him.

I asked why he wasn't leaving his stuff in his room at Gramma's house.

"She tore into me when I told her about the Navy."

"Did she kick you out?"

"Nope. She wanted me to come back there after but I said I don't expect I will and she cussed up a storm about everything she did for me and I figured it wouldn't be a good idea."

"What's she carrying on about now?"

"Because I told Mother and Daddy I enlisted before I told her."

"What did they do?"

"Mother said she was about to faint and Daddy went to get a washrag for her head."

While we waited to see where the Navy would send him, we visited the Sonora house together several times. About a mile away, the other important person in Leslie's life, the one who saved him from his Bogalusa anger, waited for us to stop by. The conversation, no matter which house we visited first, whether Raymond Avenue or Sonora Avenue, would be mostly about what happened at the other place.

Mother asked, "Are you going over to your grandmother's today?"

"In a little while. We thought she might be here."

"No, we wanted to spend time with just our kids."

It would have been nice to believe that was the whole story, but too many years, too many fights, too much competition between Mother and Gramma taught us that Leslie visiting either house first gave one an advantage over the other.

I was surprised that either of the women thought they could convince Leslie Ray to do or not do anything. He'd been doing what he chose for years. Maybe Gramma felt because she'd opened her home to him and made no demands, he'd want to stay on. Maybe Mother thought because she gave birth to him, he'd consult her about a decision as important as enlisting. Neither of those ideas made any sense in light of the facts. I doubt Leslie cared what either of them thought about his choices by then.

When he finished boot camp, we all went down to San Diego to see the Navy graduation dress parade and take the tour of the base. He was assigned to Long Beach first and nobody knew where he'd go from there. As soon as his ship docked at Terminal Island, Leslie and several buddies rented an apartment in Belmont Shore. It was tiny, with one bedroom, but since they weren't all on leave at the same time, they rotated who slept there. The living room was big enough for cots and sleeping bags, and most importantly, just down the stairs and a few steps away was the beach.

My friends and I spent weekends there when Leslie was in residence, listening to Ray Charles, drinking Paisano, and eating whatever we could afford. We made a dishpan full of potato salad, enough to feed all of us, and that was it for meal preparation—cheap wine and cheap potato salad.

The first weekend I visited the beach apartment, Leslie said the high school rule applies, that I can't date any of his friends. At Hoover none of his friends asked me out so it was never an issue. At Belmont Shore, I dated his shipmates anyway, first the misunderstood poet, Bobby, then Michael, the Elvis lookalike with perfect hair. We turned the speakers toward the window and slow-danced in the yard below.

We wore out more than one copy of *The Genius of Ray Charles*. Our friends didn't have the same reaction to the ballads and blues Leslie and I craved on that album. They asked why we couldn't listen to something happier. They called the two of us the Melancholy Twins and we all laughed because it was true.

We defended our fondness for one of the saddest records we owned, encouraging everyone to get yourself a copy of *The Genius of Ray Charles*, pour yourself a glass of something, and listen to "Just for a Thrill" or "Tell Me You'll Wait for Me" or "Don't Let the Sun Catch You Cryin'." Play those and the heart cracks a little. The more you listen, the farther you sink, so far down, there's no place to go but up, so you pick up the needle on the record player and set it down on "Alexander's Ragtime Band" or "Let the Good Times Roll" and get up and dance.

Leslie was proud of his service with the Navy Drill Team. He owned several pairs of the tight white gloves that were part of his uniform because he wore his way through them during performances. After consuming sufficient Paisano, he led us down the stairs into the yard. Barefoot, wearing shorts, and using a broom as his drill team rifle, he entertained us with his moves, insisting we all fall into line, weaving while marching to the beat of whatever song played out the upstairs window.

We spent many nights at The Hat in Belmont Shore, where jazz and atmosphere and youth were an unbeatable combination. We club hopped all over Southern California. We went to Shelly's Manne-Hole in Hollywood, the Lighthouse in Hermosa Beach, the Crescendo on the Strip and The Cellar at Breakers International Hotel in Long Beach. Curtis Counce, a superb bass player, held forth at The Cellar. We were there so often, whenever he saw us walk in, he began "Time after Time" or "It Might as Well Be Spring" or "Midnight Sun" or "Skylark." We fed the tip jar generously.

I played my part. I wore enough black eyeliner and fake eyelashes and white eyeshadow and pale lipstick to outfit the cast of a Broadway show. It's how we growing-up girls looked then, strutting into the 1960s in slim pencil skirts and high heels.

Though I looked underage, we didn't get tossed out anywhere. Leslie was a big guy, and when presented with a challenge, he was either affable or menacing, depending on the situation. He was never going to observe boundaries.

Starting a tradition that continued for years, he showed up wherever I sang, and he always brought a pretty date along, and sometimes several other couples too. He made sure I'd seen him from the stage before he was seated. Whoever approached him first, hostess or waitstaff or bouncer, Leslie asked for a message to be delivered.

"Will you ask the singer for 'Time after Time'?"

We both loved the song and it was out of my range and he knew it. I always sent back some version of the same message.

"Will you please tell the smartass who requested that song to go find himself another singer if he wants to hear it so much?"

Message received, he laughed and was shown to a seat where he remained through several sets. He never tired of the greeting ritual and repeated it everywhere I sang, changing requests from time to time, choosing only songs he knew I wouldn't take on.

On my infrequent visits to see Mother and Daddy without Leslie, there was still plenty of music and food, but conversations grew increasingly more complicated. The first time I showed up at their door in Glendale in full makeup, Daddy left me standing on the porch and said to Mother, "Fern, your daughter's here."

He tried to play like he was joking but he wasn't. He walked away when Mother said come in. It was odd he would expect to see a face scrubbed clean of makeup on a daughter who now lived on her own.

Questions were asked about every part of my life. I answered them honestly. After all the years of lying, Lord knows why I thought that was a good idea. They disagreed with everything about the way I lived, the way I dressed, the places I sang, the music I performed. After months of tension, during which I stayed away longer and longer between visits, something changed.

I was in the kitchen about to make excuses to get out of there early.

Daddy asked, "You eat yet? You don't look like you eat enough to keep a gnat alive."

"I could eat."

He was already reaching for a skillet.

"Eggs?"

"Yes please."

"What kind?"

"Over easy."

Watching him fry an egg was a ticket to the ballet. His turns were so quick you'd miss them if you looked down at your program. The man never broke a yolk. Another flame was lit to make skillet toast. No eggs since have tasted as good. No toaster ever made toast as good as the kind Daddy made in an iron skillet. There was magic in his cooking and I was still a fan. Daddy cooking while one of his grown kids sat nearby felt like peacemaking of a sort.

I heard him preach one more time. It was Easter Sunday in a giant Pentecostal tabernacle, and I thought it would be comfortable to be there, since the theme would be more "He is risen!" than "get down on your knees and repent." For Pentecostals, Easter morning is pure jubilation. In that enormous church, there were more voices in the choir than the entire congregation in some of our Southern churches. Trumpets delivered fanfares and flourishes. We sang "Christ Arose!" and "He Lives!" and "Christ the Lord Is Risen Today!"

Just before the sermon, Daddy nodded to the music director. By prearrangement at Daddy's request, the choir began "Were You There When They Crucified My Lord?"

In the South, this somber song was sung at the end of our Good Friday services, signifying sealing the body of Jesus in the tomb, but this Easter Sunday morning Daddy added it.

Mournful chords emanated from the organ. String players moved to stand next to Daddy, bringing their violins up to their chins in a Southern California megachurch equivalent of the circle of fiddlers familiar in our own small congregations. Daddy indicated we should all stand and sing together.

Were you there when they crucified my Lord
Ohhhh, sometimes it causes me to tremble

The choir repeated "tremble, tremble, tremble" exactly the way it was sung back home.

We sang another verse.

Were you there when they nailed Him to the cross
Were you there when they placed Him in the tomb
Were you there when the stone was rolled away

It was exactly the right preparation for his sermon. Daddy preached that day to an attentive audience, in spite of the fact that no one expected Easter Sunday to resemble anything like a regular Sunday, with children anticipating their Easter egg hunts and families eager to get to the special food prepared in their homes.

He stood at the front door of the church shaking hands. Some Californians commented on his accent. Some Southern transplants said they used to listen to him on the radio. That Easter service was much larger than any I'd grown up with, yet it was still the way any Sunday of my childhood looked after church, people milling around chatting with Brother Ray, but with a major difference. Gramma K was there this time. When she announced she was going, Daddy teased her about how he wouldn't get to finish his sermon because the roof would surely cave in.

I declared to Gramma afterward that the crowd was unusually attentive for an Easter Sunday and I was glad Daddy chose that day and that place to preach. He hadn't preached in a while and we didn't know at the time it would be his last sermon. He didn't announce it and he never said whether he planned it, but he didn't preach again.

Chapter 37

Love Me Tender

1961

Mother was invited to sing wherever Southern gospel fans filled large spaces, so The Joneses shined up, Vaselined and Brylcreemed, and set sail in the pink Cadillac with the fishtail fins on their way to auditoriums all over Southern California. Daddy went to every show but he no longer played guitar with her.

One day she stopped singing. She was invited to appear on the television programs of her friends. She declined. She didn't explain why, at least not to her children. Maybe Daddy, her sole confidant, could have told us, but we stopped asking him questions about that sort of thing when we left. Daddy was invited to preach on television. He declined. They never stopped making music. They sang and played and recorded in their home studio, sometimes sharing their output with the rest of us.

Daddy continued working behind the scenes on behalf of his denomination. He was glad to be instrumental in planning the growth of their sect. They compensated him well for his work, more than he'd ever made as a preacher, and hearing him talk about new churches felt like a continuation of his ministry, the planting, tilling the soil, and then the celebration of the blooming season.

He dedicated time volunteering at Descanso Gardens in La Canada where he could get lost for hours helping beautiful things grow. Daddy got a list of shut-ins from a local church. He and Gramma K cooked for them, then drove the food to their homes. Together they stopped in thrift shops buying every color and size of casserole dish, designated exclusively for their deliveries. They put the recipient's names on the bottoms of the dishes and retrieved them later to be refilled and redelivered, forming a two-person version of Meals on Wheels. The two of them discussed opening a restaurant together. They would serve only Southern food, of course. Gramma said, "It looks like if we want decent fried okra, we're gonna have to make it." They looked at potential cafe sites in Burbank, Glendale, and Pasadena, but Daddy decided against it.

Mother had an idea for a newspaper column. *The Glendale News Press* agreed, and she became a columnist.

Sister Fern continued her relentless campaign to gain control of the master reel from her recording sessions in Nashville. Randy Wood sold Dot Records to Paramount, but he remained as president for a while. The scope and size and power of her adversary kept growing, and she got so worked up when we asked it about it, we stopped asking.

By the start of the new decade, church music had completed a major transition. Brother Janway's piano set the tone many others followed, and by the end of the 1950s, it was hard to remember when hymns weren't amplified. We began with acoustic guitars, fiddles, harmonicas, and accordions, then The Joneses plugged in earlier than most. Daddy's denomination grew out of their small frame buildings all over the South and into bigger and bigger buildings.

By the end of the 1950s, so many Southern transplants lived and worked and worshipped in California, megachurches cropped up adjacent to acres of paved parking. No more muddy fields for singers to tiptoe through. Tent revivals would soon be history.

While Leslie was home on leave, we headed from our own apartments over to Glendale. He was excited about all the development in Southern California.

"You'll thank me for all those driving lessons when you get on the Golden State Freeway."

"I won't be using the freeway."

"Yes you will. Gramma'll want you to take her to Anaheim to that restaurant by Disneyland that cooks rabbit the way she likes it."

"I'm not driving her on any freeways and I'm not going to a place that cooks rabbit, so just shut up."

"Girl you better not be sayin' 'shut up' to your brother."

"You know what you are, boy? I'll tell you. You're a big ol' backslider."

"You're a heathen, Nita Faye, and ig-nernt too."

"Can't argue with that. Anyway, Gramma probably won't want to go to Anaheim anymore if you're not the one taking her."

We arrived to find Mother sitting on one of the pink chairs, playing her guitar. Leslie carried in a brown paper bag stuffed full-to-bulging with treasures we picked up from Pecos Bill's Barbecue on Victory Boulevard. I set a bowl of potato salad on the kitchen table, and Leslie said to Daddy, "Got us the pork this time at Pecos Bill's. You got any pintos ready?"

"I've *always* got pintos ready. Mama-gal made us a raisin pie too."

Mother didn't get up. She concentrated on the song she was singing. She strummed a chord and sang.

Are you lonesome tonight
Do you miss me tonight
"Nita Faye, what's the next part?"
I sang.

Are you sorry we drifted apart
She adjusted her fingering and kept going.
Does your memory stray to a bright sunny day
When I kissed you and called you sweetheart
Daddy picked up a guitar and he sang too.
Do the chairs in your parlor seem empty and bare
Do you gaze at your doorstep and picture me there
Daddy called to Leslie in the kitchen.

"C'mon in here and sing with us."

"Naw, Daddy, I told you. No Elvis for me. You want to play me some Four Freshmen or some Ella, I might consider it."

Every time it came up, they laughed, as if their differences in musical taste, once the subject of such intense discussion, were now the funniest thing.

Mother said, "I love Elvis. He sang 'Peace in the Valley' on Ed Sullivan's program."

She strummed a few seconds.

"I heard from him."

"Who?"

"Elvis. From his manager. I sent them some songs and Colonel Parker said Elvis likes them and he wants to record 'I Do Believe.'"

Leslie plopped himself down.

"When did *this* happen?"

"A while back. I said no."

"Why'd you do that?"

"Colonel Parker said Elvis won't record any more songs he can't own. I told him I couldn't sell part of a song. I won't do that again."

"What'd he say?"

"He said well anyhow they didn't want to own *part* of it. They want to buy the *whole* song and put it out without my name on it. And I said no and he won't let Elvis sing my songs."

We expected fireworks from her about news like this, but instead she asked Daddy to play. He began to noodle.

"Nita Faye, here's one you like."

I thought it'd be "Back in the Saddle Again." He never let me forget my earlier plan to marry the Singing Cowboy and whistled "Back in the Saddle" when I came around. This time he sang.

When shadows fall and trees whisper day is ending
My thoughts are ever wending Home
I joined.
When crickets call, my heart is forever yearning
Once more to be returning
Home.

Daddy said, "Your Mama's fixin' to sing. Long Beach Auditorium. The Revelators will be there too."

Mother seemed so calm as to be nearly uninvolved with this surprising announcement. She strummed. She sang.

Love me tender, love me sweet
Never let me go

Leslie asked Daddy, "You playing?"

"You know I don't play out anymore."

I asked Mother, "Coming out of retirement?"

"Just this one night. That's all."

They talked about some of the other people who'd be performing that night. It was an all-star Southern gospel lineup. They mentioned a date. I said I'll be right back, headed to the kitchen, and motioned to Leslie to follow.

I asked him, "Did you get the Ray Charles tickets?"

"Not yet."

"Well hurry up. He's only in town one night. Pasadena Civic sells out fast."

"It's the same night as Mother's singing in Long Beach."

"I *know*. That's what I'm saying. If they ask, we've gotta tell them we already have Ray Charles tickets."

"I feel like we oughta go hear Mother."

I was certain he was joking.

"Oh sure, *that's* what we should do."

He wasn't joking. I didn't want to go.

"Are you kidding? You said you'd never go hear her sing again."

"I will if you will."

I started to leave the kitchen. He could finish setting the food out on the table by himself.

He said, "C'mon. We can take our dates. Surprise her. Don't tell her we're coming."

"Why?"

"I don't know. Just don't tell her."

From the front room, her song continued.

Love me tender, love me dear
Tell me you are mine.
I'll be yours through all the years
'Til the end of time

Daddy called out.

"Nita Faye, you hear your part?"

I heard it. I went back out there and sang a third part with them.

Love me tender, love me true
All my dreams fulfill

From the kitchen came the fourth part.

For my darling I love you
Daddy said, "I hear you out there, son."
Four parts finished the song.
And I always will.

That's the last time I remember all of us singing the same song in the same place at the same time.

Chapter 38

Palm Springs

1980s

Two decades after we left them in their pink living room in Glendale, some catching up is in order. There were marriages and children for both Leslie and me and that, of course, would be a different book.

Gramma K left us in 1976 after battling cancer for years. It was a kind of cancer the doctors at UCLA said was caused by smoking.

As we took our seats inside Wee Kirk O' the Heather chapel at Forest Lawn, we sat in the family section arranged in pews on the side, Gramma's children in the first row, then us, her grandchildren, next, then the great-grandchildren. Daddy asked the minister in his remarks to liken Gramma K to Dorcas in the Bible, a person who was always helping others.

Mother spent the days before Forest Lawn squalling, keening, shaking, wailing, issuing forth all the grieving noises heard at funerals in our churches in the South.

A mantle of flowers covered the casket, which remained closed, but keeping to tradition, mourners passed by and paused. Mother went last. I thought she'd crumple, and if Daddy didn't catch her in time, she'd faint. She had a history of fainting. But without waiting for Daddy, she stood abruptly, stoic and dry-eyed, walked to the casket, laid her hand on it, and made her pronouncement.

"Mother, I will see you in the morning."

☐

The Joneses went into real estate in Palm Springs and they were good at it. They developed a loyal clientele made up of Southern transplants and snowbirds and famous and infamous personalities. Daddy did the pleased-to-meet-you handshaking, the smiling and offering recommendations about where to get good biscuits and gravy.

Mother said the heat was why she stayed inside to handle all the paperwork. She kept the details of their projects running like clockwork. The outside-versus-inside sharing of duties suited them.

When a neighbor was away, Daddy stopped by to make sure their gardeners were on the job. Many times when we went to Palm Springs we'd track him down and find him attached to a garden hose, touching up somebody else's plants.

In the courtyard in front of their own home, Daddy brought in plants with dubious forecasts for survival in the desert, and not only did they survive, they thrived. On visits we rang the bell out at the gate and made our way to the front door under a canopy of nonindigenous trees, Daddy's forest in tubs.

Mother's pink furniture kept going, covered in different fabrics in different homes. Those impressive pieces continued to assert their own personality, regularly popping overworked buttons, struggling with whatever new upholstery fabric she ordered. There was still no sign of the Maison Blanche's handiwork giving up. In Palm Springs, the chaise and chairs were covered in taupe or beige or ivory or cream or whatever the name was each year for off-white and impractical. Still formal. Still tufted.

The red Formica-topped kitchen table with the chrome-trimmed chairs fit snugly in the kitchen. Daddy still cooked in his favorite cast-iron skillet.

One room was devoted to their expanding studio, where they installed an assortment of instruments, recording equipment, microphones, speakers, and their music collections. This was the heart of their home, where they made music for themselves and where Daddy also duplicated cassettes of anything he thought would interest Leslie and me. My brother and I swapped information about the contents of the little padded envelopes we received in the mail and reported back to Daddy with our comments about music he loved that we'd never have sampled if not for him sending it.

Daddy never lost one bit of his Southern drawl and he never gave up on becoming a fluent Spanish speaker. He learned even more songs in Spanish to sing to his Doll Baby. We teased him about his pronunciation but we all enjoyed his renditions of "Sabor a Mi," "Nosotros," and Mother's favorite, "Maria Elena." We lost track of how many recordings of that song he owned. He announced he'd found a favorite version.

"Have you heard Los Indios Tabajaras?"

He put it on the turntable. It was an instrumental, so any of us could sing the words along with the bolero guitars, and some of us did. A few days after we got home, Leslie and I each received a copy of Los Indios Tabajaras music in the mail. Daddy phoned to ask if we liked it. We did, we really did.

"Your Mama wants to know if you've heard Nat King Cole sing 'Darling, Je Vous Aime Beaucoup'?"

He sent a copy. He sent copies of Ronnie Milsap's "It Was Almost Like a Song," the Sons of the Pioneers' "My Adobe Hacienda," some Mickey Gilley, Willie Nelson, and Brook Benton's "It's Just a Matter of Time" and "Rainy Night In Georgia."

When the spirit moved her, Mother took to the piano, playing gospel or boogie-woogie or blues, and when Daddy heard something he liked, he picked up a guitar and joined in. He was a rhythm guitarist, good at walking and talking and singing while strumming, but what he really wanted was to play steel guitar better.

"I'm gonna learn 'Sweet Leilani' for yore Mama. She loves High-wah-yan music."

He took his inspiration from Marty Robbins, owner of a beautiful voice and a consummate yodeler. A bit of a yodel needed to happen for a decent Southern rendition. Daddy had the yodel down, but the steel guitar playing continued to be a challenge.

☐

I stayed closest to parts of the family business, but not by design. It happened that some of my interests were also theirs, or vice versa. I moved back and forth between radio shows in Northern and Southern California.

I sang in clubs in Los Angeles and Beverly Hills while I was too young to be inside a club, just as Mother had. She and I talked about specific songs but not about the places where I sang them. When I went on the radio full-time, we found safer subject matter.

I'd just returned to Los Angeles from San Francisco to start a new radio show on KBIG. When the show was announced in the press and the moving van had already left San Francisco, as I was about to put my suitcases in the car for the drive to Los Angeles, an enormous flower arrangement arrived. The card said, "Congratulations, Nita Faye. Try not to screw it up."

I dialed from my empty flat.

A receptionist answered.

"Law offices."

"Will you put him on please?"

"Did you get my card?"

"Oh shut up, Leslie Ray."

"Where are you staying?"

"Hotel in Hollywood, near the station 'til my furniture arrives."

"See you this weekend."

"See you in Palm Springs."

My brother, the one who sketched houses and buildings and planned to design them himself, instead became a successful attorney with offices in Orange County—Brea, Fullerton, and La Habra.

In many ways we were still our younger selves. We'd each picked up additional tools for dealing with life, but when things went wrong, I still got sad and he still got mad. I wanted to make things. He wanted to make money.

He shared Mother's fear of being poor. He needed to be prosperous. I accepted all kinds of (I liked to think creative) career challenges. He barked at me for not planning ahead. I nagged him about the way he piloted his machines. He drove sports cars too fast, flew his plane in iffy conditions and landed in unlikely places. He broke bones racing motorcycles.

Everything about Leslie was magnified. He charmed a crowd whenever he chose to, and when he entered a room, someone always asked, who's that? He was a snappy dresser, lately taken to wearing tee shirts with pictures of his favorite artists, pairing them with everything from custom-tailored jackets to fishing clothes. All the shirts were in black and white or black and gray. Sarah Vaughan appeared in rotation with Ray Charles, Ella, Chet, Miles, Coltrane, Ellington, and Poncho Sanchez. Many of our family photos include singers and musicians on Leslie Ray's chest.

I lived in Northern California much of the previous decades. Leslie and I traveled back and forth visiting each other, comparing notes on our separate worlds, and still mulling over childhood. When I accepted the Los Angeles radio show, though I was heartbroken to leave my beloved flat on Green Street, it would be easier for my brother and I to spend time together with our two families.

When I moved from San Francisco I was sad to leave Glide Memorial Church behind but quickly became active in a new congregation at Little Brown Church in Studio City, a gathering of good people with a nondenominational slant, a fine preacher, and excellent music.

Though Leslie still spoke of his yearning to be a jazz disc jockey, it was always pure fantasy since he could never have made enough money in radio to be content. He became a superfan, with all his radios tuned to Jazz/KNOB out of Long Beach, soaking in every word spoken by Chuck Niles and Jim Gosa, two golden-throated announcers with ties to all the jazz greats.

When he visited me in San Francisco, my radio was set to KJAZ. While the evening fog blessed the Victorians on Russian Hill, we had wine and listened to Bob Parlocha's *Dinner Jazz* before going down the hill to Keystone Korner in North Beach or to the Marina to hear Johnny Rae on vibes at Roland's. Johnny toured with Cal Tjader, but when he was in town, he brought some of the Tjader sidemen with him to Roland's. I'd been there many times on my own or with dates, sitting just outside the circle of light around the stage, enchanted by Johnny's solos. Of course I needed to take Leslie there.

Johnny recognized me, played a chorus of "My Funny Valentine," laid down the mallets, walked over to our table, and held out his hand in a may-I-have-this-dance invitation. Of course he could.

☐

Leslie and his law partners invested in condominiums in Palm Springs and made them available to family and friends. He'd urged Daddy and Mother to spend time there, which is how our parents were introduced to the area. We were surprised when they agreed to their first visit, since Mother didn't enjoy hot weather, but eventually they bought two homes of their own across the fairway from Leslie's places.

Daddy wore his old Panama hats in the sun, and we sent him sneakers to wear in this new life. He'd never worn anything but hard-soled shoes. We had to coax him into something more casual. Finally he agreed they were better suited for his wandering, gardening, and watering enterprises, so we kept finding new and more outrageous sneakers and sandals to bring him. It took a while longer to get him into short-sleeved shirts. He'd never bought leisure clothes. He was accustomed to wearing preacher shirts, long-sleeved white dress shirts with fronts and collars and cuffs starched so stiff, assistance from a preacher's kid was often required to get cuff links situated. When the shirts were worn thin and soft as tissue, and after the collars had already been turned to extend their wearing time, only then did he adapt them for outside chores with the sleeves rolled up.

They tithed their second home to friends, inviting evangelists and musicians and pastors to free vacations. We enjoyed their updates even more when they began leasing their second home to people outside their faith. A member of The Eagles spent time there, so did Don Sherwood, a San Francisco radio and television personality who claimed absolutely no interest in religion, who stopped any conversation in which Jesus was mentioned, but loved to go over next door to chat with The Joneses about Southern music.

Daddy took on the full-time job of PR person for his Doll Baby. We received many phone calls from him that started with "Know what Mama-gal did?" He'd launch into a chapter of praise for whatever was her latest accomplishment and he believed, all these years later, that Sister Fern was pure magnificence through and through. We respected the way he felt about her. We'd learned there weren't many partnerships like theirs.

Daddy was the phone caller and Mother the letter writer. His phone calls sounded like the preacher we grew up with, with down-home storytelling, and he always ended with a reminder that he was praying for us.

Her letters should have been framed because of her penmanship. Today I see her handwriting and no matter what the document, whether it's a recipe card or notes for a song or a poem or an article she was writing, each example is decorated with all the frills she taught herself through a correspondence course and late-night study sessions. I don't think I've ever seen prettier handwriting.

During the past decades we thought we'd achieved some version of detente with them, but it was tenuous. In truth, we were no closer to accepting the way they believed and they were no closer to accepting us the way we were. Perhaps our wobbly truce had been merely geographical. It's easier not to disagree when you don't see each other often.

We visited, chatted, ate, listened to music, then without us knowing why, one or the other of them would stop speaking to one of us. The way we found out who was in disfavor was when they contacted the other one to discuss the perceived sins. Divide and conquer, deliberate or not, is a tactic employed by many families and in ours as well. When they had one of us alone, they tried to gain intelligence on the other. These are the kinds of conversations that transpired.

Nita Faye, pray for your brother. He's running around with a divorced woman. Leslie Ray, pray for your sister. She's still smoking.

Nita Faye, do you know when your brother's gonna get here? He never comes to see us unless you're here. He always says he will, but he doesn't.

Leslie Ray, I don't think that church Nita Faye goes to is preaching the Full Gospel. Maybe you should ask her if they're teaching the Second Coming.

Nita Faye, if you and your brother don't confess your sins, you're going to hell.

And this one, the big gun deployed in any conversation, aimed at either or both of us, by Mother.

You are breaking your Daddy's heart.

Our cordial shell would hold for several visits until a fracture appeared, and if someone didn't rush to mend it, the balance teetered until our relationships were in danger of falling apart all over again.

The envelopes we received in the mail changed in shape and size, stuffed with clippings and magazines and pamphlets, the kind their denomination handed out to sinners to explain how and why they should give their lives to Jesus. They subscribed us to religious publications. Leslie and I compared unwanted mail.

"Did you get [name of publication]?"

"I threw that one away."

Once in a while Daddy called to say a story Mother wrote would be in a certain magazine and he'd be sending us copies, and we'd watch for that one, read it so we could compliment her, then we went back to throwing away all the envelopes containing religious material.

[]

By the end of the 1950s and into the next decade, a steady stream of hits came out of the Quonset Hut in Nashville. Owen Bradley of the famous Nashville Bradley brothers produced hits by Patsy Cline. Willie recorded there, and so did Johnny Cash, Elvis, Eddy Arnold, Brenda Lee, and many more. Floyd Cramer had a hit with his song "Last Date." Hank Garland put out another jazz album.

Artists continued to record songs Mother wrote and royalties arrived in the mail, but still she fretted and still she believed something she recorded before any of them might have been a hit if only Dot had promoted it.

She continued to pursue ownership of her masters through decades of legal efforts and many switchbacks on the trail. Dot Records sold to Paramount, Paramount went to Gulf & Western, which went to ABC, then to MCA Universal. The modest record company out of Nashville became a Hollywood giant. She said, "These people are wearing me *out*."

But Daddy's most tenacious child, Sister Fern, remained committed to her role in the long-running drama. She said it wasn't because she was stubborn (she was) but because the Lord gave her that music in the first place. After she stopped singing her songs herself, she may have been unsure of their future purpose, but she was sure there *was* one. She'd turned down many offers to sell them so it was clear she was compelled by something more than the prospect of money.

She said, "I wish Colonel Parker wasn't so hateful. Elvis would have recorded my songs." She invariably issued her disclaimer about how it wasn't Elvis's fault. She never blamed him for her dealings with Colonel Parker. Until he died, Elvis sang the songs he learned at the Assembly of God churches in Tupelo and Memphis and at Singings wherever he traveled. He toured with Southern gospel quartets who were friends of The Joneses and recorded several albums of Southern gospel classics.

One day while I was at work in Los Angeles, a phone call came from Daddy. "Do you know what yore Mama did?"

I didn't.

"She got her tapes back from Dot."

"What? How? When?"

Daddy didn't have many details yet, he said, but he'd let us know. From what we gathered, one day someone at the label responded to one of her letters. I pictured a mountain of letters in her elegant handwriting stacked up in some back room, from which one was mercifully plucked.

Leslie and I were both in the habit of sending gifts and cards and quick notes in response to Daddy's continual publicity campaign. Was this a gift occasion? We decided it was. She sent us thank-you notes for the gifts, but instead of a big loud bang-up celebration, her subsequent mentions of the master tape were quiet. She got her tape back, but what could she do with it?

The fact that she now owned her work would have to be enough. We stopped asking about it because no one wanted to remind her of her long struggle. We'd already witnessed her heartbreak and Daddy's pain on her behalf during the 1950s when her record label hadn't cared enough to tell the world about her. Nothing anyone could do about that now. She'd brought her style from honky-tonks to church and then out of church into rockabilly.

From her current vantage point, that must seem an enormous accomplishment. She had said she would do it and she did.

Daddy never seemed to regret their move to California, and she didn't regret anything except that her recordings hadn't yet been heard as widely as she hoped. The two of them spoke often about heaven and assured us that whichever one of them left this earth first, it didn't matter, because their souls would be reunited there, and every troublesome detail about this life would be resolved.

We two came to accept that Mother was a child with unhealed wounds. She suffered from fears and phobias and perhaps serious depression, but we couldn't put a name to any of it because it would never be diagnosed.

We believed Daddy was a good man who radiated kindness to the community but remained devoted first to his faith, then to his wife, and since we didn't share his commitment, there would always be a barrier between us.

We wondered what it would be like to be regarded with favor just for being theirs, even if we were different from them. Finally we decided they did as much as they could. That was as far as we could go without stretching credulity.

During further conversations over Courvoisier (we graduated to expensive drinks when Leslie insisted on paying for everything), we came to the conclusion, dark humor fully employed, that though they didn't get the kids they needed, maybe they got the kids they deserved. What they hoped for was Bible-thumping, harmony-singing, go-along-without-protest little evangelists and instead they got us.

Daddy continued to nourish Mother in all ways. Mother continued to rely on Daddy for everything. We left them to it and went out and made our own mistakes, confiding them to each other, but refusing to believe we would end up in hell.

Another visit to Palm Springs, and after saying hello and making plans for our next group meal, Leslie and I retreated across the golf course to catch up with our real lives. Leslie picked up my suitcase and started toward the door. Daddy walked out with us.

When we reached the gate, he asked, "Leslie Ray, did you tell your sister her boyfriend lives down here now? He bought him some hotels and a baseball team and radio and television stations."

I said, "It's a little late now, Daddy. He's also got a wife."

Daddy grinned the way he did when he pulled off something silly.

Leslie patted me on the head.

"So you missed out on marrying the Singing Cowboy. Too bad, but maybe you could work at one of his stations?"

"I think I'll keep the job I have."

Daddy held the gate for us.

"Gene Autry met his wife right here, you know, at our bank."

"Well shoot, that's what I should have done then, should have been a banker."

Leslie said, "No you shouldn't. You'd have to be good with money."

"Oh, yeah. Well since there's now a Missus Autry, I'll try not to interfere when I see them around town."

"Damn nice—"

Daddy gave him the look.

"Dadgum nice of you."

Daddy asked, "What do y'all want for supper?"

Leslie said, "Whatever you feel like cooking"

I said, "Beans and cornbread and some of Mother's coconut cream pie."

Daddy said, "See you after while."

We copied Daddy's accent.

"Afterwhall."

It always made him smile.

Chapter 39

This World Is Not My Home

This world is not my home
I'm just a passin' through
My treasures are laid up
Somewhere beyond the blue
The angels beckon me
From heaven's open door
And I can't feel at home in this world anymore

Palm Springs, 1987—Ray

Years spent picking cotton in the fields as a sharecropper's son and Daddy's love of fishing and gardening took a toll. At Mother's insistence, he had several skin cancers checked. She told us he went because she begged and cried and pitched a conniption fit. Leslie and I found it impossible to take in the image of Daddy in a doctor's office.

When the biopsy results came back positive for squamous cell cancer, the doctor said there was treatment for it. Daddy told Mother he regretted going to the doctor, he'd prayed about it, and he wouldn't go back.

She was hysterical. She called each of us to confide and to ask for our help. A tumor grew on his neck, and there were episodes of bleeding when he lay on the bathroom floor for hours, not wanting to wake her. She found him there and was afraid of losing him, afraid of being alone when it happened. He wouldn't allow her to call an ambulance.

We went to Palm Springs every weekend we could from then on. Nobody said anything about how unusual that was, since we generally had trouble landing on a date when all of us could go. We didn't comment then, or ever, on his visit to a doctor. We'd given Mother our word. Not only was his doctor visit a reversal of his faith healing beliefs, but Leslie and I now knew Daddy's condition was treatable. His refusal to accept care meant we were going to have to watch him die when he didn't have to.

When we were all together, we communicated in our common language, music and food. We had peach cobbler weekends and chili weekends and Pecos Bill's barbecue weekends. Daddy ate almost nothing.

We sang all the time. We had Nat King Cole weekends and Hank Williams weekends and Willie Nelson weekends and big band weekends and Harmonizing Four weekends.

He kept practicing his steel guitar playing and laughed at himself. He put on a record he liked, overdubbed his own steel, played it back, and joked about how bad he sounded.

"That's plumb pitiful."

We went to Guitar Center on Sunset Boulevard in Hollywood, up the road from where I talked into a microphone every day, and bought him a wah-wah pedal. He was delighted.

Daddy wore a bandana around his neck tucked into a shirt collar and we were supposed to act as if this was normal. Mother told us the tumor was bigger and he said he would "let the Lord heal me or take me." Soon the awful thing was too large and too angry to hide under a bandana.

Leslie and I convened at one of his condos across the fairway, angry that Daddy made a decision that would result in us watching him kill himself and all the while we were to refrain from talking about it. His decision to die this way took us right back to childhood when it seemed every time choices were made, we lost. This time we were losing our Daddy. All these years after leaving The Glory Road, our adult logic failed and it was *our* hearts breaking.

One day when his back was turned to me and he was busying himself with his records, I asked, "Daddy, does your neck hurt?"

"Sometimes."

"Do you have something for the pain?"

"I pray."

He turned back around and his face was set in his no-more-questions expression.

We asked him to tell us more stories about his life. He agreed to record them. Mother made sure there were sufficient tapes and said she was thrilled to see him occupied with something he loved. He carried around a cassette recorder all day and talked into the mic until he grew tired. She duplicated the tapes, sending each one to us in those small padded envelopes.

Daddy's storytelling reached new heights during that year. Each time we received tapes, we had more questions. Mother said go ahead and write them down, call her, and she'd pass them along to him. Leslie wanted to know about life in El Dorado, the parts he was too young to remember.

On tape, we learned Daddy took Leslie, when he was barely a toddler, when he went to work at night in Dueft Chapel (he called it Dove Chapel) after working his regular job all day. Daddy related the details of putting the little church together, one pew at a time, and how a preacher with a baby boy ought to raise that boy up to follow in the footsteps of Jesus and how he thought it would be good for his son to see his Daddy working for the Lord.

Our colorful philosopher told us more details about plowing the fields. He laughed about the mule that was his steady after-school companion. He'd seldom talked to us about his lack of education, but in these tapes he said, without blaming anyone, he was disappointed he had to leave school so early, and in the next sentence, he absolved his parents.

He said he drank too much and took too many risks. Leslie was surprised and awed to find that Daddy once rode motorcycles. He'd never told us that. He was proud of his CCC camp service as a cook feeding hundreds of young men like him, sending money home to his family. Though he wasn't one to brag, we could tell one of his proudest moments was when he put on the gloves and knocked out the best boxer in camp in a prizefight.

His taped reminiscences generally ended with a moral, like all his stories did when we were little.

"Course I wouldn'ta done none of that if I was yore Daddy then, 'cause that's not how a Daddy ought to do."

His stories always reflected his devotion to the Lord, his love for Mother, and his respect for his parents and siblings. We never heard him say a bad word about any of them. Listening to his tapes today, it feels like Mark Twain and Will Rogers and Andy Griffith all got together to talk into a microphone about a small-town preacher's life. Mother said the questions we asked and his need to answer them kept him alive longer. None of the tapes contains a single indication he was suffering while recording them.

At a restaurant where my brother and I commiserated late into the evening, a waiter took our order. I asked for coffee please and Leslie automatically changed my order to very expensive wine, as if the costlier choice could help.

A few drinks later, Leslie said, "What if there is a heaven? Like Daddy believes?"

"What if there is?"

"Maybe we'll see him there."

One obvious flaw in that reasoning was that, according to Daddy, there wasn't much likelihood we'd get in.

Mother was losing the love of her life, and soon her children would be left with a woman who, over the years, had become even more puzzling than when we first knew her. Daddy spent his lifetime raising her and still she was dependent on him, but she'd soon be ours to deal with. After all this time, we were no closer to understanding how Daddy had managed it.

She asked if we would agree to call an ambulance without his consent. She couldn't do it. We agreed. One day we got the call. Daddy had lost a lot of blood, but he was conscious and wouldn't go to the hospital until a local Pentecostal minister arrived to pray with him.

Leslie left a courtroom, I left the radio studio, and we raced to Palm Springs.

At the hospital, Daddy was curled up on his side. His face was a reproach. He was betrayed. He was angry. He said, "This is a pitiful way for you to see your Daddy."

We wondered if he was frightened. He'd never been in a hospital except to pray for the sick. The staff took Leslie and me aside and began to question us. They asked, "How could you let him go untreated like this?"

Each change of shifts at the hospital brought more questions and incredulous reactions. Leslie took it all to mean they were disparaging about how backward our family must be. We were defensive, not just on our own behalf, but also because we were Southern kids and this was our Daddy.

The tumor was by then so grotesque someone wearing scrubs came in with a camera, planning to take a photo of it in the name of medicine. Leslie stood up. He advanced. One look at his face and the camera started backing out of the room. I don't even remember the words he said, just something like "Don't you *ever!*"

After all the years of arguments over his faith healing beliefs, with two babies in our family gone, our own childhood without medical care, when it came to Daddy in that emergency room, we were ready to be his armor, to shield him as much as possible from this new, alien environment. No battles had been won by either side. We were still unwilling to let him believe we shared his complete trust in faith healing. He would die feeling he'd failed his charge from his God, unable to reconcile irreconcilable differences of faith between him and his children.

Daddy accepted the hospital routine forced on him, remaining gracious to us after that first night. They propped him up in bed and he looked so handsome. We teased him about his pompadour, with every hair still in place and only one or two grey hairs at either temple. He looked like Daddy, sounded like Daddy, but it was clear he would be leaving soon. Brother Bruce, the Palm Springs pastor, made regular visits. If we were there when he came, he asked us to join hands with him in prayer.

Nothing destroyed Daddy's composure, though he was prodded and tested and though they connected him to morphine at our request, for what the doctor said was intense pain. Daddy had lived with this evil growth for a year and his dignity, even in this foreign environment, was unassailable.

The oncologist assigned to Daddy's case, Dr. Gary Palmer, was gentle as he came to know his patient. The staff grew protective, asking constantly if he needed something for pain. He said no. They asked us if they could give it to him anyway. We said yes. Dr. Palmer, after many talks in the family waiting room, understood how we got to this point and that we couldn't do anything but watch him die. The hospital let Mother sleep on a bed in his room.

Now within Daddy's view there was only a piece of sky framed by a window, and at one end of the room was a field of green we created, filling all available space with living plants we brought inside for our gardener.

The last morning I spent with him, raindrops spattered and sputtered against the window, trying to turn into a real desert storm. I knew he'd be right out there walking in it if he could.

I asked, "Do you ever miss the South?"

"I miss the trees. But I can't complain. I have had me some beautiful morning walks around here."

He said all his people passed away in the fall so autumn must be the Lord's harvest time for souls in his family. Daddy left us in October. After his passing, we planted a tree in his name and gathered to sing "What a Friend We Have in Jesus" and "In the Garden."

Leslie and I talked often about the way Daddy left. After many years of existing peacefully in the life he and Mother made in California without mentioning what he'd left behind in the South, we could only speculate about how it affected him. We tried to guess the depths of his remorse at leaving his calling at that church in Louisiana. He never said why he didn't pursue the ministry in California, and because we didn't share his beliefs, it seemed impertinent to ask.

Was his grief or guilt at forsaking his calling enough to convince Daddy he needed to make a stand in order to complete the circle of his life? Did he, by allowing himself to die by faith, somehow keep his own pledge to his Maker? One thing was obvious: Reverend Raymond Jones was at peace when he died. His children were not.

After all the visitors left, when it was just us Joneses sitting on the New Orleans furniture in the Palm Springs living room, Mother brought out Daddy's old briefcase. His briefcase was his traveling chapel. He kept a Bible in there and a beautiful fountain pen and nice paper with his name on it, but he also put scrap paper notes inside, brought home from wherever a thought or a scripture or a prayer came to him.

One pocket was filled with love notes from her to him, and when Daddy went to the hospital, Mother took the briefcase to his room. She also tucked inside some of his notes to her, from the many he propped up next to her coffee cup every morning. His last note to her was dated September 1987, days before he was hospitalized. It said,

> *Good Morning Doll Baby,*
> *You are the best wife a man could have.*
> *I'm sorry I woke you last night with the bleeding.*
> *Thank you for staying up and praying with me.*
> *I am having the best time with the Lord today.*
> *All morning I've been singing,*
> *"Jesus Is the Sweetest Name I Know."*

After Daddy passed, Mother existed solely inside the house. She had everything delivered. She set up a property management company in what was formerly their dining room and ran it successfully from the space where we used to eat great Southern food.

Though she finally got a driver's license, the car stayed in the driveway, and she hired people to do everything—grocery shopping, errands, delivering keys, picking up documents. She had her notary and banker come to the house when she needed them to finalize papers.

Maybe we should have noticed her retreat sooner, but we only went to visit when we felt we had to. Palm Springs was barely tolerable without Daddy there.

We returned to our lives, visiting under the weight of guilt, breezing in with dishes of things she loved, oohing and ahhing over her continual redecorating of both condos. The one next door was by then so meticulously curated, it felt as if a photographer would arrive any minute to capture the details she spent hours on, down to complete table settings which she changed often, though no one lived there.

She did most of her back-and-forth, moving things around in the two condos after dark, working into the early morning hours, always her habit. Though she didn't leave the house in daylight, she gave us the key and said to go look at what she'd done. She waited for us to return so she could ask what we liked best. There was no chance we could speak in generalities because she would go down a list until we discussed everything, so we memorized details.

Both condos had oversized bedrooms, offering plenty of space for her to stage her vignettes with multiple chairs and tables and many things on top of each table. We split up to cover everything.

"You take the back bedroom, I'll take the front."

"Don't forget to mention the ceramics on the end tables. I think those are new."

"Is that a pink flamingo? Wait, there are three of them."

"I see one in here too."

"Was this big mirror in here before?"

"Let me come see. No, I think that's a different one. What about those dishes? Last time she had Gramma K's Franciscan out."

"Which ones?"

"I'm not sure. I think Apple pattern?"

"Well she's changed it then. This is Desert Rose."

"Have you ever seen that bedspread?"

We finished our reconnaissance and returned next door to face the inquisition.

We'd been asking her to teach us some of her pie magic, and when we showed up on the appointed weekend for our lesson, she handed us aprons and rolling pins. We all laughed at our attempts to turn out something approximating her pie crust. We said this isn't easy and that she should sell her pies.

"Oh no, it wouldn't work. I like a very short crust and they'd fall apart."

We preferred her crust, which did, indeed, melt into deliciousness at the touch of a fork. We assured her we enjoyed picking up the crumbs with our fingers and hoped she'd never change her recipe.

Her pie fillings were unlike any other. Her specialties were coconut cream, raisin, and chocolate cream, though from to time she would also whip up mincemeat or a sweet and tart lemon with meringue halfway up to heaven.

It happened that each of us had occasion to go see her without the other. When it was time to drive back to Los Angeles, she walked me to the door. Instead of goodbye or when will you be back, she surprised me.

"I know you and your brother think we were wrong, the way we raised you. You do, don't you?"

I nodded yes.

"We didn't know. We didn't know about raising children. We were children ourselves."

Her tears began and I'm not sure they had anything to do with child raising. Leslie and I were probably on her list of regrets, but there might not be enough time for her to get to us because she was clinging desperately to pieces of her own memories. She wiped her eyes with one of Gramma K's handkerchiefs. She missed Daddy, she said. She was afraid, she said.

Soon after, Leslie was in Palm Springs at one of his own homes and he stopped by to take her some flowers before scooting out of there as quickly as he could. He called me in Los Angeles.

"Did Mother try to apologize to you?"

"Yes. I thought she'd faint, she was shaking so much."

"She started off the same way with me, then she was crying about her childhood and how much she missed Daddy."

I said, "I was thinking she might say something that started with 'I should have' or 'We should have . . .' or 'I'm sorry.' That might make a difference . . ."

"A *huge* difference . . ."

After that, Leslie would visit only when we both could go. He sent her gifts, which on the surface looked like an attentive son's gestures, things that would have had her bragging to Gramma K, if she was still with us, but the tokens were ways to keep from sitting across from her in person.

We should have noticed the signs. Watching her life become more off-kilter, we believed she'd become agoraphobic, complicated by several other emotional issues, and she wouldn't answer any questions that could confirm it. We offered to take her places to see about things. No. We asked if she had girlfriends. No. Did she go to church? No. Would she like to go out to eat? No. Brother Bruce visited faithfully. He must have also sensed something amiss with the Widow Jones, something in addition to burying a husband.

Without Daddy to hold her together, she was alone in their house, still the same scared teenage girl we grew up next to. She remained willful and strong-minded and resourceful about business, but she never moved a step away from her loss, even after Daddy had been gone for years.

I said to Leslie, "I'm sure it's agoraphobia."

"Why don't you ask her?"

"She might not even know what it is."

"Oh she'll know. She watches television. She reads everything. Go try it. Try asking her to go outside again."

I didn't want to and I knew he wouldn't either.

In 1995, Mother had come back from her last trip out of the house, a visit to Arkansas to see her sister, Aunt Freddie, one more time. Freddie was in the final stages of cancer. Mother took the train and hid away in a compartment. She said she hurt her ankle on the trip, maybe twisted it going up those steps they use at boarding time. During our next visit, she couldn't stand without bracing herself or leaning on something.

She didn't offer any details, but as we checked in more and more frequently, she agreed that walking was difficult, but no, she wouldn't go to a doctor. We were worried she might fall, so we pushed her to get the ankle looked at. Palm Springs had concierge doctors who came to your home. We called one. He insisted she get tested.

Tests. Consultations. The diagnosis was ALS, Lou Gehrig's disease. She'd recently begun sounding raspy, like the aftereffects of a cold. Worse still was when the full progression was explained. ALS would take her voice long before she would expire, a particular cruelty. Her voice was her definition of herself, her way out of the childhood she hated, her form of expression. And while ALS would silence the voice and take away all movement, her mind would remain intact. She would be aware of every loss.

Almost as quickly as we heard the diagnosis, that's how quickly she began to weaken. She kept a spiral notebook and pens with her for as long as she could write. She wrote down song ideas and poems and thoughts. Paralysis moved up quickly from her ankles to her legs and compromised her lower back muscles, ending any more sitting sessions even in a special chair.

Her fellow evangelists called and sent prayers. Listening to her talking with them when the diagnosis was still new, when her words were still clear enough to be understood, it was hard to believe all the horrors that were on the way. She spoke of her expected healing on the phone to other preachers, asking them to put together a prayer chain.

The preachers' conversations were the familiar language of our childhood, affirmations that surely she would not be singled out for imminent death. They called her a precious soul. Some of the preachers urged her to believe in her healing and they talked about how she would get up and walk and testify. She denied she was dying. No peace descended on her, nothing like the acceptance Daddy demonstrated. In her denial there was only panic.

We wanted to help, which meant trying to understand the contradictions in the way she lived. While she had no personal contact with anyone except business associates and had not gone outside in who knew how long, she was sad when she mentioned the name of someone she once knew who hadn't come to see her. There was no good answer when she wondered about it, so we made up stories about why so-and-so hadn't been around. We offered to call anyone she hoped to see. After a while, she said no, there was no one.

She looked at us the way a child looks when told the most remarkably unrealistic scheme will not come to pass. With a child, you explain and wait for a sign that you've been understood. With Mother, the puzzled expression stayed until the end.

ALS is a cruel fate for anyone, and for her, unimaginable to think of being without her voice. She'd relied on her voice and Daddy to make her way in the world. With Daddy gone and her voice silenced, panic settled in her eyes, which were now her only moving parts.

At the hospice, in her sunny corner room, we put some of her favorite things, feminine fragrances, a silky bed jacket, flowers everywhere, pictures of Daddy, and music. We brought tapes of her singing, and tapes of her and Daddy singing together, and they played endlessly. The staff said they loved the music and turned the volume up so others could hear it too. None of her caregivers had even been born when Fern was young and believed that people who can write songs can find immortality.

In the last months, the disease melted any extra pounds she carried and transformed her into a photograph of her younger self. She was beautiful lying there with her extraordinary skin, with her curls and waves turned platinum overnight, carefully arranged around her on a pillow.

She died exactly nine years after Daddy. Harvest time for both of them came in the autumn.

I have the last spiral notebook she filled with her script. The handwriting in it is only slightly less fancy than it used to be. Here is one page written after her diagnosis.

> *Heaven is the one and only place*
> *He could be and not be missing her*
> *And maybe even then he does?*

Leslie Ray and the Palm Springs preacher and I sat in the hospice waiting room. Leslie thanked him for all the time he spent with Mother. He said, "Fern was really something." Leslie asked if the pastor had children. Yes, he did. In fact, one of his was headed to college. Leslie talked about how expensive college can be. He took out his checkbook.

"Daddy was a preacher. We know what it's like. There's never enough money."

He wrote a check. I didn't see the amount, but from the look on the pastor's face, I assumed it was substantial. Leslie said, "Tithes."

Canyon Lake, California, 2010—Leslie Ray

When I started writing the stories that became this book, I showed each of them to Leslie Ray, since there's so much of him in here. I said, "These are my truths but they may not be yours." He said, "They're mine too." I know he would endorse this, given the numbers of times we've compared experiences. Portions of this book appear in my play, *The Glory Road*. He attended every performance. Every time we got together, he asked, "Anything new for me to read?"

Here it is, but now he's not here.

We said to him, you're going to kill yourself with that car or plane or motorcycle. When a phone rang late at night, my first thought was always about my daughter and the prayer was *please not Cathleen*, then *please not Leslie Ray*.

One night the call was about Leslie. None of his fast-moving toys was involved. He shot himself in the head. He lingered in a half-conscious state for several months and died early in 2011, but I mark the time of death from the morning he picked up that gun, July 9, 2010.

He had sought treatment for depression, perhaps too late. Hindsight begs the question about other members of the family who shared similar traits and faced similar challenges.

We raised each other, buried our parents, sat at Daddy's funeral while "Just a Closer Walk with Thee" was sung, stood by Mother's grave listening to "Precious Lord, Take My Hand," but it wasn't the loss of our parents that emptied the family vessel for me. When Leslie Ray left, he took the other half of my childhood with him.

It turns out he also took away some of the music. It's been a while, and I still haven't made it all the way through *The Genius of Ray Charles*. I'm working on it.

The Music Lives On

Mill Valley, California, 2005

When I packed up the Palm Springs house, I found the master tape from Sister Fern's 1950s Nashville sessions. Among people of faith, some say there are no coincidences. There are visions of wonder, prophecies, and answered prayers, and there are miracles, all of them attributed to the Divine. Daddy would preach the following story as a miracle. Mother would call it answered prayers.

On a Sunday morning in August, I drove around the village. Any other Sunday, I'd have walked from my cottage in the canyon to the Depot to pick up *The New York Times.* I was in the car only because I needed to collect mail from the post office box farther down the road. If I'd walked that day, I'd have missed what happened next.

Listening to *Weekend Edition* on KQED (NPR San Francisco), I heard an interview featuring Bill Moss, the founder of Capsoul, a long-dormant record label out of Columbus, Ohio, and Ken Shipley, president of a new preservation label, Numero Group. They spoke of recordings they had recently restored.

They talked about the process of remastering with the talented Jeff Lipton at Peerless Mastering in Boston. They put together some of Capsoul's early work and released it as Numero's first compilation, #001.

As the keeper of the master reel that came from Mother's studio sessions, I wanted to protect her recordings via digital mastering. I contacted Jeff at Peerless and inquired about doing that. He agreed and I flew to Boston soon after with the tape box on my lap. Once I explained what was on the tape, TSA at San Francisco International exempted it from scanning.

At Peerless, Jeff wheeled out an ancient Ampex reel-to-reel machine he kept for dealing with old analog tapes. He opened the box and found the master was tails out, meaning it would need to be rewound, a risky procedure since we'd hoped to make only one pass at it.

He protected the tape like a skilled surgeon as it went through the heads on the Ampex, and still we didn't know what we would hear, how much of the tape was viable, or what the quality would be. It hadn't been played since Dot mastered it in 1958.

We heard the music that day exactly as it was performed in Nashville decades ago. After the last note was sung, we exhaled and shared a moment of gratitude that the songs were intact. "When I Meet You" was a surprise addition that wasn't included on the record Dot released, though it was clearly marked on the original session data inside the tape box.

I left Peerless that day with a new master that already sounded much crisper than the tape. Jeff said he'd like to keep a copy and play it for a friend.

Back in Mill Valley, I received a call from Ken Shipley from Numero Group. He was the friend who heard Jeff's copy. Would I like to discuss releasing the music on their label? I respected the work they did, based on NPR's Capsoul story.

Rob Sevier, Numero's indefatigable head of research, worked for months chasing details, immersed in the music of that era, including the history of the legendary Nashville sidemen who played on the record. The booklet inside the CD box is compelling. A unique tribute in the outstanding artwork is a photo of the Bible Brother Ray studied and preached from for decades, the one he took everywhere.

Numero included the earlier album, *The Joneses Sing*, music Daddy and Mother made together. Numero's preservation is a history of The Joneses in Southern gospel, incorporating country and spirituals and church hymns and blues, moving into rockabilly, adding fuel to the rock and roll fire that swept the country by the end of the 1950s.

Fern Jones—The Glory Road, Numero's #005, launched to glowing reviews. The music turns up everywhere. It's on the radio, on television shows, in movies, on streaming services, and recently Numero Group produced a shiny new, perfectly retro vinyl version.

The movie about Johnny Cash, *Walk the Line*, features Sister Fern's song "I Was There When It Happened." When the movie was released, I made the acquaintance of Dan John Miller, who plays Luther Perkins, one of the Tennessee Two. Marshall Grant, the other half of the Tennessee Two, called to say he was writing a memoir and wanted to call his book *I Was There When It Happened—My Life with Johnny Cash*. Mother, who always kept a place in her heart for John R. Cash, would enjoy that. Rosanne Cash and Ry Cooder performed "I Was There When It Happened" at every stop during their 2019 tour.

Sister Fern was grateful for the gift of music and honored that other artists were recording her songs, but nobody was more devoted to her musical calling than Brother Ray. In the end, the things she treasured most in life were Daddy and what she was able to create.

She had good reason to believe in her songs. Long after she crossed over the River Jordan, her music is available in places that didn't exist while she was alive.

Gospel Gypsies Know

The words to most songs in the church hymnal along with some blues and country and Southern gospel and rockabilly and big, beautiful ballads.

How to find a harmony part even when you don't feel like singing.

Gravy over just about anything is a fine supper and you can make gravy from just about anything.

Gravy, part 2: When you're making gravy, you can't give up on it just because it seizes up on you. Little by little you add and you whisk. Nobody ever throws away gravy unless he's got a fortune in the bank.

Poor people eat what the Good Lord sends them.

Bacon grease has magic in it.

When digging up baby potatoes, coax them out of the ground gently, with a soft touch. Don't even try to use a trowel. Use your hands. This brings to the kitchen the tenderest new potatoes and creamed peas to feast on at supper time.

When someone is teaching you to cook a particular dish and they say, "You'll feel it when it's right," that is not always true.

Nobody's pies, then or now, compare with pies baked in the wee hours by the Musical Pie Lady.

When decorating a house with very little money, you can turn bed sheets into whatever your imagination conjures.

Baby diapers fresh off the clothesline are stiff and need to be coaxed into baby-bottom shape during the folding process.

Being the subject of town gossip when one is very young is puzzling. Nobody tells you why people talk about your family that way. You get older, find out why, and don't like it any better.

It's not being poor in a small town that'll get you discussed the most. It's when you're poor and your parents are also unusual and your family's ways don't match those of your friends.

Poor, part 2: The hardest part about being poor isn't knowing you are. It's finding out not everyone else is and that even some people engaged in church work live comfortably.

Living for the promise of heaven is hard. Living for a blue Schwinn bicycle is more practical. You can pray for the bike. You'll be promised heaven and assured that in the meantime Baby Jesus will take care of everything that is wrong down here.

Comportment is a word that comes up several times a day in a Southern preacher's home.

The End

Acknowledgments

The Glory Road arrives with a great deal of help. I'm grateful.

University of Alabama Press—Thanks to editor-in-chief Dan Waterman, acquisitions editor Pete Beatty, managing editor Jon Berry, project editor Kelly Finefrock, senior designer Lori Lynch, director of sales and marketing Clint Kimberling, marketing coordinator Blanche Sarratt, and the rest of the talented staff for masterfully wrangling the material while preserving this family's Southern "isms."

Don Barrett—The author of his own books and resident sage at laradio. com, Don is a champion for creative types. When we met, both our mothers had been diagnosed with ALS. We bonded over broadcasting and health care and writing. Don's always been generous with his resources as a motion picture executive and a broadcaster.

Carol Schild Levy and Marvin Levy—Their New York and Hollywood lives couldn't be more different from the lives in my stories. They were believers from the start and produced multiple stage performances of *The Glory Road: A Play with Music* in Los Angeles theatres.

Todd Homme—Music executive, producer, musician, composer, arranger, and dear friend, Todd is a continuing source of inspiration, advice, sly humor, and a wealth of showbiz wisdom.

Peter Stougaard—who designed *The Glory Road*'s first logo for early performances.

David Atkinson and Greg Zerkle—Both are actors and singers who directed onstage readings, gathering other talented and dedicated actors, singers, and musicians to bring *The Glory Road* to life. I'm in awe of the magic that performers can create from words and music.

Early readers—Thank you for all your comments and questions, and thanks to Pamela Meares, who's championed every project through several decades.

Curtis Correll—I met him in church in my teens when my family arrived in California in the 1950s. He remains a friend, a steadying hand, an advisor, and a mentor. It would be impossible to overstate his importance in my life.

Keeping the music playing . . .

Jeff Lipton at Peerless Mastering in Boston—who took original recording sessions on tapes from the 1950s and preserved them, coaxing them into today's formats.

Numero Group—Ken Shipley and Rob Sevier and staff. Two albums recorded in the 1950s, *The Joneses Sing* and *Singing a Happy Song*, have been remastered and released as *Fern Jones—The Glory Road* and are available wherever music is sold.

Writers and directors and producers and music supervisors—who add Fern and Ray to their projects.

NPR—Listening to *Weekend Edition Sunday* in 2005, I met Numero Group's Ken Shipley. Not long afterward, NPR aired a story about Numero's release of *Fern Jones—The Glory Road*.

Credits